THE
RESTING
PLACE

*Finding Hope, Peace, & Joy
in All Circumstances*

Carolyn McDaniel Canizales

Paperback ISBN: 979-8-218-83685-6
Hardcover ISBN: 979-8-218-83686-3

Design and publishing services by Peyton Sepeda
WildCreativePublishing.com

25 26 27 28—5 4 3 2

TABLE OF CONTENTS

It is with great joy and humility that I dedicate
this book in memory of my beloved daughter,
Shelly Rena Strickland Forston.

So much of my writing continues to be inspired not only
by my deep faith in Christ, but also by hers.

Shelly was passionately devoted to her family and friends, and
her smile radiated the love of Jesus to everyone she met.
In her illness and death, she taught us how to find not only our
rest in Him, but also hope, peace, and joy in all circumstances.

One day, we will have a glorious reunion like no other.
What a day that will be!

INTRODUCTION

WE ALL HAVE a unique story, composed of our life's experiences. During our lifetime, God helps us to weave the good with the bad and the sorrow with the joy by providing a spiritual lens, His Word, for us to see our circumstances more clearly. If we are willing to relinquish ourselves to His care, He will draw us near and strengthen us.

Throughout this book, I have woven just a fraction of my story within some of the devotions. I have written from my heart, which is full of gratitude for the many ways that my Heavenly Father has carried me through the valleys of life victoriously and given me the firm assurance that He loves me more than I can comprehend.

Toward the back of this book, a small section has been included, featuring a few devotions that honor my daughter, Shelly's memory. Before she went to Heaven, she expressed her hope that I could one day tell my story. As I see it, this is also her story – a story of profound and unwavering faith and trust in God when the chips were down. I know that Shelly would want me to convey to each of you a strong message of hope and faith in Jesus Christ. She would encourage anyone who doesn't yet have a relationship with Him to do so before it is too late, so that one day, when your time on Earth is over, you will join her in Heaven. I know she would say, *"Trust Jesus with your life and you will never regret it."*

The final section of this book holds a selection of poems I have written over the past five years. I had never written poetry, but one day during my quiet time, the first poem, "The Table," began to take shape in my mind. I am grateful that God has given me a new opportunity to further express my heart of faith, love, and devotion to Him.

It is in the Gentle Shepherd's arms that I have found my resting place, and I pray that you, too, will find rest and comfort as together we partake of these devotions. May our strength in the Lord grow abundantly as we abide in Him daily.

DEVOTIONS

FAITH AND THANKFULNESS

For by grace you have been saved through faith.
And this is not your own doing; it is the gift of God.

Ephesians 2:8 (ESV)

This morning I awoke feeling very thankful for my faith in Jesus and how that faith has shaped my life over the past years. Am I perfect? Heavens, NO! Have I made mistakes that I deeply regret? YES! More than I can say. But my faith tells me—no, it assures me through God's Word that I am forgiven, loved, and accepted by my Heavenly Father. This unbelievable gift is not because of anything I've done to earn salvation, but because of what Jesus did for me on the Cross.

We can be assured that this faith I speak of will sustain us in every difficult situation, the timing of which is known only to God. Through our unwavering trust and confidence in God, we can experience deep joy and inner peace. There is not a moment of our journey that our Heavenly Father does not see, and He desires to be fully involved in every aspect of our time here on Earth.

It's good to give thanks! Are you thankful for your faith today? I sure am! Knowing that every passing day is one we will never get back, let's make each moment count.

Prayer: Dear Heavenly Father, thank You for making a way for us to live in the light of Your love and grace. You are an awesome God! We are thankful for all You do for us as we walk this road of life. Please help us to pass Your love on to everyone we encounter in the traffic lanes of life. We pray this in Jesus' name. Amen.

LISTEN TO HIM

Then a cloud appeared and covered them, and a voice came from the cloud: "This is my Son whom I love. Listen to him!"

Mark 9:7 (NIV)

We live in a culture marinated in words! The Internet and other forms of modern media and technology are filled with a staggering amount of information. Yet, how do we know what to pay attention to? How do we know fact from fiction, real from fake, who is truthful and who isn't? After all, not everything online is real or bathed in truth!

Our answer is found in the Scripture above. God said of Jesus, "This is my Son, listen to Him." Isn't it wonderful that we have continual access to Him if we would only stop and take the time to connect? When we sit quietly without interruption, slow our minds, read and reflect on a portion of God's Word, we can sense His presence as He fills our hearts with His peace that satisfies every need we have. That is the power of the Word of God!

Friends, I hope you are as thankful as I am to have God's Word at your fingertips and for access to the One who never changes and will always be our comfort and guide. Never will we have cause to doubt the accuracy of His Word. Only He is perfect in all of His ways!

Prayer: Dear Heavenly Father, we give praise that Your Word is everlasting and Your wisdom cannot be measured. Help us to always listen to You and walk in the way You lead us. Please help us to live out Your truth in every area of our lives. We pray this in Jesus' name. Amen.

NEVER ONCE

Have I not commanded you? Be strong and courageous.
Do not be afraid; do not be discouraged, for the LORD
your God will be with you wherever you go.

Joshua 1:9 (NIV)

Have you ever had your plans disrupted due to illness or unforeseen circumstances? Of course, we have all experienced this many times. My husband and I recently experienced a big surprise—his unexpected quadruple coronary bypass surgery. As I write this, he is fourteen weeks post-surgery and recovering well. We praise the Lord for being with us throughout this journey. Our faith, family, friends, and the prayers of many have made the difference.

I don't know what you might be going through at this moment, but God does. He knows your pain, weakness, and the desires of your heart. He sees your discouragement and your fears. Do you know that during your current circumstances, you can look at life through a spiritual lens, even though you don't have all the answers to the *whys* in life? When we trust that God always has a plan much bigger than our own, never once will we be without His love, mercy, and peace. Because He is faithful and true to His Word, He will never forsake us as long as we remain in His presence, and we will always find the peace and encouragement that we long for.

Why not ask Him to come into your circumstances and bring you the peace He wants to give? Through faith in Jesus, you can live a victorious life and never be away from His care.

Prayer: Dear God, thank You for Your faithfulness and for always walking beside us through our victories and our struggles. Thank You for loving us enough to be our constant source of strength and hope. Thank You for assuring us that we will never walk alone as long as our focus is on You. In Jesus' name we pray. Amen.

HE'S STILL WORKING ON ME

And I am sure of this, that he who began a good work in you will bring it to completion at the day of Jesus Christ.
Philippians 1:6 (ESV)

Have you ever heard of the Cave of Crystals? Neither had I until recently.

The Cave of Crystals lies hidden 980 feet underground in the Naica Mine, located in the Chihuahua Desert of Mexico. According to all accounts, it is both magical and deadly. Temperatures inside the cave can soar to 136 degrees with 90-99 percent humidity. Without the protection of a special suit, anyone who enters it will die within 10 minutes.

Inside the cavern, which spans the size of a football field, enormous towers of sparkling, white gypsum crystals sprout like icicles from the walls, floor, and ceiling, creating a look reminiscent of a real-world ice palace. These stunning works of God were created slowly over many years by water dripping down or flowing into the cave.

Friends, just as the Cave of Crystals and many other spectacular places reveal God's magnificent design, He also wants to create even more beautiful and stunning works in us. Day by day, moment by moment, experience by experience, God painstakingly forms and shapes our hearts to resemble His own. It is an endeavor that takes all of our lives. Sometimes we become impatient and want Him to do the job in us all at once, but that is not how He chooses to transform us. Let's rejoice because God promises to keep working on us until we are made perfect in Heaven.

Prayer: Father God, when we see all that You have created, it astounds us. You thought of the most intricate details when You created the Earth and humanity. Thank You for loving us so much and for giving us such good things. We love You and praise You, in Jesus' name. Amen.

A DISTANT ENCOUNTER

But the fruit of the Spirit is love, joy, peace, patience, kindness,
goodness, faithfulness, gentleness, self-control;
against such things there is no law.

Galatians 5:22-23 (ESV)

On the drive to church, I saw him again. It was the man I had noticed in the same spot a few weeks earlier while stopped at a red light. The first time I saw him, my heart was stirred with empathy. This time was no different. The man was sitting in a wheelchair and had no legs from the knees down. All I could think of was the quote: "I cried because I had no shoes until I met a man who had no feet."

I couldn't help but wonder how this poor man had managed to get to the intersection. There wasn't a parked car nearby, so someone must have loaded him and his wheelchair into a vehicle and dropped him off. I wondered what percent of the money he received from passersby would be his. Was he being used by others and promised drugs or alcohol as payment? I pondered how difficult it must be to maneuver life in his shape. I know he has a story, and I can only imagine what it is. No doubt, his story begins with deep-down hurt, pain, sorrow, guilt, grief, physical abuse, or rejection. We see it plainly on the faces of the unhoused population.

While we can't solve the homeless crisis in America, we can ask the Lord Jesus Christ to help us be suitable representatives of His love and compassion. He will always place us in the middle of where He is working, if we ask Him to. He is good, and He is faithful to us in ways that are unique to each of us.

The next time you see someone on the street corner, listen closely to see if the Holy Spirit is prompting you to reach out in some way to help one who can do nothing in return. Give a few dollars, a word of encouragement, or say a silent prayer as you pass by. It will make a difference in how you perceive those who are less fortunate than you, and God will be honored.

Prayer: Dear God, so many people need Jesus. We pray that You will help us to be more aware of those we pass every day. Give us generosity and love as we encounter those less fortunate than us. Please help them to know and accept the love of Jesus through the way we treat them. We pray this in Jesus' name. Amen.

Quote Source: UTHOR: SADI, *The Gulistan, or Rose Garden*, trans. Edward B. Eastwick, chapter 3, story 19, p. 129 (1880).

I'VE BEEN CHANGED

Praise the LORD, my soul; all my inmost being, praise his holy name. Praise the LORD, my soul, and forget not all his benefits— who forgives all your sins and heals all your diseases, who redeems your life from the pit and crowns you with love and compassion, who satisfies your desires with good things so that your youth is renewed like the eagle's.

Psalm 103:1-5 (ESV)

Nothing on Earth compares to knowing God in a way that changes you. He stands ready and willing to change each of us through a right relationship with Jesus Christ. He will bring needed peace and stability to every aspect of our lives if we let Him. His ways are good, and they are everlasting.

I will remain forever thankful for how God has changed me and how He continues to do His good work in my life, making me a better representative of His Son, Jesus Christ. I pray that you, too, have been changed in this way. Always remember that Jesus knows where you are in life. He knows your burdens, your struggles, and your heartaches. He will never turn a blind eye or a deaf ear to all who seek Him. He is so faithful! His peace is the calm we can have as we walk through this chaotic world. To me, that's the Good News of the day!

Prayer: Dear Heavenly Father, thank you for changing us through Your wonder-working power! Thank You so much for walking with us and for catching us when we stumble or try to do things on our own merit or strength. We confess today that without You, we fail miserably. Thank You for loving us so much that You stand ready to continue helping us grow into good representatives of our Lord and Savior, Jesus Christ. We pray this in His name and for His sake. Amen.

MEASLES, MEMORIES, AND JESUS

Come to Me, all who are weary and burdened,
and I will give you rest.
Matthew 11:28 (NIV)

When I was around 7-8 years old, I became ill with measles. As I lay in bed, feeling miserable with a high fever, my mother would often come into my room, put a wet cloth on my forehead, and turn my pillow to the cooler underside. Since my fever heated the pillow rather quickly, it would only be a short time before Mother returned, continuously repeating this act of love as she tried to comfort her sick child.

Just as my mother loved and nurtured her children, Jesus wants to do the same for all who seek Him. His love and help are always available to us, regardless of our life stage. Wherever we are and whatever our situation, we are never too far from His reach. It is amazing how having a personal relationship with Jesus can soothe our spirits, calm our fears, and help us navigate the difficult times in life.

If you are struggling today, why not let Jesus turn the *pillow* of your life over to the other side, where you will feel the cool, refreshing stream of His Living Water. Let Him feed you from His Word and give you nourishment that points you away from the things of this world that will soon fade away. Let Him give you a life of deep-down peace and satisfaction. He never changes, and you can be assured that He cares about every aspect, large and small, of your life. Why not trust Him today?

Prayer: Dear Heavenly Father, thank You for Jesus, our Lord and Savior. We pray that You will help us turn every part of our lives over to the Lordship of Jesus Christ, trusting that His plan for our lives is perfect. We pray this in His name. Amen.

GOD WILL MAKE A WAY

But the people of Israel walked on dry ground through the sea, the waters being a wall to them on their right and on their left. Thus, the LORD saved the Israelites that day from the hand of the Egyptians, and Israel saw the Egyptians dead on the seashore.

Exodus 14:29-30 (ESV)

Just imagine well over 600 chariots coming full speed after you! What a sight that must have been for Moses and the Israelites! Exodus, Chapter 14, explains this scene as Pharaoh and his army were in hot pursuit of them. But as He always does, God had a plan. He instructed Moses to stretch forth his staff and, as he did, the waters of the Red Sea began to part, allowing the Israelites to cross over on dry land to the other side. In hot pursuit, Pharaoh's army drowned as the waters returned to normal when they were crossing over behind the Israelites. God had once again come through, done what He had promised, and rescued His people. His timing was perfect!

I couldn't help but think of the many times God rescues His children at just the right moment. He turns our sorrows into joy, resentment and bitterness into forgiveness, weakness into strength, anxiety into peace, and our stress into rest. He helps us to let go of and trust Him with those things we sometimes want to hold on to, mistakenly thinking that we have the answers. He brings us to a land of safety where He cares for us as we remain in relationship with Him. He gives us clear direction to walk on the best path forward.

If you currently find yourself standing on the shores of your own Red Sea, and you don't know what to do or how to get to the other side, please remember that God will make a way when there seems to be no way. He will part the waters, and you will triumphantly walk across on dry land to the other side, where He waits to daily guide you on this journey called life. You are never alone! The One who parts the waters is forever with you.

Prayer: Father God, in this imperfect life, there is one thing we can count on—You will part the waters of our Red Sea as many times as it takes to get us safely Home. Thank You for the peace that comes in knowing this world is not our final resting place. Help us to make the most of our day as we share the joy and peace only You can bring through Christ, our Lord and Savior. In His name we pray. Amen.

HE IS OUR REFUGE

The LORD is good, a refuge in times of trouble.
He cares for those who trust in him.

Nahum 1:7 (NIV)

Several years ago, my husband and I took a week-long cruise to the Southern Caribbean. It had been a year since our daughter Shelly had gone to Heaven, and we were still reeling from the trauma of her illness and death. Both of us were desperate for physical, emotional, and spiritual refreshment, and we needed to find the peace and refreshment that only Jesus could give.

One of the Ports of Call we visited was the Island of Aruba. While on a tour of the island, we observed a stark contrast in the shoreline between the two sides of the island. One side had a smooth and pristine beach with the whitest sand I had ever seen. The other side was rugged with angry waves crashing upon the rocky shore. Both were beautiful in a different way and reminded me of the various seasons we go through in life.

All of us love those seasons of life when the sailing is smooth and we are enjoying rest. It's the other ones we dread—the unexpected storm that hits us, and we wonder if we will survive. We recognize that God allows these challenging seasons to strengthen our faith, enabling us to rely on Jesus more deeply. As a result, when trials, heartaches, and sorrows arise, we are assured that He will be our refuge and guide. In fact, He has already prepared the way for us to make it through. In His timing, He will take us back to the smooth side of the island safely through the rough seas.

Whatever season of life you may be experiencing, be reminded that God wants to be your help and comfort through every challenge you face. He knows exactly where you are and what you need at this very moment. In His timing, He will always bring you through whatever tumultuous circumstances you face.

Prayer: Dear God, thank You for being the Master of the wind and waves. We cannot navigate the twists and turns of life without Your help. Thank You, Father, for being our protector and the spiritual compass that we need. Please keep us close as we trust You to guide us through life's troubles. May we trust and believe that our storms won't last forever; that we won't always cry out in sorrow; and that for every tempest we face, You have a good plan. We pray this in Jesus' name. Amen.

A PRICELESS GIFT

Every good and perfect gift is from above,
coming down from the Father of the heavenly lights,
who does not change like shifting shadows.
James 1:17 (NIV)

Many years ago, a man and his wife walked into my 5th-grade classroom in a small East Texas town and presented each student with a Gideon New Testament, along with Psalms and Proverbs, much like the ones distributed by Gideon and Auxiliary members today. What I remember most about that day was the kindness of the man and his wife to the students. **John, Chapter 13, verse 35 (ESV)** says the following: **"By this all people will know that you are my disciples, if you have love for one another."** I now know it was Christ's love that this man and his wife were exhibiting that day. How special that someone cared enough to share God's Word with me—a little country girl who, a year later, gave her heart to Jesus Christ for all eternity and who, many years later, serves alongside her husband, sharing God's Word through The Gideons International, just like this man and his wife did so many years ago.

Friends, we should never underestimate the power of God's Word when the Holy Spirit is leading us to share our faith with others. One Bible and one visit to a classroom continue to make a lasting impact on a little girl's heart many years later. I am grateful to still have that worn-out New Testament, and I am living proof of the truth found in Isaiah 55:11—that God's Word **will not** return to Him empty.

Prayer: Dear Lord, thank You for using this man and his wife to make a difference in my life so many years ago. Help each of us to listen for the still, small voice of the Holy Spirit as we strive to live for You in complete obedience. Thank You for giving us opportunities to share the hope of Jesus with others. To You be all glory, honor, and praise. In Jesus' name, we pray. Amen.

THE WIDOW'S MITE

Jesus looked up and saw the rich putting their gifts into the offering box, and he saw a poor widow put in two small copper coins. And he said, "Truly, I tell you, this poor widow has put in more than all of them. For they all contributed out of their abundance, but she, out of her poverty, put in all she had to live on."

Luke 21:1-4 (ESV)

Jesus was sitting in the temple when He observed the rich folks putting their large sums of money into the treasury. Perhaps some of them did so with pride and arrogance, happy for everyone to see how much they contributed. At the same time, Jesus saw a poor widow dropping two small coins into the offering box. In my mind, I see this poor woman doing her best to be invisible, hoping to move through the temple inconspicuously, not wanting others to notice her meager offering. Yet, Jesus considered the widow's gift extravagant compared to those who had given much more, because she had given sacrificially out of her poverty, and the others had given out of their abundance.

Scripture does not tell us more about the woman, but I do not doubt that she was richly blessed because of her faithfulness. Jesus looked at the woman's heart and saw that her motive and faith were pure. The value of the gift was based on what it cost her, and she gave all that she had.

Our motive for giving lies within our hearts. God will take care of those who are committed to giving Him all that we are, and that includes our resources. We give for the cause of Christ so that others will come to know Him as Savior and Lord. Whether little or much, it is rewarding to send as much as we can on ahead, bearing in mind the eternal implications for the work of God's Kingdom here on Earth.

Prayer: Dear God, I have seen You work in ways that could only have come from Your benevolent hand! Thank You for teaching us to be faithful in all things, including our financial resources. Bless those who struggle to put food on the table and provide for them according to their needs. Please help us be sensitive to the needs of others and serve as a lifeline to those in need. We pray this in the name of Jesus Christ, our Savior and Lord. Amen.

TEARS

Record my misery; list my tears on your scroll--
are they not in your record?

Psalm 56:8 (NIV)

It was just one of those days. While in conversation with a family member, I broke down, sobbing from the weight of my grief and the uncertainty of what lay ahead. In those moments I was stripped of all pretense, and my heavy heart was laid bare. Finally composing myself, I apologized, thinking I was the elder and should be showing strength instead of what I considered to be weakness. It was then that I heard the most precious words spoken to me in a long time: *"Your tears are always welcome in my home!"* How blessed we are to have a family member or friend who welcomes our brokenness into their heart and home!

As promised in His Word, one day God will wipe away every tear from our eyes. There will be no more sorrow or pain in Heaven. Until then, His Word also tells us that He records our tears on His scroll. Some Bible translations also say that He collects our tears in His bottle. What a great mental picture I have of that! Even for just myself, He must have a very large bottle! To know that we have such a personal Heavenly Father astounds and humbles me. How wonderful it is that He rejoices with us in the good times and is also attentive to every tear and sorrow we experience.

Prayer: Father God, it comforts us to know that You understand our tears. May we open our hearts to the needs of others and be the listening ear they so desperately seek. In doing so, we will be able to point them to the One who ultimately wants to wipe away every tear from their eyes. We pray this in the name of our Lord and Savior, Jesus Christ. Amen.

LIVING IN THE PRESENT

He who dwells in the shelter of the Most High will abide in the shadow of the Almighty. I will say to the LORD, "My refuge and my fortress, my God, in whom I trust."

Psalms 91:1-2 (ESV)

"Yesterday is history. Tomorrow is a mystery. Today is a gift. That's why we call it the present." Author Unknown, Quote Investigator believes this quote evolved over time.

Yesterday is indeed history. I wish I had known back then what I know now, but life doesn't work that way. We learn and grow from our experiences and past mistakes. If we allow God to shape and mold us more into the image of Christ, then we will emerge as winners for Him, despite our past poor choices. We are blessed that He is patient with us.

The past can help us see how God was working through good times and hard times, as well as through grief and sorrow. It can also remind us how far we've come on life's journey. I'm thankful for memories of the past, both good and regrettable, for they encourage me to continue allowing God to be in charge of my life as He clears the path ahead for me.

We do not know what tomorrow will bring, but through our faith and trust in the Lord Jesus Christ, we can rest in His promises, knowing there is no need to be fearful or anxious. Tomorrow will take care of itself. We have been given this day and the opportunity to make a difference for the Kingdom of God. Wherever you are, you can serve Him from your corner of the world in ways He has designed specifically for you. He will help you to carry His Good News today and in the future. That's one thing you can count on.

Prayer: Dear Heavenly Father, thank You for being the Potter of our lives—for molding and making us into more of the image of Jesus. Thank You for being patient when we wander in our own direction. Please help us always to prioritize what You want above all else. We pray this in Jesus' name. Amen.

CORRIE TEN BOOM

I can do all things through him who strengthens me.
Philippians 4:13 (ESV)

Now, here's a lady to be admired! Corrie ten Boom! Her story, as told in her book, *The Hiding Place,* and the movie of the same title, has undoubtedly blessed me and strengthened my faith. She was one of the most godly and spiritually rich individuals in Christian history.

Many years ago, my daughter, Shelly, and I were waiting at Denver International Airport for our flight back to Texas. As divine providence would have it, we had the privilege of seeing Corrie ten Boom. She was elderly even back then and was being escorted in a wheelchair down the airport concourse.

There was something indescribably glorious about Corrie's countenance that day. It was an inner beauty that radiated outward--like light surrounding her. I've never experienced anything like that and will always remember what a special moment it was. Of course, I believe it was the light of Jesus. In fact, Shelly and I talked about that very thing after Corrie's entourage had passed out of sight.

I wonder today if our light is shining for Jesus as it was for Corrie ten Boom? Do others see in our countenance something different? While I would never compare myself to Corrie ten Boom in a million years, I do know that God has promised to use us for His Kingdom if we submit ourselves to the Lordship of Jesus Christ. My goal for today and every day is to be more like Him and less like the world. I hope you will join me in that endeavor.

Prayer: Dear God, thank You for strong women of faith such as Corrie ten Boom. She will be remembered as one of the godliest women in history because she loved You deeply and followed Your example of compassion for others. I pray that even now, You are raising more people with the staunch faith, courage, and perseverance of Corrie ten Boom and her family. Raise us, Lord! This we pray in the name of Jesus. Amen.

LET GO, LET GOD

Peace I leave with you; my peace I give to you.
Not as the world gives do I give to you. Let not your hearts
be troubled, neither let them be afraid.

John 14:27 (ESV)

There are times in each of our lives when we experience moments of uncertainty and anxiety. Because we live in an imperfect world with troubles and trials, it is impossible to avoid such times. You may be wondering how we can remain calm and peaceful, even in uncertain times. For me, it is found in the meaning of the phrase, *"Let Go, Let God."*

We can take comfort in knowing that God is aware of every anxious moment we experience in life. By letting go of anxiety and allowing God to shoulder our burdens, we will never have to walk through our circumstances alone. He knows what we need and stands ready to help us. He is as close as the mention of His name, always meets us at the point of our need, sees us when we feel unseen, and brings peace to our chaos. He desires that we trust in Him to be the calm in our storm, a protective shelter of safety, and the strong shoulder we lean on. His care for us will never fail, for His Word assures us that He will never leave us. His presence is our constant companion, a source of comfort in our times of need.

As we invite Jesus into our situation, believing that His miraculous power will help us through, we will realize that each new day is a gift from above. We can then trust that our light and momentary troubles are working out for our good and His glory. He will be forever faithful, a constant in our ever-changing lives, a rock we can always lean on, a beacon of hope in the darkest of times.

Prayer: Dear Heavenly Father, without You, we could do nothing. Without You, we would surely fail. Thank You for being with us through every trial we face in this life. Give us pause to remember that our trials will not last and that it is through these times that our faith and trust in You grow even more. Help us to shine for Jesus with each new day. We pray this in His name. Amen.

THE ABCS OF LIFE

You keep him in perfect peace whose mind is stayed on you,
because he trusts in you. Trust in the Lord forever,
for the Lord God is an everlasting rock.

Isaiah 26:3-4 (ESV)

ZYXWVUTSRQPONMLKJIHGFEDCBA.

Looking at the letters above, you may be thinking that I have one of my precious little ones slapping at the computer keyboard as I write. It would certainly appear that might be the case if you didn't look a bit closer. What you see at the top of the page is a backward alphabet.

When I started school, we didn't have kindergarten classes. All children in my county began their school careers as first-graders. One of the basics we were taught was learning the alphabet. After my classmates and I were successful in this endeavor, our teacher, Miss Pratt, invited the class to go a step beyond the norm and challenged us to learn the alphabet backward if we wanted to. I accepted Miss Pratt's challenge, and only one other girl and I managed to accomplish the feat. For our reward, Miss Pratt gave each of us eleven cents, which was enough to buy a Zero candy bar at the school store. I was so excited!

Those seemingly jumbled letters might sometimes resemble our struggles at various junctures in life. If we are not careful, our minds can be easily distracted from the truly important things. I can think of many examples where we humans can be left with minds that are confused, unsure, and insecure.

For Christians, it is vitally important to maintain an open line of communication with our Heavenly Father because He desires a relationship with us. Even at times when we can't find the words or don't know how to pray, we have the assurance that the Holy Spirit makes intercession for us. He waits for us to come to Him in humility and honesty and goes to the Father on our behalf. Let's choose to focus on the truly important things and keep the communication lines open with our Heavenly Father.

Prayer: Dear Heavenly Father, we praise You for how You love us, even when our minds become jumbled with things that may distract us from living out our faith in a manner that is good and lovely. Please help us to consistently and continuously align with how You want to work in and through our lives. Give us wisdom and lead us where we can make a difference in the lives of others. This we pray in the mighty name of Jesus Christ, our eternal Lord and Savior. Amen.

LOSS

For just as the body is one and has many members, and all the
members of the body, though many, are one body,
so it is with Christ.

1 Corinthians 12:12 (ESV)

All around us there is loss. People are hurting. We've experienced it personally, and we've had family and friends who have suffered unimaginable calamities. We've seen incomprehensible losses in recent years and days, and our hearts have been broken. What do we do when we suffer or see others suffering in this way?

There's so much Good News amidst our losses. What a comfort it is to have the assurance we are never alone; that we can find God's strength to carry on, even flourish, in the midst of the hard things we encounter; and that we can go to the Father on behalf of each other.

I have heard others say that prayer is useless—that we Christians are only using it as a crutch. To them I would say, "If only you could know the peace that God will bring to your heart when you earnestly pray—when you can actually feel the prayers of others on your behalf."

There's a sweet communion that is experienced when we go to the Father in earnest prayer. I am 100% sure that He hears our prayers and that He will answer them according to His will—according to His great plan. Our job is to trust Him. To me there's no more peaceful place to be.

I'm very thankful for the unbreakable bond God provides for us with our Christian family. The communion of the saints is an excellent provision from God, and how blessed we are to support one another through prayer during times of loss and uncertainty.

Prayer: Heavenly Father, we find comfort in knowing that You are always with us. In times of loss I pray that we would seek You above all else, for it is in Your care that we will find the strength to go forward. You are our hope. You are our confidence. Be with those who mourn today. Strengthen them for their respective journey ahead. We pray that Your mighty hand will cover us as we begin this day. In Jesus' name we pray. Amen.

CHECK YOUR BAGGAGE

Come to me, all who labor and are heavy laden,
and I will give you rest.
Matthew 11:28 (ESV)

Several years ago, my husband and I flew to Miami, Florida, to board a cruise ship bound for the Southern Caribbean. Since I contingency plan and carry extra clothes in case I need them, I have always been guilty of overpacking for trips. This one was no exception.

During the cruise, I bought small gifts for the grandkids and included several large, heavy conch shells that I found on the beach in Turks & Caicos. By the time our week was over, I had collected quite a bit more than I had initially planned on taking home.

When the cruise ended, we returned to the Miami airport only to find that our luggage exceeded the acceptable weight limit. Not wanting to pay the extra fee, we began to unpack and dispose of those things we considered non-essential. As we repacked, I made sure we had all the gifts for the grand-children, including a few conch shells. Finally, after about 20 minutes of feverishly working to correct the issue, we had the weight back to 50 pounds, and the threat of an additional fee was averted.

There is another type of baggage we humans are prone to carry on our shoulders and in our hearts. Heavy bags of guilt, shame, anger, resentment, unfor-giveness, hurt, grief, disappointment, jealousy, and negativity weigh us down so much that we can barely move. But the things that hinder our relationship with God and others have no place remaining with us. In letting go, we will experience the freedom of never being encumbered by the heaviness of our emotional baggage. Checking it permanently in at the foot of the Cross will bring unimaginable peace.

I pray that all who read this have only the essential amount of luggage needed to make your trip through life more enjoyable. May you never be constrained by the heaviness of holding on to that which won't be of any benefit to you on life's journey.

Prayer: Dear Heavenly Father, through Your unfailing love, we marvel at how You stand ready to rid us of the heavy loads we sometimes carry. Father, help us to leave all things that so easily beset us at the foot of the Cross. Give us the strength never to take them up again, knowing that You sent Jesus for this very reason—that we might be free from anything that hinders our walk with You. We pray these things in the name of our Lord and Savior, Jesus Christ. Amen.

ALWAYS WITH US

And behold, I am always with you, to the end of the age.

Matthew 28:20b (ESV)

Are you facing a storm today? Jesus is with you! Are you discouraged? Jesus is with you! Have the cares of life weighed you down? Jesus is with you! In fact, Jesus will always be with you, but you have to ask Him to come along. That's all it takes. Just ask Him. Jesus came into the world for you and me. As we trust Him and believe that He is who He says He is, our spiritual eyes will be opened like parting clouds, revealing the sunlight after a storm.

As each new day comes, I am very thankful for God's promises. There's something incredibly comforting in knowing that He is always with us. Throughout Scripture, He has reassured us that He will neither leave us nor forsake us. How great it is to live within the framework of His many promises! They are incredibly comforting, bringing peace and contentment to each new day.

Prayer: Dear God, there is none like You! How thankful we are that You are always with us as we seek to trust You with every aspect of our lives. You always have our best interests at heart. Thank You for leading and guiding us for our good and Your glory. Help us to honor You in everything we say and do, all the days of our lives. We pray this in Jesus' name. Amen.

LIVING HOPE

Why, my soul, are you downcast? Why so disturbed within me? Put your hope in God, for I will yet praise him, my Savior and my God.
Psalm 42:11 (NIV)

"Our hope is not hung upon such an untwisted thread as, 'I imagine so,' or 'It is likely,'…our salvation is fastened with God's own hand, and with Christ's own strength, to the strong stake of God's unchangeable nature.'" Samuel Rutherford

More than ever before, people need hope. All of us seek a refuge—a place of protection and shelter from the storms of life. Our storms may look different and vary, but the need is there. When we look around, we see a chaotic world, and when we look within, we see anxiety. But as we look up, we will see our living hope—peace found only in the person of our Lord and Savior, Jesus Christ.

Jesus came to Earth to teach us what it would take to have eternal life. He took our sins upon Himself and died on the Cross so we wouldn't have to. After three days in the grave, He arose just as He said He would. He ascended to Heaven and is with the Father. One glad day, He is coming back for us. What a day that will be! How thankful we can be today that He is our living hope.

Prayer: Dear Heavenly Father, thank You for the hope we have in Jesus Christ, our Lord and Savior. Please help us live out Your Word in our daily lives so that others will also come to a saving knowledge of Him. We pray this in Jesus' name. Amen.

Source: Rutherford, Samuel (1600-1661), *Christian Quotes of the Day*, January 3, 2025.

LESSONS FROM THE PENCILS

As far as the east is from the west, so far does he remove our transgressions from us. As a father shows compassion to his children, so the LORD shows compassion to those who fear him. For he knows our frame; he remembers that we are dust.

Psalm 103:12-14 (ESV)

Have you ever dwelled on mistakes made in various areas of your life? Are there things that you consider failures on your part that still tug at your heartstrings?

I recently saw a little meme of two pencils that were standing side by side. The guy pencil was shorter than the girl pencil and confessed that he had made many mistakes in his life. That's a clever conversation, considering they are pencils. Of course, a pencil is just an object, but I detected a spiritual life lesson here.

As I looked at the picture and read the caption, I was reminded that our mistakes in life do not have to follow us around forever. I thought about how pencils have small erasers, but our Heavenly Father has a big one called **FORGIVENESS**. When we come to Him with repentant hearts, He will do to our transgressions as the Scripture above says. He will instantaneously remove them as far as the east is from the west and erase our sins from His mind. As a result, we are free, never having to carry around our heavy baggage of disappointment, guilt, or pain. It has been left at the foot of the Cross, and we'd be wise never to resurrect it again.

We serve a benevolent Father who loves His children greatly. He knows us better than we know ourselves and is always there to forgive us and guide us on the right path. Today, I am very thankful for such goodness.

Prayer: Dear Heavenly Father, like the pencil, we have made many mistakes in this life. We thank You for the forgiveness that is so freely given when we repent and turn from those things that are not pleasing to You. We ask that You would lay this verse of Scripture on our hearts regularly: **"Create in me a clean heart, O God, and renew a right spirit within me" (Psalm 51:10).** May we always seek to follow Jesus in all we do, sharing His Good News with those who need salvation or encouragement. We pray this in Jesus' name. Amen.

24 HOURS

He has made everything beautiful in its time. He has also set eternity in the human heart; yet no one can fathom what God has done from beginning to end.

Ecclesiastes 3:11 (NIV)

Some time ago, my granddaughter Sophie and I were enjoying breakfast together. Out of the blue, Sophie asked me the following question: *"What if, when we were born, we grew fast and only lived for 24 hours? Wouldn't that be weird? What would you do with those 24 hours, Grandma?"* Hmmm! What a profound question from this young girl. In turn, I asked her the same question. She said that was a pretty tough question to answer so quickly, but she did tell me that I'd probably be listening to music on my headphones while perched among all the birds on the electrical lines along Interstate 35. No doubt that thought came to her because we've frequently chatted about how perfectly aligned and spaced the birds sit, and we often teased that they're watching all the traffic go by without a care in the world. I remember telling Sophie that it would be fascinating to be able to join the birds just once.

Our conversation, while interesting and amusing, did cause me to think a little more deeply about what I'd do if I were given only 24 hours to live. None of us is promised our next breath, so we could all pause to reflect on that same question. Would we waste those precious 24 hours by sitting and watching the traffic go by, or would we use that time for a purpose greater than ourselves?

Our Heavenly Father is the creator not only of the world in which we live, but He is also the creator of time. Our time is in His hands. But it's ours to do with as we please. So when you feel rushed and hurried, take a moment to be still and focus on the peace God wants to give you. Offer a prayer of thanks for your many blessings. Listen to your favorite Christian music and take a deep breath of thankfulness for this intimate relationship you have with the God of the universe. Yes, He is big and powerful, but He is small enough to live within your heart. What a beautiful thing it is to know that we have all we need through Him. Even time.

Prayer: Dear God, thank you for creating the world and for being the manager of our time. You are not bound by anything, much less time. Instead, it was designed for us. Help us not to waste a moment but to be still and experience Your sweet peace. We pray these things, giving You all honor and glory. In Jesus' name. Amen.

MORE THAN AN
IMAGINARY FRIEND

I no longer call you servants, because a servant does not know his
master's business. Instead, I have called you friends, for everything
that I learned from my Father I have made known to you.
John 15:15 (NIV)

Have you ever considered how those who do not know Jesus see Christians? Do they believe that our faith is unfounded and that Jesus is just an imaginary friend? I think many unsaved people do tend to see Jesus as someone who is not real, but rather a crutch we Christians hold onto because we are weak. Acquaintances and family members alike may feel that our beliefs and practices are a waste of their time. How far from the truth they are! My heart mourns for them to know the incredible power of Jesus and His love.

I am thankful that Jesus Christ, our Lord and Savior, is not just an imaginary friend. We have felt His presence in our lives time and again, and we have seen Him answer prayers and work in ways that could only have come from Him. He promises to be with us until the end of the age, and then we are assured of a home in Heaven with Him for all eternity. He is the One we need to walk with us through the trials and tribulations we will face, because He promised He would never forsake us. His presence brings comfort and reassurance, making us feel secure and at peace. Our relationship with Jesus will never fail to bring us joy and fulfillment, uplifting our spirits and filling our hearts with contentment. No imaginary friend could ever do that for us.

Prayer: Dear Heavenly Father, thank You for giving us this Savior and friend. Help us to demonstrate by the life we lead that Jesus is not just an imaginary friend but that He is real and ready to bring joy and peace to all who will claim Him as Lord and Savior. I pray for all those who do not yet know Him—that they will be convicted and convinced that their life can best be spent as a child of the King of Kings and Lord of Lords, Jesus Christ. We pray this in His name. Amen.

THE GREATEST SACRIFICE

For God so loved the world, that he gave his only Son, that whoever believes in him should not perish but have eternal life.

John 3:16 (ESV)

You may have heard the phrase, "Winner, winner, chicken dinner!" It's often used to celebrate victory.

Speaking of chicken, I didn't know until I was an adult that my mother's favorite piece WASN'T the neck. I was touched to find out that she had only pretended to like the skinnier portion of this fowl. Chicken necks have virtually no meat on them, but our mother always ensured that her seven children were well-fed. What a sacrifice!

As my mother did for her children, many of us have sacrificed for others in various ways. Those sacrifices may not involve a piece of chicken, but we often try to make life a little easier for our friends and loved ones. Still, there's no comparison between our sacrifice for others and the greatest sacrifice known to man. God showed His deep love for us by sending His only Son to die on the Cross for our sins. Jesus willingly suffered and gave His life for everyone. Friends, that means you and me and all who were created or will ever be created. I certainly don't deserve that kind of sacrificial love. In fact, no one does. But John 3:16 clearly explains God's great love for humanity. The Good News is that Jesus, the innocent sacrifice, was victorious over death and the grave! His sacrifice has never been in vain. He is our ticket to Heaven. He is our eternal Hope.

While we wait for that moment when we'll see Jesus face to face, we can be comforted that we will never walk this journey alone. He is always with us. To this, we can rest in victory and say, "Winner, Winner, Christ died for sinners!"

Prayer: Dear Father, it is hard to comprehend the sacrifice that Jesus made for us. We are not worthy, but in great love You made a way for us to be in relationship with You eternally. Thank You for salvation through Jesus Christ. How comforting to know that He is only a whisper away. Help us to seek Him in all we do. We pray this in His name. Amen.

THE DASH MATTERS

Do you not know that in a race all the runners run, but only one receives the prize? So run that you may obtain it.

I Corinthians 9:24 (ESV)

You've probably heard the expression that it's the dash in our lives that matters the most. This is so true. Life has a beginning date and an ending date, and it's the experiences during our lifetime that shape our character, strength, patience, and, most of all, our faith.

Between our birth and death we experience times of joy, happiness, spiritual growth, spiritual struggles, tears of joy and sorrow, failure, and sometimes the fear of what lies ahead. During different seasons, the middle serves as a wilderness in our lives—a jungle of sorts. The Good News about being in the wilderness is that we grow there. God doesn't promise life to be a rose garden, but He does promise it will be worth it in the end. How thankful we Christians can be for that truth!

If we aim to finish strong, we must navigate the middle. We must find our freedom in Christ and live it to the fullest! My friends, let us continue to run our race with endurance, perseverance, and the knowledge that we do not run alone! We have each other, but more importantly, we have our Savior, Jesus Christ, who never leaves us! He strengthens us to keep the faith as we navigate each season of our lives.

Prayer: Dear Heavenly Father, You are God alone. We are thankful that You are the same yesterday, today, and forever. We are living in the middle of our lives—the dash. Father God, forgive us when we do not make the most of every day. Forgive us when we let life's burdens get the best of us. Help us to remember that it is by Your wonder-working power that we can get through each day. You bring us life, hope, and direction. And for that, we give You honor and praise and glory forevermore. We pray this in the name of Jesus Christ, our Savior and Lord. Amen.

LOVE NEVER FAILS

Love bears all things, believes all things, hopes all things,
endures all things. Love never ends.

1 Corinthians 13:7 (ESV)

A little over twenty years ago, my husband and I were in the middle of constructing our current home. Without fail, we visited the site daily to monitor the progress being made. One day, our daughter Shelly and her three children were with us at the house, and our grandchildren, Heather, Justin, and Jacob, asked permission to sign and date a corner post located in the hallway. Several days later, another grandchild, Felicia, also signed and dated the same post. As the house was completed, the walls covered that special place, but I'll always be reminded of the signatures and message of love behind the wall.

A few years after we had moved into the house, a dear friend gave us a beautiful cross based on **1 Corinthians 13:7** as shown above. Right away, I knew the perfect place on the wall to hang the cross was at the exact spot where our grandchildren had signed the post. That day, I prayed that these grandchildren's hearts, just like their signature, would always be hidden behind the Cross of Christ and that they would come to know Him in a real way.

Sometimes, whether we intend it or not, we can hide our love and kindness to others behind the walls of our hearts. It is easier and more comfortable to settle into the safety of our own lives because we don't want to get involved in sticky situations with others. However, I know that everyone we meet is fighting some battle, whether it be physical, emotional, spiritual, or a combination of all three. A smile, a hug, a kind word, or any act of kindness on our part can make a big difference. Their sorrow could become joy, their despair could become hope, and their fear could be replaced by faith.

May we always remember that we can share God's everlasting love with those we encounter, so let's not keep it to ourselves, hidden behind the walls of our hearts.

Prayer: Dear Heavenly Father, we thank You for loving humankind so much that You sent Jesus to die on the Cross for our sins. We cannot comprehend such love, but we receive it with humility. Help us to love others as we seek to shine Your light on those we encounter in our daily lives. We pray this in Jesus' name. Amen.

HE CARES

Therefore, I tell you, do not be anxious about your life, what you will eat or what you will drink, nor about your body, what you will put on. Is not life more than food, and the body more than clothing? Look at the birds of the air; they neither sow nor reap nor gather into barns, and yet your Heavenly Father feeds them. Are you not of more value than they?

Matthew 6:25-26 (ESV)

I believe that God cares not only about the big things in our lives, but also about the small things that concern us, because I've experienced His work repeatedly in my own life.

When we were on lockdown due to the pandemic, I saw God's provision and love firsthand as the recipient of kindness and generosity from perfect strangers. It was not a dire need or even a genuine concern, but one day my husband, Ray, mentioned that he wished we had cilantro for a recipe he wanted to make. Being the sweet wife that I am (hmmm) and trying to keep him out of the grocery store, I told him it would just have to wait. Later that day, a lady created a post on our Facebook neighborhood site offering free cilantro and other organic herbs from her backyard garden. I quickly responded, as did several other people. Much to my surprise, a woman who had also asked for some cilantro told the one offering it to give it to me! I was appreciative and able to pick it up from the generous gardener's porch the next morning. Although I asked both ladies if there was anything they needed that I could take to them, they declined.

Friends, the Lord does indeed provide for our needs and sometimes our wants. On that particular day, He cared enough to send Ray some cilantro from an unexpected source. The Mexican dish he made, using our gifted cilantro, was delicious! Most importantly, we recognized that God's timing is amazing!

Prayer: Dear Heavenly Father, You are the giver of all good things! You cared enough to provide a simple herb so my husband could make a familiar dish that would give him enjoyment and comfort. I praise You and thank You for being lovingly involved in the small things of our lives. It shows how much You care about every detail. Most of all, thank You for giving us Jesus Christ as the way to gain eternal life. We pray these things in Jesus' name. Amen.

LIVING BY FAITH

For I am not ashamed of the gospel, because it is the power of God that brings salvation to everyone who believes: first to the Jew, then to the Gentile. For in the gospel the righteousness of God is revealed—a righteousness that is by faith from first to last, just as it is written: "The righteous will live by faith."

Romans 1:16-17 (NIV)

Today we live by faith. If we trust and believe in Jesus Christ, have a personal relationship with Him, and seek Him through His Word with all our heart, God reveals a faith in us that leads us to greater faith in Him. **Romans 10:17 (ESV) says, "So faith comes from hearing, and hearing through the Word of God."** For Christians, true faith means that we believe and are convinced that Jesus Christ is who He claimed to be, that He was crucified for our sins, buried, rose on the third day, and ascended to Heaven, where He sits at the Father's right hand. Our faith also assures us that He will return again someday.

It's incredible how we are spiritually strengthened when we hunger after God's Word! Coming before Him with our minds clean and ready to receive His Word into our hearts is an act of faith. The Bible comes alive when we ask God to reveal it to us. In faith, we believe that God's Word holds promise and power, that He will always act on our behalf, and that His will for our lives works out for our good and His glory. It takes a strong person to allow such faith to be exercised in their life. That kind of faith brings a **"(…) peace of God that surpasses all understanding (…)" Philippians 4:7 (ESV).**

As we continue to believe in God each day, through our faith experiences we can move with joy and certainty from faith to more faith—the powerful stepping stones on our walk with the Lord.

Prayer: Father God, thank You for giving us wisdom, strength, and the faith to live according to Your Word. There is nothing to compare, and we always strive to be found serving You in our daily lives. Thank You for Jesus Christ, our Lord and Savior. We ask these things in His name. Amen.

HOW OTHERS SEE US

God demonstrates His own love for us in this:
while we were sinners, Christ died for us.

Romans 5:8 (NIV)

If you are a Christian, how do you think others see your walk with the Lord? Unfortunately many people today say they cannot tell a born-again Christian from a nonbeliever, because there is no difference in the way we live. The only *religious* thing they may notice in some of us is that we attend church on Sunday.

We should take the matter of obedience to God's standards quite seriously. God's purpose for us is to be passionate and radiant in our faith and to reach out in love to our neighbors, community, and the world. Because of what Christ did for us on the Cross, God wants to give us a burning desire to walk with Him actively and urgently.

As Christians, faithfully pleasing God is not just a set of beliefs but also our way of life so that others **will** see a difference in us. To convince a hardened and cynical world that we are better off as a result of our relationship with Jesus Christ, tell others how your faith has sustained you during challenging times. Let them know that He wants to give them peace in the midst of their difficulties, and that He is eagerly waiting for them to call upon Him. Be an encourager, because many people need to hear uplifting words that are spoken in love. As Christians, you and I are called to be the ones to speak about this kind of love to those in need of a Savior.

As we live out our faith in obedience to Jesus Christ on a daily basis, we will then begin to experience many positive changes in our hearts. God will give us the ability to show kindness and love to others in such a way that they will not see us but the radiance of Christ living in us. The most effective way to create interest in Christ and the Christian way of life is to live and enjoy it so thoroughly that others will want to know how they, too, can experience it.

Prayer: Dear Heavenly Father, we are so blessed by Your never-ending love. Help us to share that love with those around us so they will embrace Christianity without doubt or suspicion. Our greatest desire is to exhibit the light of Jesus everywhere we go and in everything we do. Help us to make a difference in our sphere of influence, we pray. We ask these things in Jesus' name. Amen.

LIFE IS NOT PERFECT, BUT GOD IS

*Trust in the LORD with all your heart and lean not
on your own understanding; in all your ways submit to him,
and he will make your paths straight.*

Proverbs 3:5-6 (NIV)

Too often Christians expect life to be perfect after they are saved. It does not happen that way. Although God wants us to have a good life, there are times when we will endure hardships that cannot be avoided. These challenges will test our spiritual character. The Good News is that through trial and testing, our faith in Jesus Christ helps us maneuver past hard times. As a bonus we will grow spiritually because of our challenges, if we allow the Holy Spirit to do His good work in us. Our job in all of this is to follow Him and, in the strength of the Lord, to be obedient. When we accept life's troubles and trials from a spiritual perspective, He will continue to shape and mold us into beautiful vessels for His good purposes.

Today Jesus is still chipping away, constantly transforming us into more of His likeness. It takes time and patience for the Potter to smooth away our flaws, but we can be hopeful and thankful for the good work He is doing in us. When we surrender our lives to God, we understand He always knows what is best for us.

Prayer: Father God, You are the Potter and we are the clay. Please do Your good work in us today, as we trust You to see us through life's ups and downs. We love You with all of our hearts. In Jesus' name we pray. Amen.

ALWAYS IN HIS SIGHT

For the eyes of the LORD run to and fro throughout the whole earth, to give strong support to those whose heart is blameless toward Him.

2 Chronicles 16:9 (ESV)

When I was a child, a young girl was lost in the woods near my home. Her parents were frantic and prayed that God would keep her in His sight until they could find her. A large search party of friends and neighbors was launched, and all were praying that they would find the girl before dark. Thankfully, she was located before nightfall and returned to the safety of her home.

We may never have been lost in the woods, but isn't it comforting to know that we have neither been out of God's sight nor have we ever taken one step that He didn't know about? Even though we may have felt lost and alone at times, He was right there all along and knew exactly where we were and what we were going through.

It seems like there are seasons or chapters in our lives that are off track from where we imagine our faith walk to be. We wonder if these times are really a part of God's plan. From my own experiences, I have found that God will use every situation we face for our good and His glory. Had I been able to skip one step of those trying times, I would have missed out on developing a deeper reliance on His help and guidance in the future.

We have never been out of God's sight, and we've never escaped from His love and care. There has never been a moment when He has said, *"That's it! No more! I'm done with you!"* He will never grow tired of teaching us His ways. He will always pursue us and give us strength and encouragement to keep going forward. That's because we are always in His sight.

Prayer: Dear Heavenly Father, You are the One we seek today. Thank You for such love that Your sight is always fixed on us. Please help us remember that very thing when we face hard times. Give us pause to remember that there is no problem too complex for You. Give us faith to know we are never alone in our fears, anxieties, and uncertainties of what lies ahead. We ask that You renew our faith and trust in You today, and that above all else, we may live in such a way that others will see Jesus living in us. We pray this in His mighty name and for His sake. Amen.

ENDURANCE

Brothers, I do not consider that I have made it my own. But one thing I do: forgetting what lies behind and straining forward to what lies ahead, I press on toward the goal for the prize of the upward call of God in Christ Jesus.

Philippians 3:13-14 (ESV)

Sometimes life gets tough, and we grow weary. Consequently, our physical and spiritual endurance often suffers. Maybe this has happened at some point in your walk with the Lord, because we are all still under construction, spiritually speaking. God continues to teach us and bring us along, and I am so thankful for that!

My prayer is that we would continue to run our race with endurance, leaving a legacy of faith for all who come behind us. May others find us faithful in showing them the lighted path to His never-ending love. May we continue to share His Word at home and around the world with those who don't yet know Him.

Finally, may we also be reminded that our Wonderful Counselor, Mighty God, Everlasting Father, and Prince of Peace will never, ever leave us to run our race alone. That's the best part and, from where I sit, awfully Good News!

Prayer: Heavenly Father, how wonderful are Your works! We praise You for being ever-present in our lives, giving us the spiritual endurance to go forward in this ever-changing world. Please help us run our race not only with endurance, but also with humility and compassion, as we strive to bring others along on this journey. We pray this in Jesus' name. Amen.

SINCE JESUS CAME INTO MY HEART

I have been crucified with Christ; and I no longer live, but Christ lives in me. The life I now live in the body, I live by faith in the Son of God, who loved me and gave himself for me.

Galatians 2:20 (NIV)

Many years ago, at the age of twelve, I walked down the aisle of my small country church and asked Jesus Christ to come into my heart. That moment still lives deep within, and I remember it as though it were yesterday. Since that day I have failed my Lord and Savior many times, although never intentionally. I have sought and received His forgiveness, and I am eternally grateful for His mercy and grace which are given so freely to all who seek redemption and restoration.

Because we dwell in a fallen and imperfect world, all of us will fail to give God our very best at times. However, when we live by faith in the One who sacrificed Himself for us, we can rest assured that He will mold and make us into a noticeable difference for others to see!

May we always strive to allow Christ to live in and through us. When we do that, I believe we will conduct ourselves a lot differently. Here are two good questions for each of us to ponder today: *How has my life changed since Jesus came into my heart? What areas of my spiritual life need more of Him and less of me?*

Prayer: Dear Jesus, when we asked You into our hearts, we gave up the rights to ourselves, to our selfishness, and to all that is not pleasing to You. Help us to honor You every day of our lives, because it is only through a personal relationship with You that we can find true joy and peace. Thank You for helping us to be salt and light in a hurting world so that others may also come to know the joy of serving You. We pray this in Your name. Amen.

THE BEGINNING AND END

Then He said to me: "It is done. I am the Alpha and the Omega, the Beginning and the End. To the thirsty I will give water without cost from the spring of the water of life. Those who are victorious will inherit all this, and I will be their God, and they will be my children."

Revelation 21:6-7 (NIV)

God is the Beginning and the End. This means He controls everything and knows every aspect of our lives, from the moment we are created to the moment we return to Him. We have every reason to trust Him, because He is who He says He is and His promises are sure and intrinsically sound.

Since we live in an imperfect and sinful world, pain, sorrow, and suffering will at one time or another affect each of us. We often grow disheartened when we are tired and weary from life's circumstances. Rarely do we understand why bad things happen as they do, but through it all, God's Word assures us that He has a plan. He is always on duty, tending to every small or extensive detail, and He will never fail us or let us down. As Christians, our job is to trust Him completely and to walk in such a way that others will see our dependence on Him. When our eternal hope is placed in the Lord, our perspective is transformed. We begin to look at life differently, knowing that the Alpha and Omega, the Beginning and the End, is always there, giving us strength for today and bright hope for tomorrow. With eternal hope, things change as we are empowered to face life's most significant challenges with courage, trust, and deep faith.

Today and every day, I am grateful for the restorative peace and joy that Jesus brings as we allow Him to continue doing the needed soul work in our lives. His transformative power brings healing, restoration, joy, and eternal hope through the precious blood of Jesus Christ.

Prayer: Dear Heavenly Father, we honor You as Alpha and Omega, Beginning and End, and praise Your Holy name. Thank You for Jesus, the One who paid our sin debt so that we might one day live in Heaven forever and ever. Help us in times of weariness to hold fast to the promises You so freely give throughout Your Word. May we be fervent torch-bearers for Jesus in all we think, say, and do. We pray this in the name of Jesus Christ, our Savior and Lord. Amen.

GOD SO LOVED THE WORLD

Jesus replied: "Love the Lord your God with all your heart and with all your soul and with all your mind. This is the first and greatest commandment. And the second is like it: Love your neighbor as yourself."

Matthew 22:37-39 (NIV)

Did you know that as Christians, we are no longer our own but are set apart and called to proclaim God's praises?

We are exhorted to love God and people, whether or not they look or think like us. No matter our differences or how others may treat us, we are called to love unconditionally. Many people might mistake this for a weakness on our part, but this is far from the truth. This is our strength!

Through God's love, mercy, and grace, we are set free to love others and share the difference that knowing Him has made in our lives. The incredible thing is that God loves all of His creation equally. His unconditional love is never dependent upon a person's current relationship status with Him. God is good, and His love endures forever.

PRAYER: Father God, thank You for loving us unconditionally and help us to love others in the same way. We need Your strength and help to do this, but we know that Your love, grace, and mercy extend beyond our abilities. We ask You to do Your work in us as only You can. Help those who feel that You have abandoned them to look into Your Word and rest on the promises found therein. We pray these things in the name of Jesus Christ, our Savior and Lord. Amen.

PASSION TO SHARE

But you will receive power when the Holy Spirit has come upon you, and you will be my witnesses in Jerusalem and in all Judea and Samaria, and to the end of the earth.

Acts 1:8 (ESV)

I'm not a very good golfer, but I do love the game. Competing with myself rather than others is usually my primary goal. Simply put, I have high expectations of myself and strive to do my best in all aspects of my life, including golf.

Speaking of golf, there was once a preacher who decided to skip church on Sunday for a round or two. On one particular Par 4, he teed off, and a big gust of wind caught the ball. Lo and behold, the ball was carried 450 yards and landed straight on the green, then dropped into the hole. A hole-in-one on a Par 4! Amazing!

As God and an angel watched from above, the angel said, "Why did you let him do that?" To the angel's question, God replied, "Who's he going to tell?"

So what good is a Par 4 hole-in-one if you can't tell anyone? That would be disappointing because we'd naturally want to tell everyone, even strangers, with gusto and great enthusiasm! We would want to shout our good news from the rooftop! To tell and retell would be our standard response to such a fantastic accomplishment.

You know…God wants us to tell others about Jesus with as much enthusiasm as if we'd made that hole-in-one. You may say that you cannot share how a relationship with Jesus has changed your life because you're too shy, don't have the proper religious education, don't know what to say, or have become too nervous to speak about such things. You may even say that your faith is very personal and you don't discuss it with others. Again, think of your response had you made that hole-in-one.

There are many reasons any one of us could give for not sharing our faith in Jesus. But you see, we don't have to do it alone. When Jesus ascended to Heaven after the resurrection, He left the Holy Spirit (third person of the Trinity) to make His home in the hearts of all who accept Him as Savior and

Lord. It is the Holy Spirit, our constant companion, who will lead us to be able to share our faith without reservation. It is He who sets the appointments and gives us the approach needed at just the right time. His timing is always perfect, and all we have to do is have a willing heart and follow His lead. He will do the rest.

Yes, golf is a great outlet for me, but sharing my faith with others is my true passion. I am shy, introverted, sometimes insecure, and not at all qualified, but God continues His work in me. One thing's for sure—He has a willing heart in mine. How about you?

Prayer: Dear Heavenly Father, thank You for equipping and empowering us to share the Good News of Jesus Christ with others. Please continue to guide us and help us to remain humble and teachable as we walk this road of life. Grant us strength and wisdom, and help us to serve You with passion and purpose. This we pray in the name of Jesus. Amen.

OUR ANCHOR IN THE STORMS OF LIFE

I lift up my eyes to the hills. From where does my help come? My help comes from the Lord, who made heaven and earth.

Psalm 121:1-2 (ESV)

God longs for us to have abundant joy and peace in our hearts, even in times of disappointment, pain, or great sadness. When we operate in our own strength, we will grow weary as things come against us suddenly and unexpectedly. Using our faith and trust in Jesus Christ as the catalyst, we must be open and willing to allow the Holy Spirit to work in and through our circumstances.

As we begin to rely on God's unwavering strength and the promises found throughout the Bible, we will be able to navigate our circumstances with the trust and assurance that God is in control. Although our sails may be battered and torn when the storms subside, Jesus, our anchor, will always keep us from sinking.

Prayer: Dear God, thank You for being the anchor that holds us together in the storms of life. You are so good to be there to rescue us when we are sinking. Your love and goodness are what we desire today. We pray this in Jesus' name. Amen.

THE FAMILY OF GOD

But he answered them, "My mother and my brothers are those who hear the Word of God and do it."

Luke 8:21 (ESV)

"In the family of God, there is a bond deep inside that binds us one to the other. It is the glue of authentic love expressing itself in caring for, clinging to, and coming to the aid of each other without strings attached. It is the River of love streaming from the bloodline of our Savior that finds, fetches, and fastens us to one another." Thelma Wells

My husband and I have been members of our church for many years. We are blessed to have a large number of Christian brothers and sisters with whom we have associated, both during the good times and the difficult ones. The prayers lifted for us and our family have made a significant difference in how we have navigated life's most challenging moments.

I pray that you, too, have a cherished spiritual connection with others, for all humans long for fellowship with one another. Because we were created to be in relationship with God and with each other, the body of Christ is a beautiful display of God's love for all humanity. We are imperfect people serving a perfect God, sinners saved by His marvelous grace, and unique individuals of various shapes, sizes, and colors, all created by our loving Heavenly Father. I pray for those who don't yet know how special God's love is and how His children find strength not only in Him, but also in one another.

Prayer: Father God, You are worthy of our praise now and forever more! We love You more than words can express, but You know our hearts. Thank You for giving us strength and comfort through our brothers and sisters in Christ Jesus, who come alongside us to share in our joys and sorrows. Help us to always look for those in the Family of God who need a little extra encouragement, as well as those who do not yet have a relationship with You. May we be salt and light in a dark world. We pray this in Jesus' name. Amen.

Source: Wells, Thelma, *Faith for a Lifetime, Daily Inspirations for Women of Faith, The Family of God,* p. 218, (2005), Published by Countryman, a Division of Thomas Nelson, Inc.

ABIDE IN HIM

*I am the vine; you are the branches. Whoever abides in me
and I in him, he it is that bears much fruit,
for apart from me you can do nothing.*

John 15:5 (ESV)

You know, friends, relationships can sometimes be messy. Since we live in a flawed and imperfect world, it is clear that developing meaningful relationships with others requires considerable effort.

What about our relationship with God? I firmly believe that our deepest desire should be to spend as much time as possible developing and maintaining our connection with our Heavenly Father. Just as hard work is involved in developing earthly relationships, so too does this require effort. On our part, it will take consistency and dedication to our great God.

We live in a fast-paced world with numerous distractions that can pull our focus away from things of God. Occasionally I have been guilty of unintentionally rushing through the time I spend with my Heavenly Father and just going through the motions of prayer and Bible study. I am very repentant of that weakness in my spiritual walk with the Lord Jesus.

I do know that He created us for a relationship through His Son, Jesus Christ. We are to come to the Father through the Son. If we abide in Christ through worship, praise, prayer, and the study of God's Word, we will develop the mutual relationship that He intended for us to have. We will then bear the fruit of knowing and trusting Him without reservation.

Friends, my prayer today is that our greatest desire would be to live out Jesus' words in the above Scripture, John 15:5. Abiding in Christ will always bring eternal implications as we develop such a sweet relationship with Him. The more time we spend with Him, the more time we will want to spend with Him. As we become more aware of His presence in our lives each day, He will then use us, His committed servants, to help Him do the Father's work here on earth. That's a "win-win" situation for us and for Him!

Prayer: Dear Heavenly Father, we come to You realizing that no relationship will ever compare with what we have with You, through Jesus Christ, our Lord and Savior. Thank You for giving us the ability to abide in You as we live out our faith each day. Help us to be consistent in spending time with You, for it is in this way that we will grow in our faith and be able to tell others what Jesus has done for us. We pray this in His name. Amen.

UNWAVERING TRUST

So they pulled their boats up on shore,
left everything, and followed him.

Luke 5:11 (NIV)

It had been a hard night's work for Simon and his fishing companions. They had caught nothing and were undoubtedly very tired and discouraged. Nearby, a great crowd pressed in on Jesus, listening intently as He taught the Word of God. Needing a little space between Himself and His audience, Jesus got into Simon's boat, with the crowd remaining on the shoreline within hearing distance.

When He finished speaking, Jesus told Simon to launch into deep water and cast the nets. Still somewhat hesitant, Simon followed Jesus' instructions and moved the boat into deeper water. Imagine the shock and excitement of these hardworking fishermen as their nets began to break from the sheer number of fish! When it was all said and done, they filled Simon's boat plus one other with an enormous catch of fish.

This scene from Luke, Chapter 5, sets the stage for Jesus to call His first disciples. It took a great deal of courage for Simon and the other disciples to leave the familiarity of their lives to follow Jesus despite not fully comprehending who He was or what His mission on Earth would involve. Their willingness to devote themselves to the work of the Lord continues to serve as a model for us as we dedicate ourselves to His ways.

May we examine our hearts, rooting out anything that keeps us from experiencing the joy of knowing, serving, and trusting Jesus. Through His Word, He will teach us to live in a way that is pleasing to Him, and He will always be with us through every situation we encounter in this life.

Prayer: Dear Heavenly Father, thank You for giving us Your Word to read, study, and meditate on. Please continue to provide us with unwavering faith and trust in Jesus Christ so that we might share His light and love with those around us. Give us divine appointments when we least expect them, for it is through the way You work that we gain more strength and joy in serving You. We pray these things in Jesus' name. Amen.

GRANDPAS CAR

I consider the days of old, the years long ago.
Psalm 77:5 (ESV)

Growing up in the country, I had no access to driver's education classes. Being the sixth child in my family, my dad was already an expert at teaching his children the finer points of learning to drive. Before Daddy could take me out on the road to practice driving in our only vehicle, a standard-shift Chevrolet pickup truck, he taught me the "H" method of how to shift the gears. After I had taken the necessary first steps, we finally got on the road. I remember Daddy telling me that I learned to drive quicker than any of my five siblings before me, and my heart smiles that I have never forgotten his words of affirmation.

A few months after I got my driver's license, Grandpa McDaniel visited us in his brand-new, white 1964 Ford Falcon Ranchero. That day, Grandpa asked my parents to let me drive him to Zwolle, Louisiana, where his wife, Ruthie, was in the hospital. Because Grandpa was 79 years old at the time, my parents didn't hesitate to give me permission to drive him where he needed to go.

The day Grandpa and I set out, with me behind the wheel of his beautiful car, was a thrill I can still feel. I was grateful for my parents' trust as I drove to Louisiana for the two-hour round trip. Our journey was a joy, with the open country roads and the unique pleasure of driving Grandpa's car. The feeling of the steering wheel under my hands, the sound of the engine, and the wind ruffling my hair are memories I will always treasure.

God is so good at giving us memories that allow us to recall key moments with our long-departed loved ones. Since I seldom interacted with my dad on a deep level, remembering his patience with me and his complimenting my driving skills is a blessing. My grandpa was always happy to see my siblings and me when we visited him, but he wasn't involved in our childhood to any great extent. Hard work was usually the order of the day back then, with little time and energy left for individual relationships.

Although these memories have stuck with me for a lifetime, they were not significant events but rather ordinary moments spent with two family members with whom I didn't often experience much quality time. I hope that we will all resolve to create more lasting memories with our family, so that one day, long after we are gone, they will understand how deeply they were loved.

Prayer: Dear Heavenly Father, You are so good at helping us remember extraordinary things from long ago that strengthen our hearts and minds. Thank You for taking us through each season of life and for helping us develop meaningful relationships with our family members and others. Give us Your wisdom as we walk side by side with others, and please support not only each step we take, but also their steps. We pray this in the name of our Lord and Savior, Jesus Christ. Amen.

WALKING BY FAITH

And without faith, it is impossible to please God, because anyone who comes to Him must believe that he exists and that he rewards those who earnestly seek Him.

Hebrews 11:6 (NIV)

I recently read a devotional, *Daily Splashes of Joy: 365 Gems to Sparkle Your Day*, written by Barbara Johnson, a Christian author and speaker. Before her death, Barbara was closely associated with the Women of Faith organization. In the devotional, Barbara related the story of Kim, a blind woman learning to depend on her seeing-eye dog to lead her safely to where she needed to go. As Kim learned to trust and rely on her furry friend, she began to experience a newfound freedom. Her steps were faster, and she could go places she had never been. She developed complete faith in her four-legged companion. Barbara compared Kim's learning to trust her dog to our spiritual journey. Because we walk by faith and not by sight, we must trust God's leading. He will never forsake us, so we are free to venture out in faith and try new things for His glory.

There is no doubt that our walk of faith is an exciting adventure. It is wonderful to see how God works in our lives and know that He is leading us purposefully. However, we sometimes face challenges such as discouragement, fear, or uncertainty regarding His will. During these times, we must walk by faith and not by sight, pray for God's direction, then remain steadfast, sure, and confident that we are always safe and secure in the Shepherd's arms.

Prayer: Dear Heavenly Father, so much of our lives is spent walking by faith. Your Word tells us that You have a good plan for us. Please help us let go of our own tendency to carry life's heavy loads. May we daily look to You for the strength to go forward and walk by faith, not by sight. We pray this in Jesus' name. Amen.

Johnson, Barbara, *Daily Splashes of Joy: 365 Gems to Sparkle Your Day*, First Edition, W Publishing Group, December 1, 2000

LISTENING FOR HIS SONG

Look at the birds of the air; they do not sow or reap or store away in barns, and yet your heavenly Father feeds them.
Are you not much more valuable than they?
Matthew 6:26 (NIV)

As I stepped outside onto the patio, some doves and a couple of birds were singing in grand harmony. Could they be rejoicing over another day they had been given? Sitting there in the stillness of early morning, I gazed upon the flower beds where new flowers and shrubs had been planted after the previous winter's ice, snow, and frigid temperatures destroyed the former vegetation. New grass had been put in to cover the bald spots caused by destructive grub worms. Things were looking up for this backyard retreat of mine.

I knew that if new foliage were to flourish, it would need to be watered regularly, fed the correct plant food, and given a little extra care and attention. That would require action, and silently, I committed to do my best.

I'm thankful for that day's reminder that God has made Himself known in nature, bringing encouragement through the song of a bird. That incident also brought to mind the realization that, as a Christian, I must regularly find my spiritual nourishment from God's Holy Word. I must be careful not to allow the *grub worms* of sin into my life. Those will come in many forms and are sneaky distractions that divert my focus away from where it should be.

Our Heavenly Father will shelter us from anything that would harm our walk with Jesus. May we always be aware of His presence in our lives and remember that He is as close as the mention of His name.

Prayer: Father God, thank You for this beautiful day that gives us pause to remember where our hope and security are found. It's in You, and You alone. Thank You for the beauty that is all around us. Help us to look for Your hand among our surroundings. It is a comfort knowing that You are always by our side. Thank You for the reminders of our need to feed upon Your Holy Word and regularly share the joy You give us. In Jesus' name, we pray. Amen.

OUR CONSTANT COMPANION

If only I knew where to find him; if only I could go to his dwelling.
Job 23:3 (NIV)

Many of us can share stories of how God has intervened in our lives at just the right time. What others might see as coincidence, we see as Divine intervention, for we know that God is with His children continually. He is our constant source of reassurance through life's twists and turns.

How wonderful it is that we can be assured of God's presence with us every step of the way, because His Word tells us that He will never leave us. And… the best part is that He's as close as the mention of His name, meaning that we can call upon Him at any moment and He will be there ready to listen and guide us.

It is comforting to know that this day was made for us, so let's face it with the joy and peace He has placed deep in our hearts as we sense His presence and walk accordingly. If your day is challenging, please remember that Jesus is only a whisper away. He will meet you where you are, and He is the friend who will never leave or forsake you. Trust Him today, for you will never regret it.

Prayer: Dear God, how wonderful it is to know that You are always with us, Your imperfect children. We are thankful for each day that we are given. Help us to always remember that You will never leave nor forsake us. We pray this in Jesus' name. Amen.

HUGS

This is my commandment, that you love one another,
as I have loved you.

John 15:12 (ESV)

"Sometimes in life, we just need a hug… no words, no advice, just a hug to make us feel better." (Facebook post, date unknown)

Recently, I went to the nail salon. To my surprise, one of the nail technicians who used to work at a previous salon I frequented now works at the current one. I hadn't seen Rosie in many months, and we both had big smiles on our faces when we spotted each other. As we greeted one another like old friends, Rosie paused work with her client, stood up, and we exchanged big hugs right there in front of everyone. It was such a sweet moment. Even though Rosie and I don't speak the same language, smiles and hugs are universal. It was easy for our hearts to connect in that manner without a word being spoken. That little encounter made my day. I was thrilled to see Rosie, and I hope she felt valued and loved just as I did through the simple exchange of a hug between the two of us.

Most people love giving and receiving hugs, and experts say that this sign of affection is excellent medicine. Let me encourage you to hug someone today if given the opportunity. Such an action on your part will make a difference not only in that person's life, but in your own.

Prayer: Dear Heavenly Father, You created hugs for us to connect in a way that makes us feel valued and loved. That love comes from You, and we thank You for such a wonderful gift! Please help us not to become so distracted with the busyness of our days that we forget the importance of sharing Your love and light with others. Please give us many opportunities to connect with others more each day. We pray this in Jesus' name. Amen.

SOMEONE WE CAN TRUST

For I know the plans I have for you, declares the LORD, plans for welfare and not for evil, to give you a future and a hope.
Jeremiah 29:11 (ESV)

Years ago, probably in the 1990s, my husband and I enjoyed watching the popular sitcom, *Home Improvement,* on TV. In the show, Tim Taylor, played by comedian Tim Allen, was characterized as a cocky, overambitious, accident-prone know-it-all.

While going down memory lane with this show, I also thought about Tim's neighbor, Wilson W. Wilson, Jr., who was often the go-to guy for solving Tim's many and frequent problems. While the two engaged in conversation, Wilson's eyes and forehead were visible only as he stood on the other side of Tim's backyard fence.

Wouldn't we all like to have a trusted and wise neighbor like Wilson on the other side of the fence who is always prepared to assist us? In reality, that usually isn't the case. But we do have Someone.

Although we have never seen the face of God, He has given us many ways to recognize Him. He possesses the most extraordinary wisdom anywhere, and He is always working behind the scenes in ways we are unaware of. He has a good plan for each of us, our family members, and our friends. Although things might not point that way, we must remain trustful, hopeful, prayerful, optimistic, and faithful to our beliefs and what we know to be His truth. He never leaves us and is always there to help us in those life situations where we need extra strength and wisdom.

We all have needs and concerns, and we often grapple with hard places in our lives. I am confident, based on God's Word, that He sees each of His children and He knows what we are going through. We will never be alone. Through Jesus and the Holy Spirit, He will bring peace, guidance, comfort, and the wisdom we need to continue letting our light shine in the darkness of any situation we face. Only He can do that!

Prayer: Dear God, we thank You for being our perfect Heavenly Father. How comforting it is to know that we can call on You at any time, day or night. I pray for all who are experiencing trying times and who need someone they can trust. May they lift their concerns and hearts upward to You, the only One who will give them security, hope, and the peace they need to go forward. We pray this in the name of our Lord and Savior, Jesus Christ. Amen.

EVERLASTING GRACE

But he said to me, "My grace is sufficient for you, for my power is made perfect in weakness." Therefore I will boast all the more gladly of my weaknesses, so that the power of Christ may rest upon me.

2 Corinthians 12:9 (ESV)

It is sobering to know how uncertain life can be at any given moment, often without warning. Yet, from my perspective, life is immeasurably priceless and rich. As I age, that awareness becomes increasingly ingrained in my mind, and I'm thankful for every moment God gives me.

Many are facing physical battles—tough seasons of life. Some of the dearest people in my life fall into that category. It's hard to accept these times unless we have a firm Anchor—the One who has given us grace upon grace. With Jesus carrying us through every battle, through every storm, and even through those days when we haven't a care in the world, we will make it through. If you're facing a tough day, please remember that God is good and His arms are always open wide to welcome you into His comfort, peace, and safety. Even though we don't understand His timing, we have His Word to assure us that it is always right.

Enjoy this day, for there'll not be another one just like it. Always look for the beauty of God's creation around you. You won't have to look far!

Prayer: Heavenly Father, Your grace is more than sufficient for our needs. We thank You for loving us so much that You poured love and grace upon us through Jesus' death on the Cross. And through His resurrection, we have been raised to walk in newness of life. We are thankful for our life in Christ, which holds eternal promises. For those who are suffering and dealing with health issues today, I pray that You will infuse them with Your supernatural strength and comfort. Give them a real sense of Your presence so they will know that all is well. We pray these things in Jesus' name. Amen.

LIFE ON THE BRIGHT SIDE

I have come that they may have life, and have it to the full.
John 10:10b (NIV)

During the years of my gainful employment, I seldom ever looked forward to Monday. I liked my job and my coworkers, so that wasn't the reason I dreaded returning to the routine I'd had for many years. Perhaps I enjoyed the freedom of a weekend more than a set routine. Looking back, it was a waste of a perfect day, as I often went to work without any expectations of having a great day. Especially on Monday! Now, my attitude on a Friday—well, that's a different story for another day.

I wonder what would happen if we awoke every day—even on Mondays—with the determination to live life on the bright side. This phrase is the title of my dear friend Mary Howell's book, *Life on the Bright Side*. Mary and I grew up together in East Texas and reconnected after many years had passed. When I was home, my sister Peggy and I often visited Mary. During those visits, we ate, laughed, cried, and prayed together. We enjoyed picnics among the tall pine trees at the local park. Peggy and I always came away uplifted from our time spent with Mary because she was an inspiration to many, and we were no exception.

As a result of injuries sustained from a fall, Mary had quadriplegia and could only use her brilliant mind. Despite her moment-by-moment physical challenges, she knew how to live life to the fullest and with joy. Mary is in Heaven now, happy and whole. She was a woman of her word, and I never doubted for one minute that she wasn't praying for my family and me daily. She once told me that she prayed for over 400 people each day—she knew the exact number. Praying was one thing she could do as she went through each day.

We need more people like my friend, Mary—the blind, the sighted, the walkers, and those who can't walk, to carry the mantle of prayer as faithfully as Mary did. I lost so much when I lost Mary's daily prayers. I will always miss her, but I am looking forward to seeing the "new" Mary when I get to Heaven.

Like Mary, let's ask God to help us live our lives on the bright side! It might just turn a dreaded Monday into a magnificent one with more possibilities than we could ever imagine!

Prayer: Dear Heavenly Father, thank You for the sweet memories of Mary Howell, who lived life on the bright side even amid her frailties. May we always rest in assurance that each day we have been given is a gift from You. Help us not to waste a moment, but to use our time sharing the light and love of our Lord and Savior, Jesus Christ wherever we go. We pray this in His name. Amen.

OUR REFUGE

Those who live in the shelter of the Most High will find rest in the shadow of the Almighty. This I declare about the Lord: He alone is my refuge, my place of safety; he is my God, and I trust Him.

Psalm 91:1-2 (ESV)

When I was growing up in East Texas, the threat of severe weather was continually on my dad's mind. Simply put, he was deathly afraid of storms.

I was very young when Daddy sought to remedy his fear of bad weather by having a *storm house* built. I remember the day some men came and began building this steel-reinforced, one-foot-thick, concrete 8-foot square. The storm house was nestled into the side of a red dirt hill by the road running past our property. It was a place where no tornado could ever reach us and a sanctuary that Daddy was counting on for our protection.

We will all experience times when we need rest and safety from the storms of life. The Good News is that we have a shelter in Jesus Christ, who will protect us every single time. To receive such security, one only needs to trust in Him. He will then take us under His wings and into the safety of His arms, shielding us from the worst of the storm.

Amidst these tumultuous days in which we live, having the assurance of such a shelter will keep our hearts and minds at peace and give us much-needed comfort in knowing that our safe place surrounds us, that no storm can destroy us, and that God will always be with us.

Prayer: Dear Heavenly Father, You are our Protector and Safe Haven through life's journey. You give hope when there is none; You bring peace when the world's noise is pressing in; and You give assurance that our trials here on earth are only temporary. Thank You for the promises found in Your Word. Please help us grab onto them in every area of our lives. We pray this in Jesus' name. Amen.

ALPHA AND OMEGA

I am the Alpha and Omega, the First and the Last,
the Beginning and the End.
Revelation 22:13 (NIV)

Today in these quiet moments, may we focus on God's power and holiness and how worthy of our praise He truly is. These and other attributes of God are almost incomprehensible. Still, we can be assured that He and His Word are the absolute truth, that He loves us more than we will ever know this side of Heaven, and that He created us for a relationship with Him through His Son, Jesus Christ. As we sit with Him, let us be extra thankful for the One who paid our sin debt--the One who purchased us with His shed blood, Jesus Christ. What a sobering and humbling truth.

Let us praise Him today! May we glorify Him for giving us life and for calling us to be His children. Though none of us deserves such love, it is a gift freely given to us by a loving Heavenly Father. We cannot work our way to Heaven; we cannot try to be moral enough; we can't give enormous amounts of money to buy our way into Heaven. Our entrance into Heaven is based on one thing and one thing only: what Jesus did for us on the Cross, and what we've done with that truth.

Prayer: Thank You, Father God, that You are from Everlasting to Everlasting, and You do not change. Help us never take for granted what Jesus did for us on the Cross. May we always glorify and praise You as long as we live. We look forward to the day when we will worship You forevermore. In Jesus' name, we pray. Amen.

THE CROSSROADS OF LIFE

Peace I leave with you; my peace I give you. I do not give to you as the world gives. Do not let your hearts be troubled and do not be afraid.

John 14:27 (NIV)

I recently heard a lady share her story of God's grace, protection, love, redemption, and restoration. One only needed to hear about the changes that have taken place in this dear sister to see firsthand and believe that God had a plan for her life. Despite the harm others caused, a beautiful child of God emerged who seeks His perfect will and guidance and leans on the everlasting arms of Jesus like never before. What a solid testament her story is to the transformative power of God's love!

Life can sometimes be full of pain, sorrow, and challenges that we don't anticipate. No doubt some of you reading this devotional have been scarred by trauma from your past. You may be navigating challenging situations at this moment, such as financial difficulties, health issues, or relationship problems. You may not understand why God has allowed you to endure such a painful experience, like the loss of a loved one or a personal crisis. Although I don't have the answer, I know what God has done for me and what He will do for anyone who relinquishes their pain to Him. His Word promises us that we are never alone, regardless of our circumstances, so He will help us to endure whatever we are going through.

If you are at the crossroads of life and must decide whether or not to trust Jesus with those things you don't understand, please remember that you are never alone. Jesus is at each crossroad we face in life. God's Word is steadfast and reliable, a testament to His faithfulness. Through Jesus, you will find a secure foundation for your life. He will instill you with His strength, confidence, and hope. He always has a good plan for each of us and will help us to choose the path that is best and most pleasing to Him.

Prayer: Dear Heavenly Father, Your faithfulness and care for Your children will forever amaze me. Your transformative power is beyond our comprehension, but we thank You for being willing to love us that much. Forgive us when we don't give You our best. Help us not to be caught up in the things of this world; rather, may we depend on You for everything we think, say, and do. Help us strive daily to live a life that is pleasing to You as You guide and direct us in all things. In the name of Jesus, we pray. Amen.

ALWAYS FAITHFUL

Your kingdom is an everlasting kingdom, and your dominion endures throughout all generations. The Lord is faithful in all his words and kind in all his works.

Psalm 145:13 (ESV)

I'm so thankful for God's commitment to the many promises found in His Word. His faithful protection and provision are ever-present even when He seems to be silent. We aren't promised detailed descriptions of God's plan for our lives, and we aren't given a "behind the scenes" tour of the many ways He is working on our behalf. But as we walk in His ways and trust Him to guide us each step along the road of life, we are assured that the final outcome will be for our good and His glory.

Let us always be thankful for God's faithfulness. Knowing that He is the perfect Heavenly Father who loves us more than we will ever comprehend in this life should give us peace and calm assurance in the depths of our hearts. He has plans for us and will never abandon us. That's some Good News to take into this day.

Prayer: Dear Heavenly Father, thank You for Your faithfulness to all generations. Forgive us when we do not live in a way that demonstrates our complete trust in Your everlasting love and care. Forgive us for those choices that tend to pull us away from the shelter of Your arms. Our heart's desire is to live in such a way that others will see Jesus shining through us. Give us strength, wisdom, and opportunities to share Your Word and our faith with someone in need today. We pray this in Jesus' name. Amen.

GOD WANTS TO HEAR YOU SING

Peace I leave with you; my peace I give to you.
Not as the world gives do I give to you.
Let not your hearts be troubled, neither let them be afraid.
John 14:27 (ESV)

I love Christian music! At one time, I was even a member of my church choir. You know, friends, it's pretty easy to sing our song on a good day, but it takes God's help and strength to give us the ability to sing on days when despair is all we see. Those aren't days that we want to sing; however, it is during these times that we must dig as deep as we can and pull a song out of our hearts. There is no doubt that God will provide the encouragement and strength needed to find our song amidst life's difficulties. I am sure of this because He has done it for me again and again in my lifetime.

Let us be encouraged by the assurance that God is at work, even in the most challenging circumstances. Whatever we may be facing, He wants to hear us sing. The Good News is that He's waiting to give us the wherewithal to do it. As we take a closer look, we'll find there are many reasons to thank Him for His goodness and for the peace He brings to us daily. That in itself is enough to sing a song.

Prayer: Heavenly Father, I believe that You love to hear us sing, both figuratively and literally. Thank You for the gift of music and for the ability that You give to songwriters, past and present, who continue to bring Christian songs to life. Thank You for old and new music, for in it we find comfort, encouragement, and the assurance that You are with us through our journey here on earth. We love You and ask that You give us the strength to sing through every season of our lives, for it is unto You that we lift our songs. In Jesus' name we pray. Amen.

SIGNS OF SPRING

The steadfast love of the LORD never ceases; his mercies never come to an end; they are new every morning; great is your faithfulness.
Lamentations 3:22-23 (ESV)

Although we don't have long winter seasons here in Central Texas, it is always a welcome sight to see signs of Spring as trees and plants begin to leaf and bloom. When God's creation exhibits an abundance of new life, I can often be found sitting outside in my swing, welcoming the birds as they announce a new season that God has brought forth.

While I do love Springtime, even better is the new life in Christ that we experience every day. His mercies are new every morning. He walks with us, leads us, and makes our way safe and secure. Great is His faithfulness! What hope that knowledge brings throughout all seasons of our lives. He is the Master of the beauty that is all around us, and I know He wants us to enjoy it and remember Him as we do.

Prayer: Dear Heavenly Father, thank You for Your faithfulness not only in bringing forth new seasons but also for being close beside us through every season of our lives. You are the One we worship, honor, and adore. Help us to move steadily along each day, serving You in all the ways that are important to You. Direct our steps to places where You are working. Give us Your heart for others who need to know Your love. We pray this in Jesus' name. Amen.

WALK ON

So do not fear, for I am with you; do not be dismayed, for I am your
God. I will strengthen you and help you;
I will uphold you with my righteous right hand.
Isaiah 41:10 (NIV)

Health experts advise that walking is beneficial for our health. It's true because I always feel better after taking a nice walk. My husband and I used to walk several miles every day, hardly ever missing the time we had allotted for such an activity. We knew we needed to be regular in this commitment to improve our health.

Do you realize that Jesus beckons us to walk with Him each day? In the process, our spiritual health is strengthened as we become more like Him. Ours is a continuous journey with the One who never fails, changes, disappoints, or leaves us. His love for us never ceases. His mercies are new every morning, and each day is truly a new beginning!

Many of you reading this hope for better days. Some need strength and encouragement, and some are tired of being tired and sick of being sick. I am so thankful that we don't have to walk this road of life alone but can go forward each day with the hope of Christ in our hearts. God is profoundly committed to us. Jesus came to rescue us, and He's as close as the mention of His name. How great is that!

How thankful we can be that there is One who never tires, grows weary, or becomes anxious. He will walk with us, whether the days are bright or the nights are dark and lonely. His name is Jesus, and He loved you and me enough to give His life for us. In doing so, He promises eternal life to all who will believe in Him and follow the path He sets for us. He is near and waiting to give you spiritual health that will encourage you to follow Him wholeheartedly.

Prayer: Dear Heavenly Father, thank You for the spiritual health You give us that keeps us going through life's difficult times. Your Word promises that You will never leave nor forsake us. Thank You for being so generous with Your grace, mercy, forgiveness, and compassion. We love You and know that You will always be with us. In Jesus' name, we pray. Amen.

GOOD NEWS AMBASSADORS

We are therefore Christ's ambassadors, as though God were making his appeal through us. We implore you on Christ's behalf: Be reconciled to God.

2 Corinthians 5:20 (NIV)

One thing about social media is that people can follow many rabbit trails. Although I do that occasionally, I try to investigate only the good ones. For instance, I follow a 78-year-old retired school teacher from Alabama named Brenda Gantt. Brenda, who started her Facebook journey during the 2020 pandemic, now has over 3.8 million followers on her "Cooking With Brenda Gantt" page.

Brenda never fails to give God all the credit for her success, for she did not aspire to have this current notoriety. It all began 5 years ago when everything was in lockdown, and she couldn't go to church. Brenda decided to make a video and post it on her Facebook page to share the finer points of biscuit-making with her church friends.

Today, Brenda continues to cook down-home southern recipes while weaving encouraging messages throughout her cooking show. I call her a *Good News Ambassador,* because she sometimes shares a Scripture and a little message of encouragement or she will talk about Jesus while she cooks. This one-of-a-kind lady has a zest for life, and her presence on social media is a God-given treasure. Thousands of people are being reached through her unique ministry, and I'm thankful to be one of them.

Like Brenda Gantt, we can be *Good News Ambassadors* right where we are. God has placed within each of us the ability to make a positive difference in the lives of others. We can rest assured that God sees us and will equip us to share His light. May we all make a difference in someone else's life this week with a smile, a hug, a helping hand, or some kind words. Shine your light for Jesus, and you and someone else will be immensely blessed.

Prayer: Heavenly Father, we long to be faithful *Good News Ambassadors* for You in everything we say and do. Please direct us to spread Your love and light to those we encounter this week. May we offer hope and encouragement to those whose hearts have been shattered by pain and loss. Thank You for hearing our prayers. We pray this in Jesus' name. Amen.

OPTIMISM AND HOPE

We have this hope as an anchor for the soul, firm and secure.
Hebrews 6:19a (NIV)

"The pessimist sees the difficulty in every opportunity. The optimist sees the opportunity in every difficulty." Sir Winston Churchill

Optimism is a choice we make—a learned skill. However, optimism and hope are more than learned skills for believers. Optimism is the belief that a better day is coming and that God has a good plan for us, regardless of our current circumstances. Hope is putting faith to work when giving up would be the easier option.

Earlier in my life, I was more of a pessimist than an optimist. I struggled to see many aspects of my life from God's viewpoint. What ultimately made the difference was an awakening of the deep faith I had received at the age of 12, when I accepted Jesus Christ as my Lord and Savior.

To change from a pessimistic to an optimistic outlook was a lengthy transformation. As I spent more and more time letting God's Word sink deep into my heart, crying out to Him in prayer, being still in His presence, and applying messages from my pastor(s) that pointed straight to my heart, I began to acquire a deeper spiritual foundation that made such a difference in my outlook on life as a whole. It was then that I was able to turn pessimism into optimism. I can never thank God enough for helping me.

Today let's choose to be optimistic and hopeful! Let us focus on the One who carries us through every battle and every situation in our lives. And when we feel the urge to give up, may we know with complete assurance that God is always there to help us in every trial we face.

Prayer: Dear Heavenly Father, there is so much pessimism in this world. Your Word is the light that we need to illuminate our pathway of life. Please give us renewed optimism for the things You love. We pray this in Jesus' name. Amen.

Source: Churchill, Winston, *Churchill By Himself: The Definitive Collection of Quotations*, September 4, 2008, Rosetta Books, Edited by Langworth, Richard.

IT'S ALL ABOUT FAITH

And without faith it is impossible to please him,
for whoever would draw near to God must believe that he
exists and that he rewards those who seek him.

Hebrews 11:6 (ESV)

During our lifetime, having faith in Jesus Christ will carry us through many difficult situations. Faith keeps us safe and secure through tough times and also brings us more joy than we can imagine. Having a close relationship with God will bring an inner peace that's almost incomprehensible, because it has to be experienced.

Without faith, we would have no hope beyond these troublesome and depressing days in which we are living. Praise God, our faith assures us that one day we will see Jesus and live with Him forever in a place called Heaven. There, we will look forward to no more tears, sorrow, sickness, death, or pain! What a glorious day that will be when we're united with those who have gone on before us.

I'm so thankful that through our faith in Jesus Christ we will experience victory, both here and in the life to come.

Prayer: Dear God, You are a faithful Father to Your children. We can never express enough gratitude for all You've done for us. Help us to live each day in such a manner that we are known as people after Your own heart. We love You and praise You for giving us peace and comfort in all aspects of our lives. We pray these things in Jesus' name. Amen.

PAY IT FORWARD

*But the fruit of the Spirit is love, joy, peace, patience, kindness,
goodness, faithfulness, gentleness, self-control;
against such things there is no law.*

Galatians 5:22-23 (ESV)

Some time ago, my husband and I visited a local restaurant for dinner. Seated in the booth behind us were three teenage boys. I would guess they were no more than 16 or 17 years old. I noticed that they seemed to be having uplifting conversations while they ate. Besides the fact that one of them was dressed in a tuxedo and the others were in jeans and polo shirts, nothing else seemed unusual about the group.

We were almost finished with our meal when the teens got up to leave. The young man in the tux walked to our booth, laid a $20 bill on the table, and said, "I want to help pay for your meal tonight." We both had shocked faces because this act of kindness had come as a surprise. All we could say was, "Thank you so much! That is so nice of you! God bless you!" I asked the young man for his name, and he told me it was Cory. Then he and his friends wished us a good night and left.

I am pretty sure that most of us have experienced "Pay It Forward" before, but when it happens unexpectedly, as it did with us, it serves as a poignant reminder that there are still good people in this world who want to do thoughtful things for others. Additionally, seeing a young person perform an act of kindness restores my faith in the youth who will be our future leaders.

It was extraordinary to receive an act of kindness from a stranger, and I am thankful to have been reminded that God uses people for good. Perhaps you won't pay for someone's meal, but there are many opportunities daily to be kind and thoughtful to those we encounter. We just need to look around us.

Prayer: Dear Father, You continue to amaze me at how You work in the lives of Your children. Thank You for Cory and his giving heart. I pray that if he doesn't know You, the dear Holy Spirit will cause his tender and compassionate heart to seek Your ways. Thank You for reminding us that You own the cattle on a thousand hills and that You love to give freely to those who seek after You. Please lead us to those who will benefit and be encouraged by a good deed done for them. This we pray in the name of Jesus Christ, our Lord and Savior. Amen.

SHARE THE GOOD NEWS

The LORD himself goes before you and will be with you;
he will never leave you nor forsake you.
Do not be afraid; do not be discouraged.
Deuteronomy 31:8 (NIV)

Having just watched the morning news on TV, I admit that what we hear daily could depress us if we let it! I am reminded of a news report some years ago that many people had fled the city of Rome, Italy, because someone had predicted a great earthquake on that date. Since we humans tend to be fearful and cautious, might we all be tempted to flee if such a prediction were made for our city?

I bring Good News for those who are searching for something other than the bad news of the day! Jesus said, **"I have told you these things, so that in me you may have peace. In this world you will have trouble. But take heart! I have overcome the world" (John 16:33 NIV).** Jesus is the One in whom we can believe. He comforts us in times of uncertainty. He always provides for our needs. Our faith and trust in Him bring the stability, security, and peace that we need to navigate the days in which we live. Because of who He is, we need not fear these perilous times. As always, God has a better plan for us than our fear and uncertainty!

Through Christ, we have been given the freedom and authority to share this Good News with those who are looking for answers. Be aware that you may be the catalyst God wants to use today to encourage those seeking an antidote for the bad news that surrounds us.

Prayer: Heavenly Father, there is so much bad news these days. If we focus on what we hear via mainstream news outlets or take to heart all that bombards us on social media, we will become anxious and discouraged. We take comfort in knowing that You are bigger than any storm we are going through, and that You will lead us safely through each perilous step. Help us to lean on You with all that is within us, knowing we will never be alone. This we pray in Jesus' name. Amen.

GOD NEVER CHANGES

For this world in its present form is passing away.
1 Corinthians 7:31b (NIV)

As a Baby Boomer, I have witnessed and experienced many changes throughout my lifetime, including space exploration, faster automobiles, amazing technology, and all of the modern conveniences a person could desire. I sometimes wonder what's next. Based on history, we know that countless more changes will come because nothing ever remains the same.

For our feelings of hope and security to remain intact in this ever-changing world, we need someone greater than ourselves to guide us through whatever transitions and difficulties we may encounter. I have Good News for you today based solely on God's Word. The verse shown above reminds us that the only constant in this ever-changing world is God.

In **Malachi 3:6a**, **NIV**, God affirms, **"I the Lord do not change."** He is the same God who spoke the world into existence and created us in His image. Our God is the God of Abraham, Isaac, and Jacob. His character is unchanging, and He longs for a relationship with us. He is the only constant in our lives--our anchor, our hope, our peace, and our rest. I'm so thankful that we have Him to steady us and guide us through our evolving world.

Prayer: Dear Heavenly Father, we are eternally thankful that You never change. Your Word stands solid and sure and is the security upon which we base our faith and trust in You. Because of Jesus' sacrifice on the cross, You made it possible for us to live with hope and assurance that one day, we will not experience a broken world or broken people. Living an abundant life through Jesus means living in His love, grace, and truth, and sharing these with others. Please help us share with those we encounter how they can experience a bountiful life on Earth and have the assurance of eternal life through Jesus Christ, our Lord. We pray this in His name. Amen.

SPEAK SOFTLY AND CARRY THE LIGHT OF JESUS

Let the words of my mouth and the meditation of my heart be acceptable in your sight, O Lord, my rock and my redeemer.
Psalm 19:14 (ESV)

Several years ago, my husband and I were having breakfast at a local restaurant. Soon after our meal arrived, we overheard a woman seated at the table next to us telling her friends how harshly she had spoken to someone she had recently invited to a dinner party. The invitee was supposed to bring a dessert but failed to show up for whatever reason. The woman went on to say that she was so upset that she called her *friend* on the phone and sharply berated her by using foul language. As she told her friends about the situation, it was clear that she was still quite angry.

As I recalled the conversation mentioned above, I thought about the power of our words. We should all consider what we say and how we say it, because our speech can build others up or hurt them deeply. Although most of us would never intentionally wound another person with our words, we sometimes speak before we think. Consequently, reflecting on our words and their impact is essential, and striving to use them for the good of others and ourselves is vital.

I firmly believe that words spoken in kindness can transform a person's life, and I will never forget the many gracious words spoken to me and the encouragement I have received throughout my lifetime.

Don't let the memory of harsh or unkind words have power over you. You are deeply loved and of great value to those around you. More importantly, you are loved immensely by our Heavenly Father, who created you for His good purposes. I pray that you will go about your day speaking softly and carrying the light of Jesus wherever you go. You and others will be better off when you do.

Prayer: Dear Heavenly Father, unkind words seem so familiar in our culture today, and that breaks my heart. Your name is often thrown around as if it were meaningless, especially by those who don't know Jesus as Savior. We pray that Your Holy Spirit will convict and redirect the thoughts of those who speak disrespectfully out of anger or mere habit. May their words of anger be replaced with words of kindness and understanding for others. Help us, as followers of Jesus Christ, to be more aware of our responses to others and always keep our hearts and minds in check with what pleases You. We pray this in Jesus' name. Amen.

DON'T WORRY

Therefore do not be anxious about tomorrow, for tomorrow will be anxious for itself. Sufficient for the day is its own trouble.

Matthew 6:34 (ESV)

Are you a worrier? Many years ago, I was full of worry and anxiety. Thankfully, the Lord has helped me immensely in that area of my life. Even still, there are times I find myself worrying or being concerned, as I like to call it. I become anxious mainly about the future as I think about my grandchildren—the adults as well as the young ones. I only want God's best for them, and that particular prayer is always at the center of my heart's cry. So when I pray, I must trust that He will answer my prayers in His timing and according to His will.

Moments of worry don't benefit us or our loved ones. We are well-served to remember that being anxious is a waste of time and energy. When we find ourselves beginning to worry, let's try giving our anxiety to the One who is more than able to handle whatever concerns us. Having His peace deep within is so much better.

Prayer: Dear Heavenly Father, You are the God who sees us. You see our worries and our fears. You see us in our weaknesses. You alone can bring spiritual strength and peace to our hearts and minds. Please forgive us when we don't fully trust You and help us to put every ounce of our faith into trusting and believing that in Your timing, You will work out our concerns for our good and Your glory. In Jesus' name, we pray. Amen.

THE IMPORTANCE OF DADS

As a father has compassion on his children, so the LORD shows compassion to those who fear him.

Psalm 103:13 (ESV)

The relationship between fathers and their children is such a vital part of the child's development. Boys desperately need a good role model in a father. It is disheartening to see so many young males without direction in their lives because they lack a father figure at home. They may have lost their dad to death or abandonment, may have never had a father figure in the home, or may be lacking a father for other reasons, thereby creating a vacuum in the family. If children are fortunate enough to have a supportive community, such as grandparents, to come alongside them and help fill the void left by an absent father, it can be a great blessing.

Girls also need to feel the security and love that a father brings to the family. When I was growing up, people didn't show much affection. However, based on what I've read, my conversations with friends who experienced less-than-perfect childhoods, and my own background, I believe that fatherly love, involvement, and affection are one of the greatest needs a child has. Because this type of love is unconditional, it is not based on performance or circumstances. Rather, it is a constant, unwavering presence in a child's life, providing comfort and security.

While your circumstances may not have been perfect, you can walk in faith, knowing you have a perfect Heavenly Father. He is the only One who will never let you down and will provide the love, affection, and peace you need. Remember, your worth and identity come from a much higher source: God and His great love for you.

Prayer: Dear Heavenly Father, please bless all fathers, grandfathers, and the many mothers who serve in the dual role of mother and father. Help them focus their lives on You in such a way that they will have a profoundly positive impact on their children. Give them the wisdom and strength to honor You in everything they think, say, and do. We pray this in Jesus' name. Amen.

GRATITUDE

Oh give thanks to the LORD, for he is good,
for his steadfast love endures forever.
Psalm 106:1 (ESV)

Sometimes there aren't enough words to express gratitude to God for what He has done and continues to do on our behalf. At other times, we may not feel like giving thanks at all. Life's circumstances tend to weigh heavily upon us, and we don't feel spiritually/physically/emotionally strong. But let us never forget that our faith in Jesus is not based on feelings, but rather on what He did on the Cross for all humanity.

Sure, there are times when we feel as though we could conquer the world! We seem to be clicking right along with nothing to distract us. Out of nowhere a situation may come along, leaving us feeling weak and vulnerable. It is during those times, especially those times, that we must continue to pray and study God's Word to regain our spiritual strength.

This world is full of sin, heartache, and pain. That's obvious to everyone. However, what we as Christians do with our faith will make a difference not only in our own lives but also in the lives of others. Showing gratitude for God's love and care will carry us through those times we find ourselves struggling in the wake of life's challenges. For it is in these situations that we learn to trust and lean on Him more. He is ever-present and longs to strengthen us in our faith walk.

Prayer: Dear God, thank You for the many blessings that have come our way. Help us to share Your love with others who need a new beginning through Jesus Christ. Give us peace and comfort in our circumstances, and let us sing a song of praise to You today and forever. We pray this in Jesus' name. Amen.

FARTHER ALONG

And we know that in all things God works for the good of those who love him, who have been called according to his purpose.

Romans 8:28 (NIV)

When I was a young girl, I would hear my daddy singing the old hymn, "Farther Along." Sometimes he would call my mother, brother, and me to gather around the piano where we would sing this and other hymns. I can still recite every stanza of all those songs, which often bring me comfort and peace.

In life there are many things we'll never understand. Although we all have questions and cannot fully comprehend God's mind, we are often able to see Him at work. At times He does give us glimpses of understanding. But when we don't have the answers, we must keep walking forward and trusting the words of Romans 8:28.

Now that I'm older, I realize even more the importance of trusting God through every challenge, trial, and battle that I may face. I truly see the importance of living in the sunshine. Our days are numbered, and I don't want to waste any of the time that I am given.

Friend, if you're currently going through a trying time, please remember that you don't have to have all of the answers. Jesus has every situation in your life covered. He has walked the road before you and will lead you safely through. Trust Him.

Remember that this world is not our final home, but while we are here, let's give God our best and let Him take care of the things we weren't meant to fully understand. One day, we will see how He sheltered and cared for us during life's darkest valleys, and we'll know that our trials only came to make us strong.

> *Farther along, we'll know more about it,*
> *Farther along, we'll understand why;*
> *Cheer up, my brother, live in the sunshine,*
> *We'll understand it all by and by.*

Prayer: Dear Father, it is encouraging to know that one day we will see clearly what You've been up to. We know You are working all things out for our good and Your glory. For now, that is enough. You are good, so we trust You in all things. Help us to have a fruitful day of life through Jesus Christ. We pray this in His name. Amen.

Source: Stevens, W.E. and Warren, Barney E. *"Farther Along." 1911*

A SOLID FOUNDATION

Everyone who comes to me and hears my words and does them, I will show you what he is like: he is like a man building a house, who dug deep and laid the foundation on the rock. And when a flood arose, the stream broke against that house and could not shake it, because it had been well built.

Luke 6:47-48 (ESV)

For some time now, I've been watching what will ultimately be a large developed piece of property just outside of our neighborhood. When finished, I suspect that we will see yet another apartment complex or a group of large office buildings. Whatever the outcome, it will be huge!

It is apparent to the visible eye that the landscape on this particular piece of property is changing and being made ready for strong and lasting foundations. Before that can occur, extensive land preparation is necessary. The first step has been finished…to clear all of the unsightly brush and scrubby trees from the property, thereby leveling the ground. That which was unnecessary and would be a hindrance to the building process has been stripped away and hauled to a recycling center. Using heavy machinery, the contractor continues to pack layer upon layer of good soil, smooths it out, and then waters it. These steps are being repeated all day long, day after day.

Another type of foundation came to mind as I've watched the progress on the above-referenced site. While it is a foundation not to be compared to an earthly one, the two do have similarities. Of course, I am referring to a spiritual foundation. What we see in this piece of property at this stage of the process is only the beginning of something far greater. The outcome takes time, the right tools, and someone who knows what they are doing.

Just as the landscape is changing on the property up the road, we can rest assured that God is continually working to shape our faith and change us in such a way that our spiritual foundation will always remain strong and unshakable. If we ask and allow Him to, He will strip us of those unsightly hindrances that would prevent us from growing in our faith. He will take them to the recycling center of His love and forgiveness, making us into someone who more closely resembles Himself.

The ground is level at the foot of the Cross, and our Heavenly Father will always meet us there. He is ready and very willing to help you and me begin building a strong and lasting spiritual foundation.

Prayer: Heavenly Father, we are thankful for the foundation of the truth of Your Word. Please help us to build on a firm foundation, one that will stand the test of time. Give us every tool that You offer so that we might always stay grounded in Jesus Christ, our Savior and Lord. We pray this in His name. Amen.

HOW GREAT THOU ART

Have you not known? Have you not heard? The LORD is the everlasting God, the Creator of the ends of the earth. He does not faint or grow weary; his understanding is unsearchable. He gives power to the faint, and to him who has no might he increases strength.
Isaiah 40:28-29 (ESV)

On that particular Sunday, the church service had just begun with the congregation singing the hymn, "How Great Thou Art." As the words to this song were lifted high in adoration to God, a beautiful sight brought tears to my eyes and deeply touched my heart. There in the back of the church, slowly making her way to a pew, was one of our dear seniors, a sweet lady whose smile had always been contagious. The main thing that caught my attention was not the fact that this precious lady was using a walker to maneuver her way into the church, but rather the joy on her face as she sang the words of the song. It was evident that this was a lady who had loved and trusted in Jesus for many years and was committed to attending church despite the difficulty of getting there. On her face I saw the assurance that she would one day stand in the presence of the One who had been her comfort, help, and hope and would hear these words: **"Well done, good and faithful servant" (Matthew 25:21).** There was no question that she was confident of the *greatness* of God.

This dear lady, who has now gone on to Heaven, encouraged me that Sunday morning without knowing it. Moments like this remind me what a wonderful thing it is to be a child of God! He is bigger than any problem or frailty we might have; He will never leave us or forsake us, whether we are young or old; His love for us encompasses more than we can imagine; we are never too old to serve and praise Him; and He alone will give us strength, wisdom, and the commitment to live out our lives in a manner that is pleasing to Him.

Prayer: Dear God, indeed, how great Thou art! Thank You for being with us throughout our lives and for the promise of eternal life through Jesus Christ, our Lord. We give thanks for the spiritual role models who encourage and inspire us. Please help us to be strong in our faith and love for others. We pray this prayer in Jesus' name. Amen.

YES, I DO!

Therefore, my beloved brethren, be steadfast, immovable, always abounding in the work of the Lord, knowing that your toil is not in vain in the Lord.

1 Corinthians 15:58 (ESV)

These days, there are countless reels and short videos available to watch online on just about any subject of interest to someone. I try to focus on those with uplifting messages and Christian values, such as Christian music, my favorite Christian preachers and speakers, and church services. It isn't because I'm perfect; perhaps I have learned, through the little wisdom I have, that what we watch, read, or listen to feeds into our minds.

Recently I watched a short video that troubled me greatly. A man stood in a mall area, then a grocery store, asking passersby a straightforward question: *"Do you believe in Jesus Christ?"* While some people answered in the affirmative, many more answered, *"No!"* Seeing so many people rejecting Jesus was heartbreaking. Their responses indicate that many people are lost in this world, and there is still much work to be done in sharing the Good News of Jesus Christ.

I often think about how those who don't know Jesus live and am mindful of two things. First, I shouldn't place spiritual expectations on those who have no idea what it is like to walk with Jesus, because they only know the things of this world that do not feed their souls. Second, except for the grace of God, there go I. All who have been redeemed by the blood of our Lord Jesus Christ have been where they are—lost.

The joy found in the heart of a Christ follower is a testament to the transformative power of faith in Him, and it should ignite a sense of hope and inspiration in our own spiritual journey. My prayer for those who do not yet know Jesus is that their hearts will be turned toward a kind and loving God who has a perfect plan for their lives. If they are ever asked again, *"Do you believe in Jesus Christ?"* may they reply with a resounding, *"Yes, I do!"*

Prayer: Dear Heavenly Father, only You can change our "No" into a "Yes!" We do not serve You to gain brownie points on Your check-off list for entrance into Heaven, nor to bring glory to ourselves or to have bragging rights for some great work we feel we've done in Your name. Instead, we realize that our righteous deeds are as filthy rags compared to who You are. May we never forget that we were once lost, just like those who have not yet found the hope and peace that come from knowing Jesus Christ as Lord and Savior. Help us to reach out to others with love, sincerity, and humility. We are thankful for the peace and joy found in knowing Jesus, and we desire that others may also discover this gift from You. We pray this in Jesus' name. Amen.

DON'T LET GO

God is our refuge and strength, a very present help in trouble.
Psalm 46:1 (ESV)

Our bout of Type A Influenza was a surprise to my husband and me, as only one month before falling ill with this culprit, we had received our high-dose flu vaccine. Needless to say, it was a shock to be physically incapacitated because we felt confident that we had acted responsibly to protect ourselves from this illness.

Thankfully, over time we recovered fully from our illness. However, many people in our circle of influence were facing more serious challenges. As we supported each of our family members and friends with prayers and anything else we could do, we encouraged them to keep their eyes on Jesus, the One who is and will always be beside them. Through every battle and every storm, there is an Anchor who will always get us safely home.

If you are currently facing situations in your life that have knocked the wind out of your sails, please remember that you are only as strong as where you place your faith and trust. I encourage you to believe that God is your strength and rest in the reality of His incredible love, power, and faithfulness. He'll do for you what you cannot do for yourself, so let Him be the source of your strength. He will see you through. Above all, don't let go of hope! It will always carry you where you need to go.

Prayer: Dear God, You alone are the source of our strength. Because of that, we have every reason to place our hope in You when we cannot see the way. Please help us to trust You fully when we find ourselves entering into a life-changing season where uncertainty reigns supreme. Help us to remember that You are the God who sees every second of our lives from beginning to end, and there's not one thing that takes You by surprise. Give us Your strength and the ability to hold on, for it is You who will do the final work in and through us by Your great power and majesty. We love You and trust You, and we thank You in Jesus' name. Amen.

GOD KNOWS NO LIMITS

*The sun stopped in the midst of heaven and did not hurry
to set for about a whole day.*

Joshua 10:13b (ESV)

The above Scripture reflects how God came through in a mighty way, giving Joshua and the Israelites victory. There is no explanation for how or why the sun stood still and did not set that day. God allowed this so that His people could avenge themselves and destroy every last one of their enemies.

We understand that God is sovereign and free to carry out His plan for our lives. He can do whatever He will, whenever He will. He is not limited by space or time. We also know that God does not follow rules. He creates them. He does not worry about political correctness, because He does whatever needs to be done for our good and His eternal purposes.

If we saturate ourselves in God's Word and ask the Holy Spirit to open our hearts and minds to what He wants us to learn, we will come to know some of His character. Many things about God will remain a mystery to us, because His thoughts are not our thoughts and His ways are not our ways. However, today's excellent news is that we do not have to understand Him; we simply need to follow Him. He will do the rest because He knows our limits.

Prayer: Father God, we desire to follow You all the days of our lives. It is You who brings peace in times of confusion, worry, and fear. There is nothing that comes our way that You cannot handle. We trust You and ask that You give us peace and rest today. We pray this in Jesus' name. Amen.

OPERATING IN FAITH

Though you have not seen him, you love him. Though you do not now see him, you believe in him and rejoice with joy that is inexpressible and filled with glory, obtaining the outcome of your faith, the salvation of your souls.

1 Peter 1:8-9 (ESV)

Do you know that we operate on faith every day without thinking about it? There are many examples, but I'll only give one. For instance, I'm currently sitting in a chair at my desk writing these thoughts. When I sat down, I didn't think twice about whether or not the chair would support me. I had faith that it would, because it has always done its job. Consequently, I'll go through my day having faith in many things I don't even think about.

A person doesn't have to be a believer in Christ to exercise this non-spiritual kind of faith. It comes naturally and helps us navigate the activities of our day and this life. But spiritual faith is a different thing entirely. Christians know what and Who the object of our faith is, because we have experienced Jesus Christ becoming real in our lives. In my case, I was 12 years old when I committed my life to Him. At that moment, my spiritual faith was born through the presence of the Holy Spirit. I was a babe in Christ, but I was His. Praise God!

It takes a lifetime to grow in our faith because God is always at work through life's varied circumstances. Our faith is strengthened through both the good and challenging times we experience. **Romans 8:28 (ESV)** states the following: **"And we know that for those who love God, all things work together for good, for those who are called according to his purpose."**

As we move forward each day, let us pray that God will use the faith He has implanted in our hearts to love and emulate Jesus more than we did the day before, for it is God's constant work in us that changes us for the better.

Prayer: Dear Heavenly Father, You are the object of our faith. Please help us to live daily in such a way that others will see Jesus in us, which is our greatest desire. Forgive us when we fail to exercise the faith You have already given us. We trust You to strengthen us as we travel through our daily walk of life. We pray these things in the name of our Lord and Savior, Jesus Christ. Amen.

FINDING OUR REST IN HIM

And your life will be brighter than the noonday; its darkness will be like the morning. And you will feel secure, because there is hope; you will look around and take your rest in security.

Job 11:17-18 (ESV)

During stressful and hurried times, I seldom express my true feelings. There is little time or opportunity to appear weak, sad, tired, or frustrated. I have come to believe that this is characteristic of many women. Deep down, we feel the need to always be strong and to give all that we have to others, which leaves little quality time for ourselves. There is no opportunity to recharge, to refocus, or to be renewed.

With more years behind me than ahead and perhaps a little wisdom now, I know firsthand that trying to be all things for all people, while hiding stressful feelings, only deceives us into thinking that we are strong. In reality, we need someone who will help carry our heavy load, listen to us, and understand where we are coming from. We need comfort. We need rest!

Today I have Good News for you! There is Someone who will bring comfort and rest, who loves us unconditionally, and who cares about what we are going through more than we can imagine! His name is Jesus. One of His many specialties is carrying the load for those who seek Him when they can't go any further. There's nothing too big for Him to handle. He relates to every aspect of what we are feeling, and He is there to love us and give rest as only He can do.

Prayer: Dear Heavenly Father, today we seek rest in You. We are confident that You will be our strength and joy through every season of life. Thank You for loving us that much. We pray this in Jesus' name. Amen.

SHAPING THE MOMENTS

Train up a child in the way he should go; even when
he is old he will not depart from it.
Proverbs 22:6 (NIV)

Have you ever considered how you, as a parent, grandparent, or great-grand-parent, are helping to shape the moments with the loved ones God has given you? More than anything else, I believe our most significant responsibility is to pray unceasingly for them. This duty is not to be taken lightly, but it is a commitment we must uphold with sincerity and dedication. Prayer is powerful! We can always have confidence in God's Word and know He hears and answers each one we lay at His feet.

Every Saturday morning, I meet with some sisters in Christ who are faithful prayer warriors. One of the prayer points we have is for our grandchildren. We pray that their mind, body, and spirit will always be protected under the umbrella of God's love and guidance. As grandmothers and great-grand-mothers, the very BEST we can do is to cover them in our daily prayers, continue to show them our love, and always strive to be good examples and spiritual role models for them.

Perhaps many of you will want to begin praying fervently for your children and grandchildren. Maybe you'll develop your own prayer points for the special individuals in your life. If you have already been doing this, please do not give up or stop! We will never go wrong by praying, because we serve a Heavenly Father who hears and answers prayer.

I pray that each of you will shape the moments you spend with your family for the glory of God. We all need a loving relationship with Jesus. Some family members have found it sooner than others, but by no means will we ever give up on the salvation of our lost loved ones. Nothing is impossible with God. Until our prayers are answered on their behalf, we will keep knocking on Heaven's door.

Prayer: Dear Heavenly Father, we continue to hear about miracles of salvation through Christ, and our hearts are filled with joy. We petition You on behalf of our family members who do not know You. Today, we humbly ask that You save them before it is too late. We know You can do it, but they must make the choice. Stir their hearts to seek Your truth. We pray this in Jesus' name. Amen.

ANYTHING WILL HELP

So shall my word be that goes out from my mouth; it shall not return to me empty, but it shall accomplish that which I purpose, and shall succeed in the thing for which I sent it.

Isaiah 55:11 (ESV)

As I approached a red light on my way home from running errands, my attention was drawn to a man sitting on the corner. Indeed, it was not an unusual sight, but something caused me to focus on this man. His face was weathered and thin, his long hair needed a trim, and he held a sign that read, *Anything will help. God bless.*

I only had a split second to decide whether to ignore this man or take action based on the compassion I felt for this stranger. I knew the light would soon turn green, so I grabbed a New Testament with Psalms and Proverbs and slipped some money between the pages. Then, as I rolled the car window down, I quickly said, "Sir, this is God's Word, and I just want you to know He loves you very much." Taking the Testament in his hand, he smiled and said, "I know He does." That was all the time I had to interact with the man before the light turned green.

What I told the man is 100% true–God loves him. Rich or poor, saint or sinner, God loves those He created, and He desires a personal relationship with them through His Son, Jesus Christ. Because of that knowledge, I knew I couldn't go wrong by giving one of God's creations His Word. Isaiah 55:11, shown above, promises that God will accomplish His purpose when His Word goes forth.

As the light turned green, I prayed that the New Testament would be used to bring a lost soul to Jesus, whether it was the man who received it from me or someone else down the line. And I thought about the untold mercy, forgiveness, and grace my loving Heavenly Father has given me all of my life. As I glanced at the man one last time through the rearview mirror, all I could think of was, *But for the grace of God, there go I.*

Prayer: Dear Heavenly Father, thank You for giving me this divine appointment with a man who needs Your grace and help. Thank You for holding the light red while I conducted Your business of sharing the Good News of Jesus Christ. Father, I know that even a brief moment such as the one I experienced is never wasted. Help us to be more sensitive to all people around us and to do what we can to encourage them in the ways You lead us. We love You and praise You in Jesus' name. Amen.

SPEAK TO YOUR MOUNTAIN

Truly, I say to you, whoever says to this mountain, 'Be taken up and thrown into the sea,' and does not doubt in his heart, but believes that what he says will come to pass, it will be done for him.
Mark 11:23 (ESV)

Jesus looked at them and said, "With man this is impossible, but with God all things are possible."
Matthew 19:26 (NIV)

No one is exempt from experiencing tough times in life. At this very moment, many people are burdened by physical, emotional, or spiritual pain. At first glance, most of us would never see the hurts of others. However, if we dig a little deeper and invest some time in one another, there is no doubt that we will find people bearing the weight of some stressful circumstance — either their own personally or that of a family member, friend, or acquaintance.

Whatever challenge(s) you are facing today, always remember that God's Word is full of promises that He will take you through every circumstance you now face or ever will face. He will give you peace as you walk through tough times. There is a light at the end of your tunnel, and His name is Jesus! He is your Resting Place, and He will see you through.

Prayer: Father God, we pray for all individuals who are hurting, wherever they may be. Give them the desire to know You and to learn of You through the many promises that are found in Your Word. Give them the hope that comes from knowing Jesus Christ as their personal Savior. This we pray in His name. Amen.

GROUNDHOG DAY

When Jesus spoke again to the people, he said, "I am the light of the world. Whoever follows me will never walk in darkness, but will have the light of life."

John 8:12 (NIV)

For many years, my sister, Peggy, and I have been blessed by our daily conversations. We laugh, we cry, and we problem-solve. I can count on one hand the times that we've disagreed about anything, and I am so thankful for our like-mindedness.

On one of my daily calls to Peggy, I began the conversation with some questions: "Hello, Sister, how are you?" "How's your day going?" "Is today Groundhog Day for you, too?" She would laugh and reply, "Yes, it's Groundhog Day again!" Being mostly in lockdown during the height of the pandemic, we were pretty much down to telling each other how many loads of laundry we had washed and dried on any given day! Our mundane chores had become a real topic of conversation!

This little joke of our repetitive days caused me to remember the 1993 movie *Groundhog Day.* In the film, Bill Murray starred as weatherman Phil Connors, who was sent to cover the Groundhog Day festivities in Punxsutawney, PA. His job was to report whether or not the groundhog, Punxsutawney Phil, came out of his den. While covering the event, something went wrong, and every morning when Phil's alarm clock rang at 6:00 a.m., it was still February 2nd. He relived the same day over and over until the calendar finally advanced.

Many of us did feel as though we were experiencing Groundhog Day during the unprecedented time of the pandemic, because in many ways we were stopped in our tracks. We had no reference point for how we would handle each day as time lengthened, and we couldn't see the light at the end of the tunnel. We were living in a time that none of us had ever experienced.

After five years, we've regained a sense of normalcy. We've all been touched deeply by illnesses and the loss of family members, friends, and acquaintances. As we go forward living each new day we are given, we can choose to make it the best day possible by praying, reading God's Word, and being kind, compassionate, helpful, and loving toward others. We can share our faith with those anxious and weary from these days of uncertainty. We can depend on the light of Jesus to help us, and we can share that light with others.

I am thankful for the time spent talking with my sister, especially during those long weeks and months when we could not meet in person. Even if we experience another Groundhog Day, we will be able to meet each new break of dawn with joy and hope, because we know the God of all HOPE! We will rest in Him. That certainly makes a noticeable difference!

Prayer: Dear Heavenly Father, we thank You for getting us through unprecedented times such as the Pandemic. Help us to give thanks each new day for all You have done for us and how You carry us through life's twists and turns. We love You and long to serve You with passion and purpose. We pray this in Jesus' name. Amen.

HIS PROMISES WILL STAND

Let us hold fast the confession of our hope without wavering,
for he who promised is faithful.

Hebrews 10:23 (ESV)

Have you ever made a promise, intending with all your might to keep it?

We are all human and will occasionally unintentionally break a promise. But isn't it wonderful to have everlasting assurance that the promises we find in God's Word will never be broken? God intends to keep His promises, for His Word remains unchanged. There are many promises found in the Bible, but some of my favorites are that He will never leave us; He will give us needed strength and wisdom; He will lead us on the best path if we allow Him to; and He will take care of us through every storm of grief, pain, and suffering. He is present in all areas of our lives and meets each of us, as different as we are, at the point of our individual needs. Whatever our situation, He is always ready to help us, give comfort, and further direct us. He has an answer for everything that concerns us.

Without a doubt, God's plans for us are the best! On our own, we could never accomplish what He wants to do in and through us. His mercies are new every morning as we strive to follow in the footsteps of our Lord and Savior, Jesus Christ. More than anything, we have the assurance that His promises will always stand.

Prayer: Father God, You are a Promise Keeper. Your Word and the many promises found therein continue to stand the test of time and will do so throughout all eternity. Thank You for giving Yourself through our Lord and Savior, Jesus Christ, so that we might be reconciled to You. In so doing, we gain access to all the promises You have made available for those who believe in Jesus. Help us to walk in the light of every truth from Your Word as we journey through this life. We pray these things in the mighty name of our Lord and Savior, Jesus Christ. Amen.

PEACE AND CONTENTMENT

I am not saying this because I am in need, for I have learned to be content whatever the circumstances.

Philippians 4:11 (NIV)

During these challenging times, many people are struggling in various ways. Having peace and contentment in the face of uncertainty or adversity is not easy. What does it take for peace and joy to become a reality in our lives? By what means are we able to counteract the enormous amount of negativity that flows so freely in our world today?

It often seems that a peace-filled day isn't possible. I can be sad, discouraged, afraid, and tired, but as I read God's Word and place my faith and trust in Him, my anxieties decrease, allowing peace and contentment to increase. Simply put, I know that God is in charge and His purposes are being carried out, even if I can't see the BIG picture. So I trust Him! For me personally, faith in Jesus is where my mind and strength are renewed, allowing me to view life in a more positive light. I trust the unknown to a known God—the One who loves us more than we can imagine and who knows our thoughts, our strengths, and our weaknesses.

My friends, if you're experiencing feelings like the ones I've described above, I want you to know that God has not brought you this far to leave you. He promises that very thing in His Word, more than once! Be assured today that He's at work nonstop on behalf of His people.

I pray that each of you is experiencing His peace and contentment today. If you're not, spend a few minutes reading the Psalms or the book of John. Talk to God, and listen for the still, small voice to guide you in all truth. Spend some time listening to Christian music. Then go about your day knowing that He is near and is working out all things for your good and His glory.

Prayer: Dear Father in Heaven, we know that it is only You who can bring the peace and contentment to our hearts for which we long. We pray that You would heal our broken world. Forgive us where we've failed You. Bring us back to Your ways and help us to live accordingly. Thank You for Jesus, who came so that we might believe, accept, and live for Him. Help us share with others the wonderful gift of eternal life that You offer through Jesus. We pray these things in the name of Jesus Christ, our Lord and Savior. Amen.

LET PEACE RULE
IN YOUR HEART

Let the peace of Christ rule in your hearts, since as members of one body you were called to peace. And be thankful.

Colossians 3:15 (NIV)

It seems that every year Christmas arrives before we know it. It passes as quickly as it appears, and recollections of the celebration will be stored away in our memory banks for yet another year.

Last year, I committed to enjoying Christmas more intentionally, so I spent more time reflecting on the goodness of God, who sent Jesus to save us for eternity. I also enjoyed seeing many beautiful Christmas light displays and preparing my home to reflect the true meaning of Christmas.

Like many special family celebrations, Christmas seems to magnify the void we feel when loved ones have gone ahead of us to Heaven. Thankfully, our family is learning, with God's help, to turn our sadness into gratitude for the love we will always feel for our departed family members and for the assurance that one day we will have a great reunion unlike anything we can imagine.

I continue to be grateful for each family Christmas, but I am most thankful for the priceless gift of God's grace and peace in my heart. The Scripture above tells us that as Christians, we have been called to a life of peace and thankfulness. The closer we are to Jesus, the more we'll be able to experience the tranquility He offers so freely. And the more we have peace about all situations in our lives, the more thankful we can be.

This year is a good time to ask the Lord to help you slow down enough to experience God's peace, not only at Christmastime but every day. I pray that you will let His gift of inner calm and emotional rest rule in your heart throughout each day and that you will give thanks for all He has done and continues to do for you.

Prayer: Dear God, when we celebrate the birth of our Lord and Savior, Jesus Christ, help us to focus more on the reason for the season and less on the commercialism of Christmas. We give thanks for the gift of family and friends and for the love and light they bring into our lives. Most of all, we thank You for the indescribable gift of Jesus Christ. Because He lives, we can face tomorrow with hope, peace, and joy. We pray this in His name. Amen.

THE LAST WILL BE FIRST

If anyone serves me, he must follow me; and where I am, there will my servant be also. If anyone serves me, the Father will honor him.

John 12:26 (ESV)

One day, the last Scripture will be placed in someone's hand. The last encouraging word of our faith in Jesus Christ will be spoken to someone who is searching for peace in their own life. The last song will be sung. The last church service will be held. There will be a lot of *lasts!* Time is short. It could be any day.

As believers, we look forward to what God has in store for us in Heaven, but while we're here on Earth running our race for Jesus Christ, may our greatest desire be to come in last! Sound strange? In this case, I believe that being last has merit and indeed eternal implications.

Let us have the desire to be that person who shares the last Scripture with someone who needs encouragement. As we share Scripture, may we never be reluctant also to share our unique story of redemption and rescue. Doing so will serve as a testimony of how God can take the broken pieces of our lives and make them into a beautiful masterpiece to be used for His glory alone.

So, yes, let us endeavor to be last in our work for the Kingdom of God. May we not stop, become discouraged, or take our focus off the prize we'll receive for completing our race. Remember that while Heaven is our ultimate home, Earth is the place where we make Jesus known. And one sweet day, we will see Him in all His glory and majesty. What a day that will be!

Prayer: Dear Heavenly Father, how we praise You and thank You for being with us through every moment of our lives. Give us the strength and wisdom to serve You with passion and purpose. May our spiritual race be run with the determination and endurance only You can provide. We pray this in the mighty name of our Lord and Savior, Jesus Christ. Amen.

WE CAN TRUST HIM

Blessed is the man who trusts in the Lord, whose trust is the Lord. He is like a tree planted by water, that sends out its roots by the stream, and does not fear when heat comes, for its leaves remain green, and is not anxious in the year of drought, for it does not cease to bear fruit.

Jeremiah 17:7-8 (ESV)

A Christian's faith in God through Jesus is about trust. In all circumstances we can trust Him to care for us. Relinquishing every aspect of our lives to His care and trusting that He always has our best interests at heart is a sure path to lasting peace and victory. He has a plan, and He knows what's best for us. He's never a day early or a minute too late. Although we may never know why certain things happen during our lifetime, we can trust that God's plan is for our good and that He ALWAYS goes before us. He promises never to leave us alone. He has always kept that promise to me. When I call, He is there to comfort and guide me in the right way. He will do the same for you if you let Him. I am praying that very thing for you today.

Prayer: Heavenly Father, through Your Word and through the many promises found therein, we have learned to trust You. Thank You, God, for teaching us that it's much easier to navigate life if we have confidence in You. Today, we ask that You empower our spirits with a new passion for the lost. Put them in our paths, I pray. As we depend on the Holy Spirit to give us those unexpected and uplifting divine appointments, please prepare us to serve You with all that is within us. These things we pray in the matchless name of Jesus Christ, our Lord and Savior. Amen.

IT'S ALL GOOD

And we know that in all things God works for the good of those who love him, who have been called according to his purpose.

Romans 8:28 (NIV)

A few months ago, my husband and I attended the memorial service of a longtime friend and dear brother in Christ. Paul was a man to be admired. He was a Marine Corps veteran from the Vietnam era, a wonderful husband, father, and treasured grandfather. He loved God and his family deeply; lived a life of positivity, even though life was not always easy; and assisted military vets suffering from PTSD to assimilate back into a stable lifestyle.

During Paul's homegoing service, his son, Donny, spoke with such deep love and unbridled affection for his dad that those in attendance were deeply moved. Donny shared that Paul repeatedly used a key phrase with three powerful words when dealing with any issue that might arise: "*It's all good!*" Regardless of family circumstances, pain, suffering, or challenges, Paul viewed life through a spiritual lens, trusting in God and believing that He was in control.

In his message to those attending Paul's memorial service, Pastor Ross Hartsfield spoke of Paul and his faith. He said, "If Paul were here today and could tell you what he is presently experiencing, I know he would tell us that it's all true." Here on Earth, Paul adopted the mindset that it's all good, knowing that whatever he was experiencing paled in comparison to the promise of what was to come in Heaven. When he stepped into eternity, his faith became sight. All that he had ever hoped for and believed was before him, even more beautiful than he could have imagined.

May we be so heavenly-minded that we don't let the troubles that come our way block the assurance that one sweet day, when we are past the trials and heartaches of this life, we will see firsthand that it has been worth it all. Then we can say with great excitement, *"It's all good because it's all true!"*

Prayer: Dear Heavenly Father, thank You for fellow believers like Paul and his family. Help us to live in such a way that others will be able to see Jesus in us as we did in Paul. We thank You for being our constant source of strength and faith. We pray this in Jesus' name. Amen.

THE CHRISTMAS GUEST

And the King will answer them, 'Truly, I say to you, as you did it to one of the least of these my brothers, you did it to me.'

Matthew 25:40 (ESV)

"The Christmas Guest" is a poem that Grandpa Jones of Grand Ole Opry fame often told during Christmas time. It's the story of Conrad, a lonely shopkeeper who dreamed that the Lord would be his Christmas guest. With great excitement Conrad carefully prepared his home for the Lord's appearance.

While Conrad waited for the Lord to visit him, three unexpected events happened. First, Conrad looked out the window and saw a beggar in the snow, dressed in ragged clothes and wearing torn shoes. Conrad felt compassion for the beggar and gave him a pair of shoes and a coat to keep him warm. Next, a knock on the door revealed a bent old lady who just wanted a place to rest. Conrad welcomed her into his home, gave her something to eat and drink, and let her rest. Finally, Conrad heard the sound of a lost child crying for help. In his concern for the child, Conrad calmed the child's fears and helped her return home.

That night, saddened that the time had slipped away, Conrad knelt by his bed and asked the Lord why He didn't come to be his Christmas guest. The Lord spoke to Conrad, telling him three times that day He had come to his lonely door. He was the beggar with cold, bruised feet; He was the woman Conrad gave something to eat; and He was the lost child on the homeless street. The Lord told Conrad that in each of those people, He had found the warmth of a friend. Conrad had expected one thing, but God chose another way to be his Christmas guest.

This poem reminds me of a time many years ago when I was hospitalized for surgery. On the morning of surgery, I received visits from two people from my church whom I had been expecting. Each prayed for successful surgery and healing over me. I was very appreciative; however, I had been expecting another visitor and was disappointed when that person didn't show up. As I mulled this over in my mind, an unexpected person came into the room. Through that visit, I heard the most beautiful and powerful prayer directed upward on my behalf. It was an amazing experience and an excellent lesson for me.

Just like Conrad, I learned that God sends to us those He chooses. He sends the unexpected to show us that He loves us in ways we sometimes don't understand and uses methods we would not have expected. I also learned not to focus my attention on particular individuals, because they will inevitably disappoint me at some point. The feeling of having been slighted by someone I looked up to soon gave way to gratitude that God always knows and does what is best for me.

I hope we will all be more aware that God has a way of sending us His best in ways we've never anticipated. May we be mindful of those He puts in our paths, and may we welcome them as our guests in whatever way is needed.

Prayer: Father, thank You for bringing the best of Yourself to us through others. Help us to be aware of the people You choose to place along our path daily. Give us wisdom to know how to help and encourage them in whatever ways are needed. We pray this in Jesus' name. Amen.

TRAFFIC STOP

For my thoughts are not your thoughts, neither are your ways my ways, declares the LORD. For as the heavens are higher than the earth, so are my ways higher than your ways and my thoughts than your thoughts.

Isaiah 55:8-9 (ESV)

It was a beautiful night as my husband Ray and I headed home from a meeting. We were only two hours away, but the drive allowed us an opportunity to share some uninterrupted time away from our busy schedules. At 10:30 p.m., our attention was drawn to the flashing lights behind us. It was obvious that we were being pulled over for a traffic stop.

The young police officer approached my side of the car. He greeted us in a warm, friendly way, then asked us the usual questions: *Where have you been? Where are you headed? May I see your driver's license and proof of insurance?* After answering his questions and digging through the glove compartment for proof of insurance, the officer told my husband that he was being stopped because he had changed lanes twice without signaling. Ray apologized, and the young man then proceeded to return to his patrol car to "check us out" on his computer. We were both hoping that no citation would be involved in this traffic stop.

Returning to our vehicle, the young man suggested that Ray remember to use his signal from now on and told us to have a safe trip home. PTL, no ticket was issued, just a warning. Ray then reached into his coat pocket, pulled out a New Testament, and offered it to the officer. The young man happily accepted this gift, stating that he usually kept a small Bible in his patrol car, but didn't seem to have one with him at that time.

As we drove off, I silently said a prayer for this young policeman, knowing what thankless and dangerous jobs first responders often have. I prayed that God's Word would not return void in this situation. I commented to Ray that the traffic stop might have happened just so that particular police officer would receive the Testament, for we didn't know what God was up to in his life. Ray agreed with my line of thinking.

Because we have seen firsthand and heard testimonies of those affected by the life-changing Word of God, only He knows for sure how many lives that one little New Testament will touch. The young officer may be reading it himself, sharing it with someone in need of spiritual help as the Holy Spirit directs, or sharing Jesus, the Hope of the world, with someone he arrests.

There are numerous exciting possibilities for that one little New Testament, and I firmly believe that we were placed in the midst of where God was working so that He might be glorified. These are the moments when we know that God will use us to share our faith through the Gospel of Jesus Christ, if only we make ourselves available, even during traffic stops!

Prayer: Heavenly Father, thank You for the traffic stops of life where we have unusual opportunities to share Jesus with the world. Help us to always be sensitive to the Holy Spirit's leading in sharing Your message with others. Please be with all first responders and keep them safe in the arms of Jesus. Show Your love in ways that only You can do. This we pray in the name of Jesus. Amen.

WORRY

But seek first the kingdom of God and his righteousness,
and all these things will be added to you.

Matthew 6:33 (ESV)

I could have written a book on worry and anxiety many years ago. My thinking was consistently negative, and I didn't seem to know how to change my thought patterns. While I understood that circumstances had thrown me into a pit of despair, I did not fully seek God's help to rid me of this destructive stronghold on my mind. At the time, I didn't recognize how negative my thinking was. I worried about every aspect of my life, from finances to illness. I was addicted to worry and had allowed fear and anxiety to distract me from living an abundant life in Christ. That distraction alone hindered me from giving God my best.

I am thankful that with God's help and to His glory, I walked out of my pit of worry and anxiousness. It was not sudden, but over time I learned to rest more comfortably in the arms of my Shepherd, Jesus Christ. Somewhere along the journey, I realized that I was thinking more positively about my life, and my fear, worry, and anxiety began to diminish. Even though there are occasional times when worry does sneak back into my mind, the difference now is that I have given all my concerns over to Jesus Christ.

Because God is faithful to care for His children, we do not have to let worrisome thoughts interfere with our days. We belong to Him! He is the only one who can bring us the real and lasting peace we desperately long for in this life. He can certainly handle all that concerns us today and always.

Prayer: Dear Heavenly Father, thank You for being ever present to take our worry and anxiety upon Your shoulders. In doing so, You free us to be a better representative of what Jesus did for us on the Cross. Give us peace, comfort, and the assurance that You are working out our story for Your good purposes. May we always shine for You. We pray this in the name of our Savior and Lord, Jesus Christ. Amen.

BRAND NEW DAY

Yet this I call to mind and therefore I have hope: Because of the LORD's great love we are not consumed, for his compassions never fail. They are new every morning; great is your faithfulness.

Lamentations 3:21-23 (NIV)

When I was growing up in East Texas, we didn't have any air conditioning. I can still remember those sleepless, hot summer nights. To make it worse, if possible, there were always a few mosquitoes flying around in the dark. We children knew they'd find us before the morning light. Thankfully, we survived despite the less-than-desirable conditions. These are warm memories now, but at the time we didn't see things quite that way.

Despite my childhood memories of the uncomfortable heat and my present-day existence in the high temperatures of a Central Texas summer, today is a brand-new day! This day was ushered in by none other than our Heavenly Father, Himself—God Almighty, the Creator of the universe and each one of us. And I'm so thankful that He saw fit to give us a beautiful day.

I hope that each of you will begin this new day by giving our Heavenly Father a personal invitation to be active in your life; that you will seek His guidance as your day progresses; and that you will share His love with those you encounter. May today find you serving Him in all ways. He is ever faithful to shower us with His love and mercy as a new day dawns, and He is always faithful in giving us yet another opportunity to experience a new beginning.

Prayer: Heavenly Father, thank You for each new day. Some may be do-overs, but in Your love, grace, and mercy, You allow us to begin again and again. We thank You for showing us how faithful You are through the many blessings bestowed upon us. Help us to honor You with our time and talents while here on Earth; to tell others how a relationship with Jesus Christ has changed our lives; and how they, too, can experience eternal salvation by placing their faith and trust in Him. We look forward to whatever today holds, for we know Your loving hands have fashioned it. Give us Your wisdom and guidance in all things. We pray this in Jesus' name. Amen.

EVERLASTING WATER

But whoever drinks of the water that I will give him will never be thirsty again. The water that I will give him will become in him a spring of water welling up to eternal life.

John 4:14 (ESV)

I have always loved to be near, around, or in the water. Whether it's hearing the roar of Niagara Falls, the sound of ocean waves, or the trickle of a stream, the result is always an incredible peace that rests my mind and soothes my soul.

Today I am reminded of the eternal *living water* referenced in Scripture. Jesus offers this water to each of us if we will surrender our lives to Him. His is the only water we can partake of that will quench our spiritual thirst and give us eternal life when our time here on Earth is gone. While we wait for that glorious day, we will be given peace and joy that can only come from a powerful God who loves each of us more than we'll ever realize.

How thankful we can be today for the promise of eternal life through the *living water* Jesus offers each of us so freely. Drink plenty of this thirst-quenching, everlasting water today, and your heart will never be the same.

Prayer: Dear God, we can never thank You enough for the eternal living water that You give us through faith in Jesus Christ. We are undeserving, but in love You made it possible. Help us to drink freely of Your Word as we find our joy and peace through Jesus. We pray this in His name. Amen.

SPIRITUAL EYESIGHT

I pray that the eyes of your heart may be enlightened in order that you may know the hope to which he has called you, the riches of his glorious inheritance in his holy people, and his incomparably great power for us who believe.

Ephesians 1:18-19a (NIV)

Now and then something reminds me of my age. My energy level is excellent most of the time, thanks in part to the young people and sweet babies in my family with whom I spend a lot of time. However, there are occasions when our bodies do give us hints of the maintenance we need.

Such was the case a few months ago when I scheduled a long-overdue eye exam appointment. After a thorough examination, I was relieved to hear that I only needed surgery for cataract removal to correct my poor eyesight.

Since seeing the eye doctor, I've thought a lot about my maternal grandmother Smith. Grandma lost her eyesight due to glaucoma at the age of 60-something. Because I was so young, I only remember her being blind. She lived with my aunt and her family about five miles from my home, and occasionally, Grandma would come to visit us for a day or so. I admired how carefully and slowly she maneuvered her way around the house. It must have taken a lot of faith and fortitude for her to adjust to total blindness after having had sight all those years.

I am thankful to have had a BIG improvement in my eyesight after surgery. But more than just better eyesight, I pray that the Lord will always help me to improve my spiritual eyesight. I pray that He will open the eyes of my heart so that I might always see Him more clearly, love Him more dearly, walk with Him more steadfastly, and serve Him at every opportunity. I pray the same for my family and friends who know Him.

For those who do not yet have a personal relationship with Him, I pray that the spiritual film will fall off the eyes of their hearts and that they will experience the inner peace and freedom that can only be found in knowing Jesus Christ as Lord and Savior.

Prayer: Dear Heavenly Father, today I pray that You would open the eyes of our hearts and give us spiritual eyesight to see the needs of those around us. May we never be spiritually blind to living out Your Word. Holy Spirit, please lead and guide us, for we know there are many hurting souls. We pray these things in Jesus' name. Amen.

PEACE

Peace I leave with you; my peace I give you.
I do not give to you as the world gives. Do not let your hearts
be troubled and do not be afraid.

John 14:27 (NIV)

Peace. Ahh! Isn't that what we all want? How can we reduce our focus on fear and worry? How can we look at God's long-range plan for our lives rather than focusing on these troubled times in which we live? How can we find lasting peace?

None of us is exempt from the struggles of this life and the fear we sometimes feel as a result of our struggles. From personal experience, I can testify that we can have lasting peace if our focus is in the right place. There's only one place that I have found such peace, which results in less and less fear of anything that will come against me, present or future. It is through my sweet relationship with Jesus Christ that I find peace.

Through our commitment to God and our reliance on Him to guide us through each day, we can rise above the hard places in life. Rather than our circumstances blinding us, we will see that there is no need to fear. With God's help we will understand the words found in **1 John 4:18a, ESV: "There is no fear in love, but perfect love casts out fear."**

When the veil of pain and sorrow is lifted from our eyes, we'll see a brighter and clearer picture of God's love and peace all around us.

Prayer: Heavenly Father, Yours is the only peace that we desire. Thank You for giving us all that and more. To know that Your love reaches into the depths of our souls brings not only peace but sweet joy. Help us to live in such a way that we shine the light of Jesus to a lost and dying world and that we exhibit peace amid the challenges we face today. We pray this in the name of Jesus Christ, our Lord and Savior. Amen.

GOD'S WORD

You will seek me and find me,
when you seek me with all your heart.
Jeremiah 29:13 (ESV)

When I don't spend time in God's Word, I feel as though something is missing–and it is. We cannot truly get to know another person or maintain a relationship unless we spend time with that individual. So it is with God's Word. How can we know God unless we spend time reading life's instruction book–God's story–the Bible? How can we know the wonderful promises contained in His Word if we don't first find out what they are? How can we have peace that passes all understanding and joy unspeakable unless we know Him in a personal way?

Many people claim they don't believe in God, but I wonder if they have truly searched for Him through His Word and the many promises it contains. If you seek Him, you will find Him. That I know with certainty. And, if you do not know the Lord Jesus Christ as your Savior, I pray that your heart will seek Him while He may be found.

Prayer: Dear Father, Your Word is a lamp unto our feet and a light unto our path. It never changes or goes out of style. While today's culture may indicate otherwise, Your children know Your voice and follow You instead of the world. Help us to live in such a way that others will see Jesus in us and that they will seek You with all of their heart. We pray this in the name of Jesus Christ, our Lord and Savior. Amen.

SERVE WHOLEHEARTEDLY

Serve wholeheartedly, as if you were serving the Lord, not men, because you know that the Lord will reward everyone for whatever good he does, whether he is slave or free.

Ephesians 6:7 (NIV)

Having previously worked in a public school system for 27 years, I can assure you that each day was an adventure. To put it mildly, there was never a dull moment! Some days passed smoothly, but others were not enjoyable! On any given day, there could be stray bats flying down the halls, disruptive children refusing to follow instructions, or an estranged parent attempting to remove their child from the school without the legal right to do so. Although I loved my job and the campus staff dearly, there were days when the dentist's office sounded like a more appealing alternative than being at work.

During moments like the ones described above, I genuinely tried to show love and compassion to others when presented with stressful situations. However, there were days when my patience would wear thin, and my frustration would show. Perhaps those around me could not see even the slightest characteristic of Christ living in me during those moments. If that were the case, then I was relying on my own strength and not doing my job *as unto the Lord.*

This week, let us resolve to devote ourselves to others, serving them joyfully, enthusiastically, and with earnest commitment. May we go the extra mile whenever possible and show patience, kindness, and love. Above all, let's remember that Christ living in and through us brings light to the world. Accordingly, we will experience God's peace for striving to create this type of environment in the workplace, at home, or in our communities.

Prayer: Father God, help us to joyfully serve You with love and kindness, knowing that we are Your representatives here on Earth. Fill us with Your power and strength each day, so that others may see Christ living in us and want to follow Him. Give us strength and patience as we go about Your business in our daily lives. We ask this in the precious name of Jesus Christ. Amen.

TAKE TIME

Be still, and know that I am God. I will be exalted among the nations, I will be exalted in the earth!
Psalm 46:10 (ESV)

I do love the quietness of a morning when I haven't let my own *busyness* stand in the way of being still before God. I'm so thankful for another day—one more day to get up and show up for Jesus.

As I write this, I'm looking at one of the rose bushes outside my window, and I'm thankful they are the *easy ones* to grow! Even though I don't have a green thumb, I appreciate the beauty I see and hear all around me. Nearby, the birds are singing a beautiful melody with such gusto! I am reminded that they have no worries, no fears, no anxiety. If God cares for them **(Matthew 6:25-34)**, He will care for us in the same way. He is able to do **"(...)immeasurably more than all we ask or imagine, according to His power that is at work within us" (Ephesians 3:20 NIV)**.

We have a perfect Heavenly Father who loves us more than we could ever comprehend. May we take time to find rest in gratitude for all He has done for us and for all He intends to do. His love and care for us will never fail.

Prayer: Dear God, thank You for the beauty and quietness of a new day. Help us to stay alert with our eyes wide open in gratitude for the many blessings You bestow upon us. Thank You for the peace and joy that come when we are settled and abiding in our Savior, Jesus Christ. We pray this in His name. Amen.

HE CAME FOR US

For we do not have a High Priest who is unable to sympathize with our weaknesses, but one who in every respect has been tempted as we are, yet without sin.

Hebrews 4:15 (ESV)

Talk about having friends in high places! Isn't it great to know that we are serving a God who knows what it's like to walk in our shoes! Being a child of the King, we may go boldly to the throne and find grace and strength to help in times of need.

Jesus Christ, God in human form, came to the Earth, yet He never lived outside God's perfect will. The Bible says He was tempted in every way we are; yet He never gave in to temptation, had an impure thought, or did anything to displease His Father. He was flawless, sinless, and perfect.

So why did Jesus come to Earth as God in human form? Was it to give us the very best set of principles ever? No. Though they were the greatest teachings ever given, He came here for more than that. Did Jesus come to set the perfect example of how a man or woman should live? Yes, He came to do that and much more. Did Jesus walk the Earth merely to do miracles and heal people? While He always reached out to people in need, that was not His primary purpose. C.S. Lewis aptly expressed this idea in his book *Mere Christianity*: "The Son of God became a man that men might become sons of God."

God became a man so that we might become His children. Now that is something worth celebrating!

Prayer: Dear Heavenly Father, what a marvelous plan You had for the world. Sending Jesus on such a rescue mission was costly, but He obeyed You fully. We can never repay Him for dying on the Cross for us, for we were the ones who deserved to be there. Help us to live according to Your precepts so that others will see Jesus living in us. Please guard our hearts and minds daily as we face trials and temptations that often come our way. We pray this in Jesus' name. Amen.

Lewis, C.S., *Mere Christianity*, Geoffrey Bles, published July 7, 1952, adapted from a series of BBC radio talks made between 1941 and 1944.

WALNUTS

For I am sure that neither death nor life, nor angels nor rulers, nor things present nor things to come, nor powers, nor height nor depth, nor anything else in all creation, will be able to separate us from the love of God in Christ Jesus our Lord.

Romans 8:38-39 (NIV)

When I was a child, Christmas and New Year's Day were special celebrations for my siblings and me. We didn't have many extra things, but we never complained because we somehow knew our parents were doing their very best to provide for seven little children. But......during the holidays, my parents somehow managed to pull out all the stops for us. There was always delicious food from my mother's kitchen, and our dad would buy bags of fruit, mainly apples and oranges, for us to enjoy. The Washington Red Delicious apples always seemed to be bigger and juicer at Christmastime.

Daddy would also purchase bags of mixed nuts, which is where my love for walnuts began. Presently, I eat walnuts almost every day. For me, consuming them is about the health benefits, for sure, but even more so, it's about the warm and secure feeling of *being home* that I experience every time I indulge in them. Strange, I know, but it's like going back in my mind and heart to a happy time from my childhood.

It's amazing what will bring cherished memories and joy to us if we only take the time to remember. I'm thankful that God has given us these remembrances that will always hold a special place in our hearts.

Prayer: Dear Heavenly Father, the love You give us through the simplest of things brings great joy. You don't miss a thing! Thank You for the lessons You teach us through the everyday things of life. Help us recognize how You are always at work and give us pause to honor and praise You in all things. We pray this in Jesus' name. Amen.

GOD KNOWS HOW WE FEEL

Come to me, all who labor and are heavy laden, and I will give you rest. Take my yoke upon you, and learn from me, for I am gentle and lowly in heart, and you will find rest for your souls.

Matthew 11:28-29 (ESV)

Have you ever been so distraught that you blamed God for your circumstances? I know many people who have.

Once during a small group meeting, one of our friends shared how he was going through a tough time. He said he found himself standing in the middle of his living room and yelling at God. Do you think God was shocked and didn't know how to handle that situation? Of course, He wasn't! God knows how we feel.

At times our spirit breaks from the heavy load we bear. It is then, when we are the most vulnerable, that God stands ready to guide us and to give us His strength. As we come to Him with a humble and trusting heart, we will experience His overwhelming love and peace.

Through all of these times - the good, the bad, and the ugly - God is faithful to stand by us. Just as a family member or dear friend is at our side no matter what happens, our Heavenly Father is always available to jump in and actively work to make things better for us. Our part? We must exhibit our faith and trust that He is there and that He will give us His hand to hold while we walk slowly forward. He will always carry us through the rough places of life. We can be confident of that very thing.

Prayer: Dear Heavenly Father, thank You for making a way for us when we are weary from the cares of life. We trust that You know what is best for us in every situation, and that You have a good plan and purpose that we cannot always see. It is through our faith in Jesus Christ that we can continue to move forward each day. Thank You, Father. In Jesus' name we pray. Amen.

OPEN THE EYES OF MY HEART

I pray that the eyes of your heart may be enlightened in order that you may know the hope to which he has called you, the riches of his glorious inheritance in his holy people, and his incomparably great power for us who believe.

Ephesians 1:18-19a (NIV)

I am very thankful for having been raised in a Christian family. Despite its imperfections, it was in that home where I was taken to church and taught that having faith in Jesus needed to be my top priority in life. How thankful I am that the spiritual eyes of my heart were opened at a young age to find eternal life, hope, peace, and joy. I have failed many times, but Jesus has always been there to forgive me, set me straight, and help me keep my focus on Him.

Let us pray for those who have not yet found that relationship—that their eyes will be opened in a miraculous way. If only they could know what they are missing by not looking at life through a spiritual lens. Jeremiah 29:11 tells us that God has a plan for each of us that is good and perfect. It is a gift given in great love and begins in the heart, where one's pride is surrendered in exchange for His plan.

Prayer: Heavenly Father, we praise You and we thank You for making a way for us to inherit eternal life. We fully know that it is not through our own works that we are saved, but by Your grace alone. Father, today and every day, we humbly ask You to continue doing a work in us that will enable others to see the light of Jesus shining brightly through us. We praise You and thank You for hearing and answering this prayer. In Jesus' name, we pray. Amen.

FINDING REST

Come to me, all who labor and are heavy laden, and I will give you rest. Take My yoke upon you, and learn from me, for I am gentle and lowly in heart, and you will find rest for your souls.

Matthew 11:28-29 (ESV)

In the above Scripture, Jesus tells us that He will give us rest. He helps us slow down, take a breath, and trust that He is not silent to our present concerns, because sometimes life can be excruciating.

Before I retired from the local school district, I often came home physically and emotionally drained. Life on a school campus can be challenging at times, but it is also very rewarding.

I was reminded of my own times of exhaustion when a teacher friend messaged me asking for prayer. My friend is a strong Christian and a seasoned high school teacher, but her work week had been so overwhelming that she had given serious thought to quitting her job. In addition to assuring her that I would be praying for the circumstances surrounding her school challenges, I felt she could best be served by my encouraging her to rest. The next day, my friend let me know that she had completed her lesson plans (one of the pressing tasks she needed to do) and was about to take a long rest. At that point, she was much more positive about what her upcoming week would look like. Praise God for that!

Friends, let's remember that God meets each of us, as different as we are, at the point of our need. Whatever our situation, He is there to help, give comfort, and direct us. God loves us, and we can meet with Him at the foot of the Cross, where we will find rest for our souls. Meeting regularly with Him will ensure that we are spiritually nourished for anything that comes our way.

Prayer: Dear God, You are the God who sees us. You are big enough to rule this mighty universe, yet small enough to live within our hearts. We praise You and thank You for being as close as the mention of Your name. When we feel overwhelmed and in need of rest, You are always present to bring us peace and comfort. We love You and praise You for all You are to us. In Jesus' name, we pray. Amen.

THE LORD IS PEACE

Peace I leave with you; my peace I give to you.
Not as the world gives do I give to you. Let not your hearts
be troubled, neither let them be afraid.

John 14:27 (ESV)

Jehovah Shalom – The LORD is Peace. Where is God in our plight or pain? Where is He when we feel that life is not going the way we wanted? Where is He when we feel all alone? Friends, He is with us and will bring peace, not fear, to our hearts. Throughout the seasons of life, it is through our faith and trust in Jesus that we experience His presence, peace, and faithfulness at every step.

The truth remains that God's peace will be with us through every circumstance. Our struggles in life will change, but our focus should remain the same. God is the author of our story, and He has not yet finished writing it.

Prayer: Dear Heavenly Father, how comforting it is to know and experience the peace You bring to every situation that we have ever faced or will ever face in life. You are not only a loving Father, but also a very generous One who lavishes Your grace upon us. We thank You and can never repay the debt of love we owe. We commit to praising and honoring You completely all the days of our lives. We pray these things in the name of our Lord and Savior, Jesus Christ. Amen.

DON'T DOUBT YOUR USEFULNESS

And the LORD turned to him and said, "Go in this might of yours and save Israel from the hand of Midian; do not I send you?" And he said to him, "Please, Lord, how can I save Israel? Behold, my clan is the weakest in Manasseh, and I am the least in my father's house."

Judges 6:14-15 (ESV)

Like Gideon in Judges Chapter 6, we may doubt what we can accomplish for the Lord. It is easy to come up with varying excuses instead of actively participating in where God is leading us and what He wants to do in and through us.

Self-doubt will hold us back from being all God wants us to be. During my young adult years, I struggled with that very thing, having little confidence that God could use me in any way. I found excuses, just as Gideon did. Eventually, over time and through various experiences, God brought me to the realization that there is nothing I am capable of doing on my own, but with Christ living in me, I can accomplish much.

How then can we rid ourselves of doubting our usefulness to the Kingdom of God? It is imperative to focus on what God thinks of us, rather than what we think of ourselves. Day by day, as we communicate with God through prayer and the study of His Word, He will help us to overcome our doubts and fears. It is He who goes before us, carving out the path we should take. Our job is to allow the Holy Spirit to lead and give direction. We will then have the knowledge and assurance that we are not alone in our walk of faith. God does have a plan for us as we reach out to others and strive to do His will.

We are called to be the hands and feet of Jesus Christ as we live out our faith. Remember, His strength is made perfect in our weakness. He will give each of us the confidence that we need for a productive day of serving Him.

Prayer: Help us, Father, never to doubt our usefulness to Your Kingdom. You have gifted each of us in ways unique to who we are. May we live out our faith in Jesus Christ by sharing His Good News with those whose paths we cross, even today. We pray this in His name. Amen.

TOUGH TIMES NEVER LAST

When I thought, 'My foot slips,' your steadfast love, O LORD, held me up. When the cares of my heart are many, your consolations cheer my soul.

Psalm 94:18-19 (ESV)

Isn't it wonderful that God knows every anxious moment we experience in life? It is impossible to avoid tough circumstances, for they come to all of us. But the Good News is that we don't have to be alone during those times, because we have Jesus to see us through each moment of uncertainty. He is as close as the mention of His name, He meets us at the point of our need, He sees us when we feel otherwise unseen, and He brings peace in the midst of chaos. Why can I be so sure of this? Because He's done it for me countless times during my lifetime.

In His Word Jesus gives a rock-solid promise: **"Peace I leave with you; my peace I give to you. Not as the world gives do I give to you. Let not your hearts be troubled, neither let them be afraid" John 14:27 (ESV).** You have Someone who can see you through those seasons of struggle and discord in your life. He knows what you need and stands ready to help you. Be assured that when you call upon Him, you will begin to experience a deep peace that only He can give.

God loves you more than you will ever know. Today and always, He wants to walk beside you. The key is to call on Him, invite Him into your situation, and trust that His wonder-working power will help you safely navigate through whatever challenges you face.

Prayer: Heavenly Father, You are the God who sees every aspect of our lives. You are working on our behalf even when we can't see or feel it. Help us to lean into Jesus and trust His heart for us. Thank You for giving us such love. We pray this in Jesus' name. Amen.

WHAT DOES CHRISTMAS MEAN TO YOU?

For unto you is born this day in the city of David a Savior,
who is Christ the Lord.

Luke 2:11 (ESV)

What does Christmas mean to you?

From my earliest memories, it seems I've always known the true meaning of Christmas. My siblings and I were taught about Jesus from childhood, but truthfully, as a little girl, I didn't have the maturity to fully understand the Greatest Gift of all until I was a bit older. I did like the idea of Santa and always looked forward to the gifts he brought on Christmas Eve, which was our traditional time to celebrate. In addition to receiving presents, we shared a delicious meal, after which we built a roaring fire outside to pop fireworks!

Even though I have always loved the festivities that surround the Christmas season, I am thankful to have learned at an early age that the true meaning of Christmas is NOT about opening presents. It's about inviting Jesus, the greatest gift ever given to humanity, into our hearts. When we have His presence deep within, then our perspective and priorities will change to the point that He will always have first place in our lives.

Prayer: Dear Heavenly Father, thank You for the greatest gift of all—our Lord and Savior, Jesus Christ. There is nothing that could ever give us peace and joy like our relationship with Him. Please help us to shine brightly for You. We pray this in Jesus' name. Amen.

LEST WE FORGET

The thief comes only to steal and kill and destroy. I came that they may have life and have it abundantly.

John 10:10 (ESV)

It had been a wonderful weekend of spiritual renewal. The meeting was amazing, and the fellowship with Christian brothers and sisters was the icing on the cake. Shortly after returning home, I came down with a terrible upper respiratory infection. I felt discouraged on those tiresome days, not knowing the outcome of my health issue. After a trip to the doctor and several days in bed, I finally returned to my energetic self.

One of Satan's specialties is to bring us down even further when we are not feeling well. He knows our specific weaknesses and how to plant unhealthy thoughts, words, and actions into our minds to temporarily remove our focus from our faith. What do we do? Our only response should be not to take his bait. While I was sick, I continued with my daily quiet time, which included reading God's Word, praying, and writing inspirational thoughts. I also listened to uplifting Christian music.

I have lived for many years, for which I'm very thankful. Along with age often comes a little wisdom. I have found that through life's hard times and challenges, Jesus offers us an abundance of His joy, peace, strength, hope, guidance, and wisdom, as well as an intimate relationship with Himself. Lest we forget, our part is to trust Him and move in His direction. He's so good at taking us right where we are and lifting us up. Any setback we experience will be temporary as we walk in step with Him. Over our lifetime, our story will have its mountains and valleys, but God will be with us every step of the way.

Prayer: Dear Heavenly Father, thank You for leading us through the dark valleys of life, only to bring us out on the other side more in love with You. Thank You for protecting us against the enemy's schemes. Help us always to be aware that Satan is working overtime in these last days. Lest we forget, may we stay focused on our faith in Jesus Christ and the glorious riches of our life through Him. Forgive us when we fail You, and continue to bring us closer to the truth of Your Word. We pray this in Jesus' name. Amen.

BLESSINGS FROM GOD'S HANDS

Give thanks in all circumstances, for this is the will of God in Christ Jesus for you.

1 Thessalonians 5:18 (ESV)

I love waking in the morning and being reminded how blessed I am, even though I've had many heartaches and trials during my lifetime. I honestly don't know what I would do without the strength and encouragement found through a personal relationship with God, through Jesus Christ. The assurance found in Him, His love, and His Word, serves to strengthen us for whatever we may face in the days ahead. He has proven His faithfulness in the past, so there's no reason to doubt Him now.

If difficult circumstances have found their way to your doorstep, try your best to find the blessings in them. One blessing I know for sure is that Jesus is with you every step you take in going forward. He will not leave you; He will not forsake you; He will see you through safely and completely. You have His Word on that. Rest in Him today.

Prayer: Dear Heavenly Father, You are the God who sees us—the One who has numbered every hair on our heads. You know our weaknesses, our strengths, our sadness and sorrow. You know what and when we need something even before we ask. You are a personal Father who will never leave us nor forsake us. In times when we are presented with life's challenges, it is You who longs to step in and help us through the difficult circumstances that we encounter. Thank You for watching over us and for giving us all we need to get safely through life's battles. We pray this in Jesus' name. Amen.

WE NEED A SAVIOR

For all have sinned and fall short of the glory of God,
and are justified by his grace as a gift, through the
redemption that is in Christ Jesus.

Romans 3:23-24 (ESV)

"Have you ever thought about what a Christian is? Christians are people who have shuddered at the awfulness of their sin. They have seen sin for what it is: willful rebellion against the rulership of God in their lives. And in turning from their sin, they have embraced God's only means of dealing with sin: Jesus." Kay Arthur, Facebook Post, 2023.

Even as a 12-year-old child, I knew I needed a Savior. I will never forget that Sunday night when my friend Charlotte and I walked the aisle of our little country church and asked Jesus to come into our hearts. I felt the change immediately. Since then, I've had a lifetime of growing and learning to lean more and more on Him; of trusting that He works out all things for my good and His glory; and of coming to believe beyond a shadow of a doubt that despite my faults and failures, He loves me more than I can comprehend.

Had I been spiritually mature at a young age, perhaps I would have avoided some of life's pitfalls and hard knocks. However, I've been drawn closer to Jesus through those tough times, so I can only thank Him for never letting go of me. All I know now is that God is good; He has a plan for each of us; He is with us if we seek Him; it's up to us to choose to follow Him; and it's in His loving care that we will find unexplainable peace and rest. I am eternally grateful for His goodness and pray that each person reading this also follows the Savior of the world, Jesus Christ. He waits for you and is as close as the mention of His name. I pray that you will give your heart to Him, even now. You will never regret it.

Prayer: Dear God, we give thanks today for Your never-ending love and patience. Thank You for guiding our footsteps as we walk this journey called life. Most of all, we thank You for eternal salvation through Jesus Christ. Help us to pass our faith along to those around us and lead us to be Your witnesses everywhere we go. We pray this in Jesus' name. Amen.

LIVING WATER

Have you not known? Have you not heard? The LORD is the everlasting God, the Creator of the ends of the earth. He does not faint or grow weary; his understanding is unsearchable. He gives power to the faint, and to him who has no might he increases strength. Even youths shall faint and be weary, and young men shall fall exhausted; but they who wait for the LORD shall renew their strength; they shall mount up with wings like eagles; they shall run and not be weary; they shall walk and not faint.

Isaiah 40:28-31 (ESV)

I am so thankful that Jesus provides a wellspring of living water, which is the perfect place to renew our physical, emotional, and spiritual strength daily. While we may become parched in a dry land—a very draining season of life—we are never without the refreshment of His living water.

Just as we need water to hydrate our bodies constantly, we must also drink regularly from God's Word, pour out our hearts through conversation with Him (prayer), and encourage one another. God will renew us daily as we lean upon Him. He will guide us to be a blessing to others along the way, thanks to our own life experiences. We need not waste our tough times or keep them to ourselves; instead, we are called to offer words of hope and encouragement to others as the opportunity arises.

Jesus is always there to guide, provide for, and protect us! Many people need to hear this Good News. Why not watch for those types of opportunities today as the Holy Spirit leads you.

Prayer: Father God, while our bodies need rest, You neither sleep nor slumber. How comforting to know that You have a watchful eye on us at all times. Help us today to honor and serve You with gladness. Place others in our path that we might share all that Jesus offers them. Prepare their hearts with the desire and conviction that Jesus will save them from their old way of life. This we ask in the name of Jesus Christ, our Lord and Savior. Amen.

WORDS

Let the words of my mouth and the meditation of my heart be acceptable in your sight, O LORD, my rock and my redeemer.

Psalm 19:14 (ESV)

When reading Psalm 19 and focusing on verse 14, I am reminded of the power of our words. It wasn't a new revelation to me, but rather a little nudge to park here for just a moment.

"Let the words of my mouth (...)" Our choice of words makes such a difference in the lives of others as well as our own. Words can tear down, and they can build up. Words can wound or they can heal. Words spoken harshly to another can certainly be forgiven, but they are not easily forgotten. We must always strive to choose our words carefully. I certainly need reminders of how much the words I speak and the way I say them can affect others each day.

Because we are all human, we've been on both sides of this equation. We have been injured by someone's thoughtless or harsh words and no doubt have wounded others in the same way. Whether or not the words were spoken impulsively or defensively makes no difference. Someone was hurt.

How do we go forth with kind words that build others up? We do it day by day, trusting our good, good Father to arm us with His strength and the love of Jesus in our hearts.

Every morning and night for several years I have prayed **Psalm 51:10, ESV, "Create in me a clean heart, O God and renew a right spirit within me."** Sometimes I fail. However, my heart desires to always focus on Him, to have a clean heart before Him, and to allow His Spirit to work in my life so that His love will shine forth from me in such a way that He will have found me faithful in all things. So whether I use a lot of words or just a few, I pray that my heart will always be centered on Him. May this be your prayer today, as well.

Prayer: Gracious Father, our words are of great importance to You. Please help us to think before we speak in harshness or anger, and give us a heart that is willing to forgive those who use their words to wound us. Ultimately, what matters most is that we keep our hearts clean before You. Thank You for helping us in yet another way to abide in You. We pray this in Jesus' name. Amen.

HIS HEART REJOICES

The LORD your God is in your midst, a mighty one who will save;
he will rejoice over you with gladness; he will quiet you by his love;
he will exult over you with loud singing.

Zephaniah 3:17 (ESV)

I love God's Word! It gives direction, soothes my soul, and has strengthened my walk with the Lord Jesus time and time again! Yet, what I gain from God's Word is only scratching the surface of how much He loves each of us and how His heart rejoices when we abide in Him.

When we fail to live as we should, God's heart breaks. Just as we feel sorrow when we see others hurting and seemingly helpless to rise above their circumstances, He must grieve as He watches us struggle with the consequences of our poor choices. God has the power to lift us out of our pit of despair and pain if we call out to Him with repentant hearts.

So when you don't know where to turn, it's Jesus who is ready and waiting to walk with you, pour His love into you, and help you stay on the path where you will reap eternal benefits. I don't know of a better place to be than resting in our perfect Heavenly Father and His Word.

Prayer: Dear God, words fail to convey just how much we love You and Your Holy Word. It is life to our sometimes dry spiritual bones. Your Word is alive! Thank You for showing up every time we open our Bible. Help us to live out our faith standing on Your promises, for they bring peace to us in such a sinful and fallen world. We want to make a difference for Jesus, so please give us Your wisdom and love for everyone we meet. We pray this in the mighty name of Jesus and for His sake. Amen.

A NEW NORMAL

But blessed is the one who trusts in the Lord, whose confidence is in him. They will be like a tree planted by the water that sends out its roots by the stream. It does not fear when heat comes; its leaves are always green. It has no worries in a year of drought and never fails to bear fruit.

Jeremiah 17:7-8 (ESV)

Patsy Clairmont, best known for her association with the Women of Faith ministry, has an amazing story. Once traumatized by the thought of going outside the boundaries of her home, she wasn't experiencing life to the fullest. Her life was anything but normal when the Lord pulled her out of the awful pit Satan had kept her in for so long. God had a great purpose for her life, gave her a new direction, and loosed her from the chains that had held her imprisoned in her own home. I believe that Jesus rescued Patsy for people like me and other women who have been blessed by her messages of hope and encouragement.

You may be feeling that your life is anything but normal. While you aren't suffering from agoraphobia like Pasty Clairmont did, you are experiencing heartaches, grief, and pain. There's a little bad news, but some REALLY good news to follow! The bad news is that because we live in a fallen world, we will never be without the presence of abnormalities. We will be tried and tested as long as we are in this imperfect and sinful world. However, the Good News is that we have the assurance of a new day that is coming when Jesus will right every wrong and gather His flock to give us a normal and exciting eternal home in Heaven. We can be at peace knowing that in God's house, all things will be made normal. One sweet day, we will experience all that Heaven has to offer, and it will be marvelous!

Prayer: Heavenly Father, in You, there is life, breath, and normalcy. You hold us and all things together. Thank You for loving us that much and for the promise of a better day to come. Until then, please give us Your strength so we might continue serving You in all that we do. We pray this in the name of our Lord and Savior, Jesus Christ. Amen.

WHAT'S THE USE?

Therefore encourage one another and build each other up,
just as in fact you are doing.
1 Thessalonians 5:11 (NIV)

Some time ago, my young granddaughter Sophie and her dad went camping at her favorite spot–Jellystone Park. With its Yogi Bear theme, the campground offered a range of fun activities, including a swimming pool, water slides, a giant trampoline, arts and crafts, and more, all designed with children in mind.

On the way to drop Sophie off at school the following Monday morning, I wanted to hear more about her weekend away. I asked if she had met any other children while at Jellystone. She said, "No, I wasn't there long enough. It takes a longer time to form a friendship." I could tell that this sweet girl, who values her friendships with others, had been doing some thinking.

Wanting to impart a few quick words of encouragement to Sophie before we arrived at school, I told her it has often been said that people come into our lives for a reason, a season, or a lifetime, and that meeting someone for two days or even two minutes can often make a difference for them and us. I emphasized to her that God created all of us to have a relationship with Him and with others, and that He stands ready to guide her in developing healthy and meaningful relationships throughout her life.

Yes, many interactions and relationships with others can be brief. Regardless, I hope that all of us will find God's purpose behind each one and trust Him to use them for our good and His glory. And the next time Sophie goes camping, I hope that she will find a friend with whom she can share the excitement of a fun-filled weekend.

Prayer: Dear Father, we love You because You first loved us. Thank You for the wonderful relationship we find in You. We need and welcome the unconditional love that You offer to all whom You have created. Help us to live in such a way that we aren't fearful of reaching out to others for Your name's sake. Help us to trust You as we pray for our children and grandchildren, that they may always choose godly friends. May their relationships bring glory to You in all things. We thank You and pray these things in Jesus' name. Amen.

JESUS, LIGHT OF THE WORLD

When Jesus spoke again to the people, he said, "I am the light of the world. Whoever follows me will never walk in darkness, but will have the light of life."

John 8:12 (NIV)

Lately, it seems we need an extra serving of God's light in the world. These days can be very discouraging, if we let our minds dwell on the scenes of hate and evil we see and hear daily. But here is my peace today: Things change—culture changes. Our situations sometimes change. But God will never change! His mercies are new every morning, and He has already walked the path we are about to take.

Friends, don't let the darkness of the world discourage you or slow you down in doing what you are called to do as a Christian. We are never too old to serve Jesus in the ways specific to where we are in life. And we are indeed called to pray hard for our families, country, and world. May we continue to let Him lead us through this challenging time in our lives, knowing that His light can only be as bright as we allow it to be through our faith and action in serving Him. Never forget that His light will always outshine the darkness, for darkness is only the absence of light. Because we carry that light within us, may we shine so that others can see Jesus. If we don't, they may never find a Savior who will give them peace, the ability to live an abundant life now, and assurance of a home in Heaven when they leave this old, sinful world.

Prayer: Dear Lord, I am so thankful that You are the Light of the world, You are all-knowing, all-powerful, and You do not change. You have equipped those of us who already know Jesus as Savior and Lord with Your light. Please help us remain more determined than ever to share the message of Jesus with others. Please help those who do not yet know You to have the desire for a relationship with You. In doing so, they will experience the inner joy and peace only You can bring. This is our prayer for a lost and dying world today. Help us not grow weary, angry, or disillusioned about our mission here on Earth. This we pray in the name of Jesus. Amen.

DIVINE INTERRUPTIONS

"For my thoughts are not your thoughts, neither are your ways, my ways," declares the LORD.

Isaiah 55:8 (ESV)

Don't you love it when you've got your entire day or maybe even your whole week planned? Things seem to be going smoothly, and you're in *full speed ahead* mode! Suddenly, with little or no warning, something happens to change those plans you had locked into your mind.

It happened to me on a Monday morning; I awoke with a terrible toothache. The entire left side of my face was in excruciating pain. I called my dentist's office and was able to schedule an immediate appointment. With just a short exam, I was informed that I needed a root canal and a new crown! This was not welcome news, and I thought to myself, *No, God, this was not in my plans for this week!* It was in that moment that I thought of the above verse of Scripture and was reminded that God was in control, which helped to ease my anxiety.

At the dentist's office, I had the opportunity to share my faith in Jesus with two women, and previously, with a young woman at the grocery store. Had I stayed on my planned schedule, I would not have been at either place on that particular day. There is no doubt that God rearranged my plans to allow these three *divine appointments*, even though they were not on my schedule. The miraculous thing is that the pain subsided long enough for me to be able to share with these folks. Thank you, Jesus!

When we begin to feel concerned about the inconveniences life throws our way, perhaps we should remind ourselves that God may be bringing these challenges into our lives so that we will learn to rely more fully on Him and less on ourselves. He can then work in the lives of others by placing us in their path. When we recognize the importance of God's divine interruptions, we will be comforted in knowing that He is always working in our lives, even though we cannot see the big picture.

Prayer: Father God, Your plan is always best! We don't always see it that way, but then You, in great love and compassion, remind us that You are in the driver's seat of our lives for our good and Your glory. How can we argue with that? Help us to serve You with a passion for others who don't know Jesus. In His mighty name, we pray. Amen.

LESSONS OF THE DOVE

Now when all the people were baptized, and when Jesus also had been baptized and was praying, the heavens were opened, and the Holy Spirit descended on Him in bodily form, like a dove; and a voice came from heaven, "You are My beloved Son; with you I am well pleased."

Luke 3:21-22 (ESV)

As I settled down for some quiet time, I heard a dove coo from the rooftop of the house. Another one, several houses down, answered.

I always think of the Holy Spirit when I hear or see a dove. Perhaps these special birds are there to remind us to be thankful for waking up to another day with wonderful possibilities and to allow ourselves to be led by God's plan for us that day. How comforting to know that God hears and answers us when we commune with Him. The doves serve as a poignant reminder of that truth.

It is comforting to know that God's faithfulness and mercy are new every morning, and His grace is sufficient for all our needs. He is the initiator of every good thing. During the hard times, He carries us through and gives us hope. Think of how He reaches for us in acceptance and love and shows Himself faithful time and time again, even though we are imperfect and a work in progress! He is for us! May we, in gratitude, desire to walk in the recognition of His great love today.

Prayer: Dear Heavenly Father, there is none like You! Your power and majesty cover the whole Earth, and we give You praise and glory. Forgive us when we don't take the time to see You in our daily lives, for we know that You are always there waiting to commune with us. May we remember the gentleness of a dove and conduct ourselves accordingly as we strive to do Your will in all things. We pray this in Jesus' name. Amen.

GOD IS WITH YOU

The LORD your God is with you, he is mighty to save.
He will take great delight in you, he will quiet you with his love,
he will rejoice over you with singing.
Zephaniah 3:17 (NIV)

During our time on Earth, we experience both elation and immense heart-ache. We live through circumstances we'd never have imagined that require every ounce of faith and strength we have, and then some. Although situations may differ, we are all in the same imperfect boat called life. As Christians, we aren't flawless by any means, but we try to be image-bearers of our Lord and Savior, Jesus Christ.

There is so much Good News today, even though we are tempted to focus only on the negative things that surround us. I am very thankful that God has not changed and never will. His character, His Word, and His love for us remain steadfast. That's enough to bring peace, no matter where we are in life at this moment.

I am grateful for God's willingness to extend His hand of mercy, grasp ours, and bring His peace and direction to the forefront again and again. Through every burden, every care, and every trying circumstance, we can see His hand guiding and strengthening us. May we never feel far away from His love and care.

Prayer: Heavenly Father, You are present in every breath we take, every thought we think, every song we sing, and we have learned that it is only You who can bring us lasting peace. Thank You for Your great love and thank You for making a way for us to bridge the gap with You. It is through Jesus Christ, our Savior and Lord, that we have been gifted a hope that offers peace beyond measure and an assurance that this isn't all there is to life. We have an eternal home not built by human hands but fashioned from the hands of a loving Father who thought of every detail, small and large. For this and so much more, we thank You. This we pray in the name of Your Son and our Savior, Jesus Christ. Amen.

THE LOVE OF GOD

For I am convinced that neither death nor life, neither angels nor demons, neither the present nor the future, nor any powers, neither height nor depth, nor anything else in all creation, will be able to separate us from the love of God that is in Christ Jesus our Lord.

Romans 8:38-39 (NIV)

In the many words I've written over the years, I could never fully describe how deeply God's love touches me. It's hard to convey the richness of this message to others. It is simply something that has to be experienced. Although I am fully aware of how undeserving I am of that much affection, I am eternally grateful to know that I am unconditionally cherished. God's arm of love and forgiveness is long and always there.

Today I've been thinking of the timeless old hymn "The Love of God." I've always loved hearing it sung. Perhaps the third verse describes how I feel as a writer. There could never be enough ink produced, paper made, or pens available to write about the love of God. Rich. Pure. Measureless. Strong. The songwriter did his best, too, and to his words, I say, "Amen." What hope we have wrapped in God's never-ending love.

Prayer: Dear Heavenly Father, Your love supersedes our wildest imagination! We have only the language we have been given to express our love and appreciation for all that You mean to us and for the many blessings bestowed upon us. Please help us to share Your love with those around us. We pray that You will lead those we encounter, through the power of the Holy Spirit, to a lasting relationship with Jesus Christ. We pray these things in His name. Amen.

Source: Lehman, Frederick M., *The Love of God* (1917), Faith Publishing House, 1987, Timeless Truths, page 484.

FINDING SHELTER

Be merciful to me, O God, be merciful to me, for in you my soul takes refuge; in the shadow of your wings I will take my refuge, till the storms of destruction pass by.

Psalm 57:1 (ESV)

Have you ever been caught in a situation where you needed to find shelter? If you saw a thunderstorm approaching while you were on a long hike in an unfamiliar location, you would undoubtedly seek a shielded location for protection from the elements. Thankfully, I have always had a physical shelter—a safe place that I call home.

Often, I have needed to find protection from the storms of life's circumstances that raged around me. During those times, my need has been to find spiritual shelter. Sometimes I have tried to handle this situation myself before seeking the restful, secure, and loving comfort of my Lord. Before I wandered too far, God would turn my eyes back to Him, and I would run to the beautiful safety of His presence.

On the many occasions when I have desperately sought the comfort and shelter of God's presence, I have never been disappointed. His Word gives me hope, strength, and peace. Deep love for my Heavenly Father and Jesus Christ, my Savior, has transformed how I handle difficult situations. The power of prayer and the ability to go to Him and share my hurts and fears assures me that He is listening and answers according to His will for my life and those around me.

If you need God's shelter due to the circumstances around you or if life seems to be spiraling out of control, remember that you have a Savior—Jesus Christ. He is the One who brings peace and hope and who shelters you from any storm you may face now or in the future. He is the master of calming storms.

Prayer: Father God, thank You for sheltering us from the storms of life. Through Jesus we can always rest safely in the Shepherd's arms. Help us trust You always, knowing Your love for us is beyond comprehension. We pray this in Jesus' name. Amen.

MINI-SERMONS

The LORD is near to all who call on him,
to all who call on Him in truth.

Psalm 145:18 (ESV)

Today I awoke humming a timeless old hymn that I learned to sing as a child. Through the inspiration of the Holy Spirit, these songs were brought to life and ingrained into our hearts and minds.

Much like mini-sermons, the old hymns offer spiritual strength and rest, reminding us that we have an anchor for our souls. They lift us closer to God and speak life, help, trust, and faith to us. They inspire us to stay strong in our faith, knowing that a better day is coming because we are in Christ Jesus.

Through these mini-sermons in song, we will always have God's promises that are steadfast and sure. Nothing can compare to the peace He brings. May we find that quiet place of rest near to God's heart today. For sure, there's no better place to be.

Prayer: Dear God, the timeless hymns inspired by gospel writers through the Holy Spirit give us much-needed rest in You, because we long to always be near to Your heart. It is in that place where we find peace, rest, and security. We ask that You help us point others to Jesus as we represent You, so that they may discover the richness and eternal value of knowing Jesus Christ as their Lord and Savior. This is our earnest plea, and it is our only goal. We pray these things in Jesus' name. Amen.

INDEPENDENCE DAY

Blessed is the nation whose God is the Lord.
Psalm 33:12 (NIV)

Independence Day is a time of celebration, marked by neighborhood parades, backyard barbecues, and picnics with family and friends. This time of celebration also brings forth great patriotism in our country and reminds us how truly blessed we are as a nation. Even with our challenges and disagreements, we remain a land made up of many hardworking and decent people. May we never forget that the freedom we enjoy today has been paid for over the years by brave men and women who have fought to keep our country free. We owe them such a debt of gratitude.

The United States of America was founded on the principles of liberty and democracy, and the Statue of Liberty is a symbol of that hope for a better world. In **John 3:16 ESV**, Jesus speaks these words: **"For God so loved the world, that He gave His only Son, that whoever believes in Him should not perish but have eternal life."** Therefore, as the Statue of Liberty's torch lights the way to freedom, all who choose to accept Jesus Christ as Lord and Savior, following Him at all costs, will gain a soul that is liberated. Because of the Cross, we are set free to live a life of faith and trust in Someone much bigger than ourselves, and we are assured of an eternal home that is waiting for us when we leave this world.

Prayer: Dear Father, Creator of the world and of all who are in it, we acknowledge Your sovereignty. It is You, and You alone, whom we trust. Thank You for placing us here in the United States of America, the land that we love. Forgive us, Lord, for we have drifted so far off the course that You intended. Please heal our land and unite us under Your banner. Help us to show Your love to those around us. We pray this in the name of our Lord and Savior, Jesus Christ. Amen.

HIDE AND SEEK

But the LORD God called to the man, "Where are you?" He answered, "I heard you in the garden and I was afraid, because I was naked; so I hid." And he said, "Who told you that you were naked? Have you eaten from the tree that I told you not to eat from?"

Genesis 3:9-11 (NIV)

Most of us have played the game of Hide and Seek with our children and/ or grandchildren when they were young. Much of the time we already knew where they were hiding before we called out to them and began our search. We only pretended not to know the whereabouts of their *secret* location. Finally, with giggles and delightful squealing, we exposed their hiding place and the game was over.

In the Scripture referenced above, God came looking for Adam, even though He already knew where he was. Adam and Eve were hiding out of shame because they had disobeyed God's specific command not to eat from the tree of the knowledge of good and evil. Unlike the game of Hide and Seek mentioned above, God was not playing games with Adam and Eve.

So it is with all of God's creation. We sometimes play Hide and Seek with the LORD, not realizing that the game is futile. Because you see, God knows where we are at all times. He knows our hearts and our innermost thoughts, and we cannot hide from Him.

Our Heavenly Father wants to change the attitudes and actions of our hearts, but we must first come before Him in humility and honesty, exposing our true selves. That is not always easy, because sometimes we don't like to admit that we need His help.

Each day we have a choice to make. We can continue playing the useless game of Hide and Seek with God, or we can look to Him through faith in Jesus Christ for our strength and guidance. We can choose a hope-filled life with eternal benefits by being honest with God and coming to Him just as we are. Making this decision each day gives us the peace and assurance that we are always in His loving care.

Today, let's make the choice to seek God for direction, comfort, and peace. May we choose to follow Jesus at all costs and cease the useless game of Hide and Seek with Him. He wants to be found, and once you find Him, you will never be the same.

Prayer: Father, bless each person reading these words. Help us to put away our game of Hide and Seek with You. May we live in obedience to Your Word and keep nothing hidden from You so that others will see transparency in our daily lives. Help us always to be a living testimony of Your faithfulness and love. In Jesus' name, we pray. Amen.

THROUGH IT ALL

When you pass through the waters, I will be with you; and through the rivers, they shall not overwhelm you; when you walk through the fire you shall not be burned, and the flame shall not consume you. For I am the LORD your God, the Holy One of Israel, your Savior.
Isaiah 43:2-3 (ESV)

What a powerful promise that amidst trials and hardships, Jesus will always be our source of strength. It is through these times that we will learn to depend on His Word and rely more fully on Him as our help.

God does not always bring us around storms but walks with us through them so that we might learn to trust Him more fully. As the words to the song "Through It All" say, "If we never had a problem, then we would not know that God could solve them, nor would we know what faith in Him could do."

May we continue to lean on and trust Jesus as He directs us in ways that we could never have imagined. I pray that He is the source of your strength today.

Prayer: Dear God, thank You for staying beside us through the tough times. Help those who may be going through challenges to rely fully on You for their strength. May they place their trust in Christ alone. In Jesus' name we pray. Amen.

Source: Crouch, Andrae, *Classics, Vol. 1,* Through It All, 8-17-1993.

GOD'S UNCHANGEABLE PROMISES

God did this so that, by two unchangeable things in which it is impossible for God to lie, we who have fled to take hold of the hope set before us may be greatly encouraged. We have this hope as an anchor for the soul, firm and secure. It enters the inner sanctuary behind the curtain.

Hebrews 6:18-19 (NIV)

Have you ever promised someone you would do something, only to fail to follow through on it? I have. It's not a good feeling to let others down, especially if what you've promised is essential to the other party.

The Bible is full of God's promises. And you know what? Unlike us, God never breaks a single promise. I am so thankful for God's faithfulness and trustworthiness, because it is on His promises that I rest my head at night. I sleep peacefully knowing there is nothing too difficult for our great God. When the morning comes, I can begin each new day holding onto God's promises, as well.

Resting in the assurance of God's faithfulness will always bring us comfort. There is no circumstance in our lives that is beyond the outstretched hand of our Savior. He's as close as the whisper of His name, and His love and care are limitless and always available. We are never alone. I don't know about you, but that is very comforting to me.

As you read this, my prayer is that you will always have the assurance of God's unchangeable promises, and that you will carry them with you each day and night.

Prayer: Dear God, You are the God who never changes, nor do You ever fail to keep the many promises that are so beautifully written in Your Word. Help us to rely on You and You alone for our peace, rest, and guidance. We know that when we walk with You, we will never walk alone. Thank You for loving us that much! Lead us to share the Good News of Jesus Christ with others in our daily lives. We pray this in the matchless name of the One who died for our sins, Jesus Christ. Amen.

PLANS

Many are the plans in a man's heart, but it is the LORD's
purpose that prevails.
Proverbs 19:21 (NIV)

Hardly a day goes by that I don't speak with my sister over the telephone. Although Peggy and I live six hours apart, we remain grateful for our ability to communicate with each other as often as possible. During our daily conversations, we usually ask each other, *"What are your plans for tomorrow?"* Following the question, we will then take turns sharing what's on our agenda for the next day. Some days are more eventful than others, but we always have plans in place.

It is good to make plans for the future, but let us always hold our plans out to God with an open hand, remembering that He is ultimately in charge and may change our course whenever He sees fit. We must trust Him for the outcome, because He is wise and His plans will always work out for our good and His glory. He wants to lead and help us stay on the right path, but we must be willing to give Him authority over our lives through faith in Jesus Christ. When we do, we can have full assurance that He is guiding us in the direction that is best for a steady and meaningful relationship with Him. His ways and His plans are simply the BEST.

Prayer: Dear Heavenly Father, You are the Maker of Heaven and Earth and are very wise. Because of Your great love for us, You have planned for our past, present, and future in ways known only to You. You have given us the freedom to choose whether or not we want to include You in our daily decisions. Forgive us when we try to carve a path on our own, for we have no strength or wisdom without Your help. Thank You for loving us and guiding us each day. We pray these things in the name of Jesus Christ, our Savior and Lord. Amen.

SEEK LASTING THINGS

The LORD does not look at the things people look at. People look at the outward appearance, but the LORD looks at the heart.

1 Samuel 16:7b (NIV)

Around the world there are poverty-stricken nations whose people are suffering and dying from starvation, even at this very moment. Having spent some time in a third-world country on mission trips, I have seen poverty firsthand. It was an experience that changed my life forever and altered how I view my possessions. Although I consider these *things* to be a blessing, they do not last or satisfy my soul.

How important are material possessions to you? It is not wrong to accumulate worldly goods or even wealth, but how we view and use our possessions does make a big difference. The Bible teaches us the following truths:

The things we have accumulated in this life are not our own. Everything that we possess has been given to us by a loving God. He has given us intelligence and the ability to work in a job that provides an income. In turn, this enables us to access the necessities of life for ourselves and our families. God has blessed many of us beyond the basic necessities. What do we owe Him in return? I believe that we owe Him our commitment to be good stewards of what we have been given.

Who we are is not determined by what we have in this life. God does not care about the size of our bank account, the kind of house we live in, the brand of clothes we wear, our popularity with the crowd, or any of the things that others see on the surface. Rather He looks to see if we have a heart like His. He seeks people who are willing to give of their time, talents, and resources to spread the Word that Jesus Christ came to seek and to save those who are lost.

When we learn to be content with what we have, we can rest in the knowledge that there is more to life than material possessions. When we die, we will take nothing with us. Whatever material possessions we have accumulated will remain here on earth for others to dispose of. While we are here, why not invest in something that will last? If we can think less about material possessions and more about how we can serve God, we will begin to make a difference in the lives of others. Remember, we have all we need. His name is Jesus.

Prayer: Dear God, You are the source of our peace and contentment. Thank You for loving us that much. Help us never to set our sights on temporary things, but give us the ability and wisdom always to lay up our treasures in Heaven. You are the eternal source of our salvation through Jesus Christ. We love You and praise You for the many blessings You shower on us each day. We pray these things in Jesus' name. Amen.

WONDER WORKING POWER

To the thirsty I will give from the spring of the water of life without payment. The one who conquers will have this heritage, and I will be his God and he will be my son.
Revelation 21:6b-7 (ESV)

It is inevitable that in life we will have times when we grow tired and weary due to a myriad of physical, emotional, or spiritual causes. But when our hope is placed in the Lord, things change. We view life differently because we know that God is always present. Not only is He giving us strength for today, but also bright hope for tomorrow.

We often don't understand why things happen as they do, but God has a plan through it all. He is always on duty, tending to every small or large detail. As Christians, our job is to trust Him and to walk in such a way that others will see Who it is that we depend on through every season. Sometimes that's hard, but it's the safest and wisest thing to do.

Today and every day, I'm thankful for the restorative peace and joy that Jesus brings to those who trust Him enough to let go and let Him do the needed work in their lives. There is hope, peace, and joy in His wonder-working power.

Prayer: Heavenly Father, You alone have the keys to life, breath, and strength. Thank You for being there for us in all ways, at all times, and through all circumstances in life. Please forgive us when we fail You, and help us walk in such a way that others will see Your wonder-working power at work through our lives. We pray this in Jesus' name. Amen.

OF GREAT WORTH

Beloved, if God so loved us, we also ought to love one another.
1 John 4:11 (ESV)

Terri, the sweet lady who had manicured my nails for several years, was not at the salon that day. Instead, she had taken the day off to be at the funeral home due to the death of her mother. Because Terri had spoken about her mom at previous appointments, I was saddened to hear the news of her passing.

Terri and I became friends on my first visit to see her. At the end of the visit, I gave her a copy of God's Word, which she said she would read to practice her English. After that, our friendship seemed to be one of mutual love and respect for each other. Sometimes Terri cried because of cruel words that had been spoken to her as a child. Once we even cried together, for her story broke my heart. I always listened, did my best to encourage her, and felt honored that she trusted me enough to acknowledge the pain she was still feeling, even after many years.

Because of the bond Terri and I shared, I felt strongly that I should go to the funeral home to pay my respects that afternoon. When I arrived, I was warmly greeted with big hugs and tears by Terri and her niece, who also worked at the salon. I silently thanked God for the nudge He had given me to visit with them that day.

Terri retired three years ago. Although she and I were different in many ways, I believe that our loving Heavenly Father brought us together for a brief period, all for His good purposes. He sees great value in Terri's worth, and I pray that she experienced the love of Jesus through me.

I urge you to be on the lookout for your own Divine Appointments, because you will find them in many of your daily routines and activities. You are the hands and feet of our Lord and Savior, Jesus Christ, and He wants to use you for His good purposes. All He needs from you is a willing heart, and He will do the rest.

Prayer: Dear Heavenly Father, we thank You for placing others in our lives with whom we can share Your love. I pray that You will keep Divine Appointments on our calendars, and may we make an eternal difference in the lives of others. Help us to always serve others with gladness and Your joy in our hearts. We pray this in the name of our Lord and Savior, Jesus Christ. Amen.

SPIRITUAL FEET

How beautiful on the mountains are the feet of those who bring good news, who proclaim peace, who bring good tidings, who proclaim salvation, who say to Zion, "Your God reigns!"

Isaiah 52:7 (NIV)

When I was growing up, there were seldom shoes on my feet. I just loved going barefoot! During the summer months when my brothers and I were out of school, we never wore shoes. I cannot tell you how many rusty nails and grass burrs (stickers) we stepped on. Those were some painful experiences, physically speaking! However, I was never deterred from repeating my country-girl habits. To this day, I still go barefoot in the house and am very thankful there are no rusty nails or grass burrs to dodge!

Do we have compassionate, kind, tender-hearted, loving feet that carry us to places where we can serve the Lord? How are we to put our feet into action during these unprecedented times? Many things could hinder us—our modern-day rusty nails and stickers. However, we can take comfort in the fact that God always has a plan and is ready to make a way for us to serve Him passionately as His Spirit directs.

If we are willing, He is able. Each of us has a unique role to play in His plan. May He use us, individually and collectively, to tell the old story in some way today, for His glory alone.

Prayer: Heavenly Father, how thankful we are that You give us opportunities to be the hands and feet of Jesus. May we serve You passionately by helping those who need both physical and spiritual assistance. We pray this in Jesus' name. Amen.

A NEW BEGINNING

A new commandment I give to you, that you love one another:
just as I have loved you, you also are to love one another.
By this, all people will know that you are my disciples,
if you have love for one another.

John 13:34-35 (ESV)

Some years ago, my husband and I attended a Christmas Pageant at a large church in the Houston, Texas area. The play was a modern-day version of the Prodigal Son, a story that resonated deeply with us. It was a powerful narrative of faith in God, unconditional love, and unrestricted forgiveness, which are themes we all grapple with.

Despite the busyness of the Christmas season and frequent visits with friends and relatives, the husband and wife in the play were lonely for one family member. Michael, their oldest son, had left home five years earlier to pursue a life of sin and rebellion. Since that time, his Christian parents and other family members had longed for him to come home and prayed fervently for his return. Their only desire was to welcome Michael home and make up for lost time.

Meanwhile, Michael, who has squandered his resources, is living in a homeless shelter and feeling lost, alone, and hopeless. He is quite certain that he can never be reunited with his family because he caused them so much pain. Little does he know that God is about to orchestrate the most joyful family reunion!

As the story ends, Michael returns home to his family. With God at the center of their lives, Michael's family demonstrates the transformative power of unconditional love and forgiveness. This act of mercy from his family not only enables Michael to have the new beginning he so desperately wants but also fills us with hope and optimism for our lives.

I think I can safely say that all of us have wanted a new beginning at one time or another, and we have all been in need of unconditional love and forgiveness from others. I pray that we will seek whatever new beginning we might need, and be willing to show others the same love and forgiveness that Jesus extended to each of us. We all know someone who needs a new start, so with God's help and guidance, let's love, forgive, and encourage our brothers and sisters.

Prayer: Father God, every day You give us the chance to start all over again. You are so generous with Your love, grace, and mercy. Help us to seek Your will as we embark on each new day. May we make a difference in someone else's life today. We pray this in Jesus' name. Amen.

BLUE JEANS WELCOME

Listen, my dear brothers and sisters: Has not God chosen those who are poor in the eyes of the world to be rich in faith and to inherit the kingdom he promised those who love him?

James 2:5 (NIV)

The church service began, and as we stood for the first song, I excused myself to make a quick trip to the restroom. I walked into the foyer and noticed two church members engaged in warm conversation with a young man. He was dressed in jeans and a t-shirt, and nothing seemed unusual about him. While I wasn't privy to much of their conversation, I did overhear the young man saying, *"I don't have any nice clothes to wear to church."* Immediately, the church members reassured this man that nice clothes were not a requirement to attend our church and that he was dressed just fine. Upon returning to my seat, I noticed that the young man had seated himself just a few rows in front of us.

When the invitation was given at the end of the service, this same young man walked down front to have one of our pastors pray with him. I couldn't help but feel thankful and excited at the same time! Wow! God did that! With a lot of thoughts running through my mind, one thing I knew for sure was that this young man was not there by accident, and the couple who spoke to him in the foyer were placed there at just the right time to assure him that he didn't need to be dressed up to attend our church.

It is with gratitude to my parents that I was taught to recognize Sunday as a special day—the Lord's Day. At a young age, I also learned that I should *dress up* for church. My best dress was always starched and ironed for Sunday church services. This was my upbringing, and I carried those habits into adulthood. I taught my daughter to dress her best for church, and she, in turn, taught her children the same.

Even though I still try to look my best for church, things have changed, and others may not have the same background or family teachings as I did. Therefore, I will not judge them for what they wear. May we desire to keep our eyes focused on the author and finisher of our faith, Jesus Christ, so that we will be good role models for our children, grandchildren, great-grandchildren, and all young people. May we lay aside our preferences and return to the true heart of worship. Only God can bring us to that point through the work of the Holy Spirit within us, for He is so much bigger than our preferences. This is where I want my focus to lie. How about you?

Prayer: Dear Heavenly Father, we are not our own and have been bought with the precious blood of Jesus Christ. Help us be Your obedient children so that we might radiate Your love to others. Help us not to miss what You want to do in our lives for Your good purposes. In Jesus' name, we pray. Amen.

POWER SOURCE

For this light momentary affliction is preparing for us an eternal weight of glory beyond all comparison, as we look not to the things that are seen but to the things that are unseen. For the things that are seen are transient, but the things that are unseen are eternal.

2 Corinthians 4:17-18 (ESV)

Even in Central Texas, winter temperatures can drop quite significantly. Sometimes the power goes out in the midst of a winter storm, leaving us to navigate an unexpected situation. Our once-reliable power source has become, at best, temporarily unreliable. But there is another power source—a spiritual one in nature that we must stay connected to for a life of power through Jesus Christ. God has given us all the tools necessary to maintain our spiritual power running smoothly.

As Christians, we've been given the Holy Spirit, who works to renew our minds so that we might be more like Jesus. The comfort He brings gives us hope and peace. He even intercedes on our behalf when we don't have the words (Romans 8:26-27). I love that! His convicting power is essential in the daily lives of all believers.

Reading and studying God's Word are excellent strategies to employ to stay connected to our spiritual source of power. As we focus on His Word, which serves as our roadmap for living the Christian life, we are given detailed routing instructions from a biblical perspective.

By utilizing God's arsenal of spiritual tools, we can also perform the much-needed maintenance checks on our spiritual life. Being regularly plugged into the power source of our faith will help prevent us from stumbling into many of life's pitfalls. We'll walk confidently forward, trusting God in every area of our lives, when we fix our eyes and hearts on the One who is always with us. God, who holds the keys to everlasting life, will fill us with His peace. I pray that you are firmly connected to the ultimate and everlasting spiritual power source.

Prayer: Dear God, we love You and thank You for Your 100% reliability as the greatest Power Source ever known. We take comfort in knowing that You are with us in all situations and that we need not fear or grow anxious, whatever our station in life. Help us to trust You more and more and lead us to share with others what You've done for us through our relationship with Jesus Christ. It is in His name that we pray. Amen.

STANDING FIRM IN OUR FAITH

Only let your manner of life be worthy of the gospel of Christ, so that whether I come and see you or am absent, I may hear of you that you are standing firm in one spirit, with one mind striving side by side for the faith of the gospel.

Philippians 1:27 (ESV)

Christians come from diverse backgrounds and religious affiliations, but there is one common denominator that unites us—our faith in the Lord Jesus Christ.

We are children of God who have much more in common than our differences. While we may wear dissimilar hats in our daily lives, we are bound together as servants of the Most High King. We may be at various ages and stages in our lives, but our spirits are united by our Heavenly Father, who created us and chose us to be His children.

God had a plan for us before we were created, and He has given us eternal life through our faith in Jesus Christ. Wherever you are in your faith journey, please know that God is right there in the midst of it. He knows where you are in this stage of life. He knows your thoughts, your strengths, weaknesses, struggles, successes, and the desires of your heart. He hears your prayers and the cries of your heart when you are tired, discouraged, and weary. He knows when you want to give up. He knows when you desire solitude, even for just an hour!

Sometimes, our busyness can begin to overwhelm us. We may feel as though we can no longer juggle our responsibilities as we once could. At other times, we are blindsided by a storm that blows into our lives in the blink of an eye, when life is already complicated enough. Now this!

I have encountered each of these crossroads during my walk of faith, and were it not for God and others, I know that I would not have had the strength to move forward. Standing firm in our faith requires us to take action. We must believe that God is who He says He is; that He will do what He says He will do; that we are who God says we are; and that His Spirit is alive and working in us.

So you see, our faith comes down to belief. Today I pray that each of us will hold on to the nail-scarred hand of Jesus. In doing so, we will move forward with the courage and assurance that He is always with us and will realize how much He helps us.

Prayer: Dear Heavenly Father, You are our perfect Father. When we are weak, You are strong. Thank You for giving us the hope and peace in our lives that we desperately need. We desire to follow our Lord and Savior, Jesus Christ, at all costs and in every situation we face in this life. Help us, we pray, to be His ambassadors each day. We pray in His name. Amen.

FOLLOW HIM

So the sun stood still, and the moon stopped, till the nation avenged
itself on its enemies, as it is written in the Book of Jashar.
The sun stopped in the middle of the sky and delayed
going down about a full day.
Joshua 10:13 (NIV)

Have you ever doubted that God could help you get through life's challenges? In situations where you have needed Him to come through in a big way, have you sought Him out to do that which you cannot do? If you have doubt, we only need to look at the above Scripture to be sure that He is in control of everything, both large and small.

Joshua, Chapter 10, illustrates how God came through in a mighty way, giving Joshua and the Israelites complete victory. Science cannot explain how or why the sun stood still that day and did not go down. God orchestrated this extraordinary event so that His people could avenge themselves and destroy every last one of their enemies.

As Christians, we know God is sovereign and free to carry out His plan for our lives. He can do whatever He will, whenever He will, and for whatever His great purpose. He is not limited by space or time. His Word tells us that His thoughts are not our thoughts and His ways are not our ways (Isaiah 55:8-9), but we are given many pictures of a loving Heavenly Father whom we can trust. His promises are many, and He is faithful to keep every one of them. As we trust and follow Him, we will find that He is with us every step of the way.

Prayer: Heavenly Father, today we lift our hearts before You in gratefulness for Your care over us. May we follow You all the days of our lives. Please help us to use this day for Your glory in all that we think, say, and do. We pray this in Jesus' name. Amen.

LESSONS FROM A KING

Josiah was eight years old when he became king, and he reigned in Jerusalem thirty-one years. His mother's name was Jedidah, daughter of Adaiah; she was from Bozkath. He did what was right in the eyes of the LORD and walked in all the ways of his father David, not turning aside to the right or to the left.

2 Kings 22:1-2 (NIV)

Josiah was only eight years old when he became King of Judah, after the assassination of his father. Josiah's father, Amon, and his grandfather, Manasseh, were evil kings and led the nation of Judah far away from God through idol worship. Despite his challenging upbringing, Josiah chose a different path and devoted himself to God at an early age. Because of Josiah's devotion to God, he stands out as one of the godliest kings in Judah's history. Though he lived in dark times, he wholeheartedly sought the LORD and led his people to do the same. God graciously responded by blessing Josiah with peace, spiritual renewal, and success.

I have heard many testimonies of mighty men and women of God who grew up in difficult circumstances and had never heard of Jesus; however, something happened that made their hearts ready to seek Him. Many speak of someone in their generational line praying for them. In some Middle Eastern countries, we hear accounts of Jesus appearing in dreams and other unconventional ways to those who are steeped in false religions. We must never forget that God, through the work of the Holy Spirit, seeks out the lost. Nothing is impossible for Him, nor is anyone beyond His hand of mercy and compassion. He is the only God who pursues His creation so that we might become His children through faith in Jesus Christ. What a gift we have been given!

Prayer: Dear Heavenly Father, I love how Your Word comes alive when it is read. Your power, love, and mercy are remarkable and will never compare to anything we find outside of a relationship with Jesus Christ. Thank You for reminding us that our circumstances never hamper You from knocking on our heart's door. Please help us to stand firm like King Josiah and never waver in our faith. We pray this in the name of Jesus Christ, our Lord and Savior. Amen.

SEEK GOD'S SHELTER

God is our refuge and strength, a very present help in trouble.
Psalm 46:1 (ESV)

On the many occasions that I have desperately sought the comfort and shelter of God's presence, I have never been disappointed. His Word gives me hope, strength, and peace. The deep love I have for my Heavenly Father and Jesus Christ, my Savior, has made a significant difference in how I handle difficult situations. The ability to go to Him in prayer and share my hurts and fears assures me that He is listening and that He answers according to His will for my life and the lives of those around me.

If you feel the need to seek God's shelter due to situations that are presently surrounding you, or if there are circumstances in your life that seem to be beyond your control, remember that you have a Savior, Jesus Christ, who wants to bring you hope and peace. He will shelter you from any storm that you may face now or in the future, because He specializes in calming the storms.

Prayer: Father God, thank You for sheltering us from the storms of life. Through Jesus, we can rest safely in the Shepherd's arms at all times. Help us to trust You always, knowing that You love us beyond comprehension. We pray this in Jesus' name. Amen.

SUPERNATURAL VICTORY

The three companies blew the trumpets and smashed the jars.
Grasping the torches in their left hands and holding in their right
hands the trumpets they were to blow, they shouted, "A sword for the
LORD and for Gideon!" While each man held his position around
the camp, all the Midianites ran, crying out as they fled.

Judges 7:20-21 (NIV)

The above Scripture gives an excellent example of how God worked supernaturally through Gideon—a man who wasn't the bravest warrior, but who chose to obey God's instructions on how to defeat the enemies who threatened his people.

The Israelites were not serving the LORD God as He had commanded. Consequently, they found themselves in circumstances that threatened their destruction. Because of their disobedience, God had given them up to their enemies for seven years. In chapters 6 and 7 of the book of Judges, we see that the Midianites were encamped all around the Israelites and were attacking on every side. Because of their vulnerable position, the Israelites ran to dens, caves, and safe places in the mountains to hide.

Twenty-two thousand of Gideon's fighting men had already left in fear of the enemy. Only ten thousand men were remaining who were willing to fight. God instructed Gideon to reduce the number of men who were to go into battle with him to three hundred. Furthermore, God only required that three things be taken into battle by each man: a trumpet, a torch, and a clay pot (pitcher). Imagine what the men thought when Gideon instructed them to take nothing into battle except those three things. There was nothing that even remotely resembled a weapon fit for battle; a tremendous faith was required as they faced at least one hundred eighty thousand Midianites.

In addition to the three bizarre weapons for battle, God told Gideon that he and his warriors were to shout the following phrase over and over: **"A sword for the LORD and for Gideon!"** When the three hundred trumpets blew and the men began shouting this phrase over and over, the Midianites became so confounded and confused that they started killing one another. Those who did not die at the hands of their men fled from the scene of the battle.

What was God's purpose in doing this? He wanted the Israelites to understand the source of their victory. He wanted them to see that it was not their substantial numbers that had enabled them to fight and defeat the enemy, but rather His strength and power that had made the difference between victory and defeat. With only a handful of men and no real weapons available, what a sight that must have been as the battle began and ended with a mighty victory for Gideon and his small band of warriors!

The Good News is that we, too, have God-given weapons at our disposal to fight our enemy. God has given us everything we need to be victorious and free from any circumstance that keeps us from wholeness in our lives and a successful spiritual walk with the Lord. He has given us His Son Jesus, the Holy Spirit, His Word, our faith, and our trust in Him. He has also given us others who are available to encourage us during times of difficulty. Most of all, He has given us His love. No matter what our situation, we have the assurance that He will never leave nor forsake us and that we are never alone. He will always fight our battles for us if we allow Him to. Just as He did with Gideon, God will work in supernatural ways in our lives as we live in obedience to His Word. There is no limit to what we can overcome when we are walking in the strength and power of God.

Prayer: Dear Heavenly Father, how Your Word comes alive when we read and study it! Thank You for men like Gideon, from whose experiences we can learn and grow in our spiritual journey. Trusting You is the only way to victory over the challenging life situations that come our way. Through every season of life may we follow You, knowing that the battle belongs to You and we will be victorious through our faith in Jesus Christ. We pray this in His name. Amen.

GOD'S TIMETABLE

See, I have engraved you on the palms of my hands;
your walls are ever before me.

Isaiah 49:16 (NIV)

During our walk of faith, we have all questioned God's timing in certain situations. Of course, we would prefer that He answer our prayers instantly. However, we must remember that God has His own perfect timetable, because He knows what we need and when we need it. Who better to determine how and when to act on our behalf than our Heavenly Father, who created us?

Scripture offers us profound reassurance when we feel that God has forgotten us. Just as He told the children of Israel in the above verse that He had not forgotten them, how comforting it is to know that He remembers us and hears us when we pray. He constantly acts on our behalf, even when there are no outward signs of an answered prayer.

In times of uncertainty, God's Word assures us that He has heard our prayers. He is the perfect Father and will always care for His children. Rest assured that your prayers will never go unheard.

Prayer: Dear Heavenly Father, You are an awesome God! Thank You for being our comfort and stay during all seasons of life. Help us to trust Your perfect timing in all circumstances. May we always remember that You are the one constant we can always depend on. In Jesus' name, we pray. Amen.

THE MESSAGE NEVER ENDS

The grass withers, the flower fades, but the word of our God will stand forever.

Isaiah 40:8 (ESV)

My husband and I live in the city and have a small backyard. Over the years, we have experienced several harsh winters and much of the grass has died. Spring 2025 seemed like the perfect time to spruce up our outdoor space, so we pressure-washed the patio, ordered a small outdoor furniture set, added some new grass, and hung decorative lights along the fence. We have enjoyed many relaxing evenings outside with family and friends in this updated space. I have also found time to read, write, and pray as I listen to the doves softly cooing and the birds singing their melodious songs of joy.

Yes, our backyard looks more inviting, but the Scripture above tells us that **"the grass withers, the flower fades (…)"** Nothing on earth is eternal, for God has created a life cycle for everything. However, we can take encouragement and comfort from the last part of **Isaiah 40:8,** which tells us that **"(…) the Word of our God will stand forever."** It is the infallible and inerrant guidebook to a life filled with hope, and it assures us that there is more to life than what we now see and experience.

God has given us His Son, Jesus Christ, so we might have the eternal hope of glory when we leave this imperfect world. I am thankful that His message will never be outdated or irrelevant to those who call Jesus Christ their Savior and Lord.

Prayer: Dear Heavenly Father, how we love You and Your Word. When we need guidance, Your Word lights our path, showing us the way to go. When we need comfort, Your Word is a lamp unto our feet, giving us peace unlike anything this world can offer. Your Word assures us that we are never alone and will always have Someone who guides us through this life until we reach the other side in glory. Thank You for Jesus Christ, our Savior and Lord, who rescued us from sin and promised eternal life in Heaven when we leave this world. We pray this in His name. Amen.

MORE THAN ENOUGH

Lord, you have been our dwelling place in all generations. Before the mountains were brought forth, or ever you had formed the earth and the world, even from everlasting to everlasting, you are God.

Psalm 90:1-2 (ESV)

When I reflect on the many years of my life that have now passed, I am grateful that God has helped and protected me through His mercy and goodness. He has provided more than enough for my needs during seasons of struggle, hardships, and times when I didn't know which way to turn. He has guided me toward what is best for me, even when I didn't always give Him my best. It was through those challenging times of grief and sorrow that He comforted me in a way no one else could have. I can never thank Him enough for loving me that much!

Regardless of where we are in life, God will meet us at the point of our need. As we remember all He has done for us in the past, we are encouraged and strengthened with renewed hope for the future.

Today will be a brighter day as we keep our hearts and minds on the main thing, which is following the way that leads to peace and comfort, no matter what comes our way. Our Lord and Savior, Jesus Christ, is as close as the mention of His name.

Prayer: Father, we thank You for being more than enough. To know that You are with us when we face challenges in life brings peace and hope for better days ahead. It is during those hard seasons that we can face our struggles knowing that we are never alone. Please help us to always honor You in all we do. We pray this in Jesus' name. Amen.

TURNING LEMONS INTO LEMONADE

I lift up my eyes to the hills. From where does my help come?
My help comes from the LORD, who made heaven and earth.

Psalm 121:1-2 (ESV)

As I sat in the theater watching the movie, I was deeply touched by the true story of the main character's unimaginably complex life. Seeing the depiction of how he suffered such deep physical and emotional pain, as well as total rejection by his family members, was very sobering. As the story concluded, it was clear that this man had turned the lemons of his life into lemonade. He became a writer and singer, using his pain to testify to the faithfulness of God in leading him out of such depressing life circumstances.

This movie encouraged me to continue doing something I love — write. It inspired me to continue transforming my pain into something useful through heartfelt written thoughts, such as the ones in this book. Lines from the movie were just the encouragement I needed to put aside the many doubts and fears I felt from time to time and to trust in the only One who truly knows me.

I continue to write in my own style and from my heart. In many ways, it serves as my spiritual and emotional therapy. I have given my heart and mind to the Lord and asked Him to use them to encourage others and to bring glory to Himself. God is so good—completely trustworthy and faithful! I continue to lean heavily on Him, knowing that it is He who sustains me every moment of every day. He is ever faithful and always there to help each of us.

I'm wondering if there's anything in your world —pain, sorrow, grief, health issues, fear, family issues, unforgiveness, uncertainty, decisions that need to be made, discouragement—that weighs you down. If so, I pray that you will look up, reach out to God, and trade your burdens for His peace. Jesus will meet you right where you are. He's always on duty and is ready and willing to help you make sweet lemonade out of those lemons in your life.

Prayer: Dear God, we thank You for never letting us go. Thank You for helping us turn the lemons of our lives into something beautiful and pleasing to You. Help us share the sweetness of our faith with those who need encouragement or are in need of a Savior. All we need to do is look around, and we see how much others need you. Give us words and the opportunity to serve You in this manner as long as we live. We pray this in Jesus' name. Amen.

SHARE YOUR STORY

*The LORD is near to the brokenhearted and
saves the crushed in spirit.*
Psalm 34:18 (ESV)

Every person on earth has a unique story, a narrative of immense power. Some stories have more chapters, and some reveal nearly insurmountable obstacles, but somehow the ability to overcome them has triumphed. Your story, no matter how big or small, can inspire and uplift others.

Never be afraid to share all or parts of your story to encourage someone else. I've always wanted to sit down with the unhoused population and listen to their stories. I suspect there would be much heartache, sorrow, and pain involved, and perhaps some good memories of days gone by. I care about the circumstances that led to their situation, for each is someone's child, spouse, father, mother, grandfather, grandmother, or friend.

Friends, many people are struggling these days and in need of encouragement. Ask God to use your story of redemption or brokenness and His faithfulness to encourage someone else. I know with certainty that He will never refuse to work in and through us when we have that desire. I suspect that our stories are more valuable than we know.

Prayer: Dear Heavenly Father, You are a merciful and loving God who wants us to tell others how Jesus has changed our lives. Give us pause to know that our story has value, not shame. Thank You for giving us such love and mercy. We pray this in Jesus' name. Amen.

THOUGHTS FOR A NEW DAY

I am the Alpha and the Omega, the first and the last,
the beginning and the end.
Revelation 22:13 (ESV)

While we don't know what each day will hold for us, we can rest firmly and securely in knowing that God is the same as He was yesterday, as He is today, and as He will be forever (Hebrews 13:8). He does not change (James 1:17; Malachi 3:6), He will keep His promises and He will always be with us. From Genesis to Revelation, He is the same. He is the author and finisher of our faith (Hebrews 12:2). Therein lies our peace.

Today is a new day, and I pray that Jesus will meet each of you wherever you are in life. Our needs are diverse, but how thankful we can be that our Heavenly Father is never at a loss about anything we may be going through. Since He is all-knowing, nothing we encounter in life ever comes as a surprise to Him. He has already been there, because He goes before us. May we seek His strength, wisdom, and guidance to live in such a way that others see Christ, the hope of the world, in us. May we always walk with the assurance that we belong to Him, and because of that, may we hold securely to His unchanging hand throughout our day and beyond. It's the safest place to be.

Prayer: Heavenly Father, thank You for the gift of life and for helping us to see that it is only through Your love, grace, and mercy that we can face these days in which we are living. I pray that peace will prevail over strife and goodwill will triumph over evil in the days ahead. May each person reading this message trust and believe that You are in control, even when circumstances seem to dictate otherwise. We love You and thank You for our Lord and Savior, Jesus Christ. It is in His name that we pray. Amen.

JUST AS I AM

I have been crucified with Christ. It is no longer I who live, but Christ who lives in me. And the life I now live in the flesh I live by faith in the Son of God, who loved me and gave himself for me.

Galatians 2:20 (ESV)

Have you ever bought something "As Is?" For instance, "As Is" on a real estate listing is equivalent to saying, *Buyer beware. Home may require further significant investment.* The seller is unable or unwilling to spend additional money to repair it or make it more attractive, so any necessary repairs or desired improvements will be the buyer's responsibility after the purchase is completed.

I find it remarkable that when Jesus died on the Cross, He paid the highest price for each of us, regardless of our condition. He willingly purchased us with His blood. We were bought "as is"—imperfect, with many faults and flaws, and whether we want to admit it or not, there is a need for renovation in all of us. The Good News is that He loves us enough to continue shaping us into a more beautiful reflection of Himself. We are His work in progress, but no transformation project is too big for Him.

Prayer: Heavenly Father, we can never thank You enough for the gift of Jesus Christ. His death on the Cross was substitutionary because it should have been us. Please continue to do Your good work in us that we might represent You well here on Earth. We ask this in Jesus' name. Amen.

A MOTHER'S LOVE

*She is clothed with strength and dignity; she can laugh
at the days to come. She speaks with wisdom,
and faithful instruction is on her tongue.*

Proverbs 31:25-26 (NIV)

*"A mother is the truest friend we have, when trials heavy and sudden fall upon us;
when adversity takes the place of prosperity; when friends desert us; when trouble
thickens around us, still will she cling to us, and endeavor by her kind precepts
and counsels to dissipate the clouds of darkness, and cause peace to return to our
hearts." Washington Irving – Quotes About Mothers, A-Z Quotes*

Being a mother is not just about giving birth; it is an unending divine
appointment filled with love, sacrifice, and dedication. Motherhood brings
wonderful moments of joy and sometimes unimaginable moments of heart-
ache and pain. But it's worth everything we have to put into it.

As I witness the young moms in my sphere of influence who have been
blessed with multiple children, my love and respect for them only deepens.
I had the honor of raising only one child, and it was sometimes tough, but
these moms are truly remarkable. They're exhausted, yet they continue to
push forward.

Whether you're a stay-at-home mom, a working mom, a single mom, a mom
of one, a mom of multiples, or a grandmother helping to raise your grandchildren, your strength and resilience are extraordinary. Please know that you
hold a special place in my heart, and I pray that you realize the enormous
difference you are making in the lives of the children in your care. You are
shaping your children into who they will become in the future. Keep up
the good work and remember that you are seen and loved by our Heavenly
Father much more than you will ever know.

Prayer: Dear Heavenly Father, there is no question that motherhood is one of Your most extravagant gifts. The love You have planted in our hearts for our children is unmatched by any other. There are joys, sorrows, and times when we grow weary from the load of serving as a mother, but You are always there to help us. I pray that all who read this will reassess their role as mothers. For those struggling with the responsibilities of motherhood, please offer them a renewed sense of love and understanding. Thank You for being with us on one of the most incredible journeys a woman could ever take. We pray this in Jesus' name. Amen.

WHAT FUELS YOUR DAY?

No, in all these things we are more than conquerors through him who loved us.

Romans 8:37 (ESV)

I've often heard it said, *"Today is what we make of it."* I believe that's true. If we choose to fill our minds with negativity, hate, bitterness, and unhappiness, that's what will fuel our day! If we allow God's love, forgiveness, compassion, kindness, and mercy to fill us today, then we will look for the best in others rather than the worst. We should never forget that everyone is fighting some type of battle. So instead of judging or misinterpreting others' motives, let's ask God to give us His eyes to see them.

As followers of Christ, we are fueled by faith even when it feels like we are running on empty or others have deserted us or even when we grow weary. Joy sustains us in all circumstances and through all seasons because the joy of the Lord is our strength!

Friends, let's make the most of this day we've been given by our gracious and eternal Heavenly Father. With our head up, shoulders back, and a smile on our face, may God's love fuel this day in such a way that we'll see and feel the difference in our daily walk with Jesus and our interactions with others.

Prayer: Father God, we love You and thank You for being the source of our joy, whether we're in the valley or on the mountaintop. We pray that You will fill us with Your love so that we might pass the light of Jesus on to those who are fighting their own battles. We pray this in Jesus' name. Amen.

BUILD YOUR HOUSE
UPON THE ROCK

*Everyone who comes to me and hears my words and does them,
I will show you what he is like: he is like a man building a house,
who dug deep and laid the foundation on the rock. And when a
flood arose, the stream broke against that house and could not shake
it, because it had been well built.*

Luke 6:47 (ESV)

Over the years, I have been blessed beyond words to have had "strong-in-the Lord" pastors whose uncompromising messages from God's Word have helped strengthen my spiritual foundation. Through personal time with the Lord, regular prayer time, Bible studies, small groups, mission trips, Christian music, and serving in special ministries with others of like mind, God has put His Word into my heart so that I might steadily develop a stronger spiritual foundation, held firmly and securely by my Lord and Savior, Jesus Christ.

The Good News today is that God is continually working to shape our faith and change us in such a way that our spiritual foundation will remain firm and unshakable. If we ask and allow Him to, He will strip us of those unsightly hindrances that would prevent us from growing in our faith. He will take them to the recycling center of His love and transform us into someone who more closely resembles Himself and someone who will not be ashamed or afraid of sharing the Good News with others as often as He allows.

Remaining steadfast and confident in Jesus, taking advantage of the tools He provides for our spiritual growth, and living a life focused on Christ will enable us to stand firm on our spiritual foundation through every season and every circumstance that lies ahead. I will always be a work in progress, but I am so thankful for His love and care throughout my lifetime. I owe Him a debt I can never repay, but thanks be to God, Jesus loved me enough to pay that debt for me.

The ground is level at the foot of the Cross, and our Heavenly Father will always meet us there. He is the Rock on which we stand. He is ready and willing to help you and me begin or continue building a strong and lasting spiritual foundation.

Prayer: Dear Heavenly Father, thank You for helping us to strengthen our foundation of faith in Christ every day. Forgive us when we fail to honor You as we should, and help us to live each day according to Your principles. We pray this in Jesus' name. Amen.

WITH HOPE, THINGS CHANGE

Rejoice in hope, be patient in tribulation,
be constant in prayer.
Romans 12:12 (ESV)

Presently we live in an imperfect and sinful world; consequently, pain, sorrow, and suffering affect each of us. We often grow disheartened when we become tired and weary from life's challenges. Rarely do we understand why bad things happen as they do, but through it all, God's Word assures us that He has a plan. He is always on duty, tending to every small or extensive detail of our lives.

A committed relationship with Jesus is the catalyst that holds us together in times of difficulty. When we have the everlasting hope found only in Jesus, our perspective on our present earthly life and our future eternal life is transformed. We begin to see life through a spiritual lens as God empowers us to face our most significant challenges with courage, trust, peace, and deep faith.

I am forever grateful for the peace and joy that Jesus brings to us as we allow Him to continue doing the necessary soul work in our lives. His miraculous and transformative power that brings healing, restoration, joy, and eternal hope is a priceless gift.

Prayer: Dear Heavenly Father, we don't have enough words to tell You how much we love and appreciate all You have done for us. Thank You for Jesus, who paid our sin debt so that we might one day live in Heaven forever. Help us in times of weariness to hold fast to the promises You so freely give throughout Your Word. Please help us be fervent torch-bearers for Jesus. We pray this prayer in His name. Amen.

NO ORDINARY DAY

This is the day that the LORD has made;
let us rejoice and be glad in it.

Psalm 118:24 (ESV)

In the busyness of life, it often seems that days, weeks, and months fly by so quickly that we struggle to find time for rest. So, how can we remedy the need to slow down and appreciate the moment?

I think we have to focus on one day at a time. Not thinking too far ahead, but making the most of each day, is a strategy that works for me. Of course, I do make plans and work on projects, but I try to remember that God has gifted me with this day. Beginning each day with the Lord by reading my Bible and praying helps me to develop an attitude of gratitude for waking up and being given another day to serve the Lord and my family.

What's your day like today? It may seem like an ordinary day, but in God's eyes it is a day that you have been given to make a difference in the lives of others. We have this moment in time, and God will use us in some way if we let Him. Be on the lookout for opportunities to serve God and others, and then carry them through with all your might. Find time for rest, balance your day, and let the ordinary become the extraordinary. We will look at life much differently and experience greater joy if we ask God to help us live from His perspective rather than our own.

Prayer: Dear God, You are the Giver of Life and the Author of all our days. We confess that we've unintentionally wasted some of our days. Please forgive us for that oversight. We truly value each day that we are given, for we know our time is in Your hands. Please help us to make the most of each day as we listen for Your voice. Give us the wisdom and opportunity to share our faith in Jesus with others we encounter. Thank you for hearing and answering. We pray this in the name of our Lord and Savior, Jesus Christ. Amen.

DEEP CLEANING

Create in me a clean heart, O God,
and renew a right spirit within me.

Psalm 51:10 ESV

Recently, I was sitting on the floor of my closet working on a project. Gazing around, it was evident that my closet needed to be purged of the accumulation of many items that would never serve any purpose. At that moment, my mind shifted as it often does. I began thinking of how we hold on to many things that are not useful: anger, hurt, bitterness, resentment, unforgiveness, disappointment, shame, guilt, fear, or anything else that robs us of our joy.

Did you know that inner clutter can become such a part of us that, for whatever reason, we can't let it go? We may even be aware that no purpose is served and no benefit is derived from holding on to it, so it is puzzling why we cling to something that causes pain, sorrow, or unsettling memories.

The Good News is that all of us can experience freedom if we allow God to help us choose to surrender this unnecessary clutter to Him. Throughout His Word, God has promised that if we cast our burden(s) on the Lord, He will sustain us, free us from anxiety, and give us gladness and joy. This reassurance of God's help and the promise of joy through faith can bring comfort and peace to our hearts.

If you are holding on to anything in your life that hinders you from experiencing a more joyful heart, I pray that you will decide to release this type of clutter today. With prayer and faith, we can find the strength and guidance to release emotional clutter. The joy-filled heart that comes as a result will give us a different perspective on life.

Prayer: Dear Heavenly Father, today we give You thanks for being our strength and hope. We are grateful that You are always there to help us rid ourselves of unnecessary clutter in our lives. Please give us Your wisdom as we go about our day, that we may honor You in all that we do and say. This we pray in the name of Jesus. Amen.

HE IS WITH US

If only I knew where to find him; if only I could go to his dwelling.
Job 23:3 (NIV)

Many of us can share stories of how God has intervened in our lives at just the right time. What others might see as coincidence, we see as Divine intervention, for we know that God is with His children continually. He is our constant source of reassurance through life's twists and turns.

How wonderful it is that we can be assured of God's presence with us every step of the way, because His Word tells us that He will never leave us. And… the best part is that He's as close as the mention of His name, meaning that we can call upon Him at any moment and He will be there ready to listen and guide us.

It is comforting to know that this day was made for us, so let's face it with the joy and peace He has placed deep in our hearts as we sense His presence and walk accordingly. If your day is challenging, please remember that Jesus is only a whisper away. He will meet you where you are, and He is the friend who will never leave or forsake you. Trust Him today, for you will never regret it.

Prayer: Dear God, how wonderful it is to know that You are always with us, Your imperfect children. We are thankful for each day that we are given. Help us to always remember that You will never leave nor forsake us. We pray this in Jesus' name. Amen.

REDEEMED

In him we have redemption through his blood, the forgiveness of our trespasses, according to the riches of his grace.

Ephesians 1:7 (ESV)

Because we are all human, there are mistakes and failures along life's road. We sometimes make poor choices that are not pleasing to our Creator. The Bible calls this sin. Mentioning sin is becoming more and more unpopular in today's politically correct society and even in many churches. But this word is used repeatedly in God's Holy Word, because God has never, nor will He ever, condone sin.

Through our faith in Jesus Christ, we can replace the unpleasant-sounding word "sin" with one that gives comfort, assurance, hope, and peace: redemption. Redemption is the process of being rescued or brought back to the safety of the fold and a place of rest in the shadow of the Almighty.

How wonderful to know that God loves us enough to rescue us repeatedly when we fail Him. In human thinking, we might compare it to a parent who has gone through many difficult situations with a wayward or rebellious child. Any loving parent will freely welcome that repentant son or daughter home. This is what God does for us. Jesus, our Shepherd, cares for His sheep, and He will always rescue those who have gone astray and return them to the safety of the fold.

I am thankful that I have been redeemed and am not the person I used to be. Even more importantly, I am grateful that I am not yet who I will be, for God is not finished with me yet! I pray that all reading this devotional can say the same thing.

Prayer: Dear God, thank You for the gift of redemption through Your Son, Jesus Christ. We are very grateful for Your presence as we navigate this life. You are everything we need. Please bless each person reading this message and bring hope and restoration where required. Give peace and comfort in every situation that might arise in our lives. We pray this in the name of Jesus Christ, our Savior and Lord. Amen.

HE MAKETH NO MISTAKE

One God and Father of all, who is over all
and through all and in all.

Ephesians 4:6 (ESV)

I recently read about a pastor in Mississippi in 1932 named A. M. Overton. Rev. Overton had a wife and three small children. His wife was pregnant with their fourth child, but when it came time for delivery, there were complications. Sadly, she and the baby died. During the funeral service, the officiating preacher noticed that Rev. Overton was writing something on a piece of paper. After the service, the minister asked him about it, and he handed him the paper with a poem he had just written. Rev. Overton, who was grieving intensely, penned the poem saying that God does not make mistakes. His strong faith enabled him to look beyond deep sorrow as he focused on the goodness of God.

Even with all of the world's problems today, we can trust with steadfast assurance that God has never made a mistake, nor will He ever! Our faith and trust in Him will keep us firm and unwavering during those times we don't understand. That's really something to be thankful for every day.

Prayer: Dear Heavenly Father, even though life is uncertain and unpredictable, we take comfort in knowing that You have never made a mistake. While we don't always understand Your timing or Your ways, Your Word assures us that trusting You is the only way to live the Christian life victoriously. We believe that You will never leave or forsake us, no matter what circumstances we face. Thank You for such love and care. Please help us to encourage those in our sphere of influence who are hurting or weighed down by grief and pain. We pray this in Jesus' name. Amen.

DARK TIMES NEVER LAST

For our light and momentary troubles are achieving for us
an eternal glory that far outweighs them all.
2 Corinthians 4:17 (NIV)

"Most of the time, God doesn't reveal what's next—and we can't begin to antic-ipate what the future holds. But most of us never learn to walk by faith until we walk in the dark. So, if it's dark, keep walking and trusting. Every step you walk with Jesus will lead you to where He has planned for you to be." Jennifer Rothschild.

Jennifer Rothschild, a Christian author and speaker for women's conferences, has been blind for many years. She knows firsthand the truth of her state-ment because she walks in physical darkness every day.

Although we may not be physically blind, we have all experienced spiritual dark times in our lives. If we allow it, they will teach us much about trust-ing and leaning on the only One (Jesus) who has and will always carry us through. It's all about trusting Him first, embracing whatever His plan for our life involves, and then walking in faith toward it. As we apply God's Word to our lives, there is peace in knowing that we are in His hands.

God is so good, and I'm thankful that He is always with us to help us over-come spiritually dark moments in our lives. Walking in the light of Jesus is by far our best option. He is ever faithful and will never fail to help us during our challenging seasons of life.

Prayer: Thank You, Heavenly Father, for always being there for us. You turn our dark moments into days of sunshine through Jesus, who died for our sins. Please help us look to You when we doubt, grieve, or feel discouraged. May we remember Your many promises to love and care for us, to direct us, and to strengthen us. We love You and can never thank You enough for the many blessings brought to us through Your grace and kindness. This we pray in the name of Jesus. Amen.

Source for quote: Rothschild, Jennifer, *Facebook Post*, November 12, 2018.

A LASTING LEGACY

O God, from my youth you have taught me, and I still proclaim your wondrous deeds. So even to old age and gray hairs, O God, do not forsake me, until I proclaim your might to another generation, your power to all those to come.

Psalm 71:17-18 (ESV)

If we are believers in Christ, our greatest desire should be to pass our convictions on to the next generation, so that those who come behind us will have our legacy of faith. As we pray for our children, grandchildren, and great-grandchildren, we must ask the Lord to guide them in His ways and to help them understand that money, status, and other worldly possessions will never truly satisfy them and are only temporary at best. Only God and His Word will last.

I believe that as parents and grandparents, we can make a difference in the lives of those we care about. There's no stopping place when it comes to serving the Lord, and we never grow too old to tell others about Jesus. We are imperfect and have made mistakes along the way, but we can and must continue to make an eternal difference at every stage of our lives.

Life is short and eternity will be long, so let us continue to be a light shining in the darkness for those we love, which should include family, friends, and every person whose path we cross each day. May all who come behind us find us faithful.

Prayer: Dear God, thank You for loving us more than we can comprehend and for being at our side during all seasons of life. We couldn't have done it without You. Forgive us when we fail You and help us to live in such a way that we truly do make a difference in the lives of our family members, friends, and everyone we meet. We pray this in the name of Jesus Christ, our Lord and Savior. Amen.

RUN THROUGH THE WRINGER

Cast all your anxiety on him because he cares for you.
1 Peter 5:7 NIV

When I was a young girl, I often helped my Mother wash load after load of laundry in our old Maytag wringer-type washing machine. One day, Mother and I were in the smokehouse getting started on the wash. Mother leaned over the machine, and her long hair got caught in the rollers of the wringer as they turned. Thankfully, I found the switch and stopped the motion of the rollers. We then had to reverse them and back Mother's hair out, which took some doing. Understandably, Mother was a bit shaken but relieved to have all her hair still attached to her scalp.

Back in the old days, we used an expression when we were tired: *I feel like I've been run through the wringer.* Now we know where it comes from! Mother was able to relate to that phrase literally, having experienced the physical and emotional toll of the incident in the smokehouse.

Do you ever feel like you've been *run through the wringer?* Do the ups and downs of life get to you? Do you see all the crazy things happening in the world, and wonder if it will ever get any better? Are you tired of being tired? There are many challenges in this imperfect life, and we can become physically, emotionally, and spiritually exhausted. But in the midst of it all, there is hope.

The comforting news I want to share with you today is that there is Someone always ready to bear your burdens, bring you peace of mind, and be with you through every challenging season of your life. There is a light at the end of your dark tunnel, and His name is Jesus. He is the One who will lift you up when you're down, bring peace to your troubled heart, and give you the strength to keep going.

Jesus came to give us an abundant life, even when we feel we've been *run through the wringer.* When we find ourselves in His loving arms, He will comfort us, provide us with the rest we need, and bring sweet peace to our hearts. His presence in our lives can transform our exhaustion into strength, our despair into hope, and our turmoil into peace.

Prayer: Heavenly Father, thank You for helping us when we struggle with the cares of this life. Without You, living a victorious life here on Earth would be impossible. We thank You for Jesus, our Savior, who gives us daily victory. Please help us to pass our faith along as the Holy Spirit provides us the opportunity. We pray this in the name of Jesus. Amen.

CALLED TO GREATNESS

You are the light of the world. A city set on a hill cannot be hidden. Nor do people light a lamp and put it under a basket, but on a stand, and it gives light to all in the house. In the same way, let your light shine before others, so that they may see your good works and give glory to your Father who is in heaven.

Matthew 5:14-16 (ESV)

Do you know that as a Christian you are called to greatness? In 1 Samuel, Chapter 16, we find the amazing account of how David, an ordinary shepherd boy, was chosen by God to be King of Israel. David is the only person in the Bible referred to as **"a man after God's own heart" (1 Samuel 13:14).** Although David sinned greatly, suffered for those sins, and failed more than once, He sought forgiveness. God knew his heart and called him to greatness.

As imperfect as we are, God loves us so much that he does not focus on our looks, what kind of clothes we wear, our bank account balance, the size of our home, or our popularity with the crowd. He looks deep within our hearts to see if we are a person after His own heart. He does not call great people, but He calls ordinary people to be great, so that He might receive all the glory.

Through our faith in Jesus Christ, God calls us to be men and women after His own heart. When He calls us, He will equip us and bring something extraordinary out of our walk with Him.

Prayer: Dear Heavenly Father, we know that it is Your good plan for us to love and serve You all the days of our lives. Although we may not see ourselves as being called to greatness, we want to serve You with willing hearts in obedience to Your divine guidance. Our greatest desire is to leave a legacy of faith in Jesus and love for others as we journey through this life. This we pray in the name of Jesus. Amen.

HE'S IN YOUR BOAT

But he was in the stern, asleep on the cushion. And they woke him and said to him, "Teacher, do you not care that we are perishing?" And he awoke and rebuked the wind and said to the sea, "Peace! Be still!" And the wind ceased, and there was a great calm.

Mark 4:38-39 (ESV)

Have you ever slept through a storm, only to hear others tell you the next day how fierce and frightening it was? Being one who sleeps soundly, I've done that on more than one occasion.

In the passage of Scripture above, Jesus had undoubtedly had a tiring day, as He had spoken to thousands of people along the shoreline of the Sea of Galilee. Now He was getting some much-needed rest there in the back of the boat. But when the storm arose, the disciples were clearly frightened. The waves were so fierce that water was coming into the boat, threatening to sink it. All they wanted was to get to the other side, which was looking pretty doubtful.

Imagine how those on board the boat felt, seeing Jesus peacefully sleeping as the storm raged around them. How relieved they must have been as He rebuked the winds and calmed the waves. No doubt, their fear was gone as quickly as the winds and waves subsided, and they marveled at what had taken place before their very eyes.

Is there something in your life today that threatens to sink your boat? Do you feel you're about to be overcome with waves of circumstances you can't control? I don't know what your storm might be, but I do know that in this imperfect world of flawed people, we all experience times where we feel the heaviness that comes from situations we didn't want or ask for. Consequently, our particular storms and the ensuing pain they bring weigh us down.

There is Good News, though! Jesus will always be with us, whether we're heading through stormy weather or the waters are calm and the sailing is smooth. I pray that you will discover His peace that passes all understanding. Until you've experienced it, you'll never understand it. But once you do, your life will never be the same.

Prayer: Dear God, how mighty You are as You help us to safely navigate through our storms in life. We would definitely sink were it not for You. Your power is unfathomable, and because of that, You bring peace to all situations—if we ask You. Lord God, please help us to stay close to You, for we need Your wonder-working power daily. We pray this in Jesus' name. Amen.

GOD'S STRENGTH

*For who is God, but the LORD? And who is a rock, except our
God?—the God who equipped me with strength
and made my way blameless.*

Psalm 18:31-32 (ESV)

As Christians, we are not exempt from experiencing days that leave us spiritually depleted and discouraged. However, when we find ourselves in the depths of discouragement, we can turn to the unwavering power of God's Word for strength. Throughout the Bible, we find that the many promises of His constant care provide the assurances that we can carry into life's uncertainties.

Relying on God's strength is the only way we will be successful in fending off times of discouragement. Even when those episodes occur, they won't last long because we have God's ever-present help to move us forward in the right direction. Amid life's trials and storms, Jesus is with us every step of the way, and His presence is a perpetual source of comfort and security. What may be hidden from our sight, He sees! When we ponder the future, we can rest in the knowledge that He plans it for our good and His glory.

Let us always look to our Heavenly Father for the fortitude to endure our tough days. May His Word be our anchor, guide, and source of strength today and always.

Prayer: Dear Heavenly Father, You are the God who knows our every thought and the weakness of our human frame. None of us is exempt from times of discouragement and weariness. But it is through Your mighty power, love, and mercy that You equip us with the needed strength each day. Thank You for making a way for us to find peace and rest through Jesus Christ, our Lord. Help us to keep our gaze continually fixed on You. We pray these things in the Holy name of Jesus Christ. Amen.

THIS WORLD IS NOT OUR HOME

And the world is passing away along with its desires, but whoever does the will of God abides forever.

1 John 2:17 (ESV)

One Sunday morning while at church, I noticed how some of our congregants had aged noticeably before my eyes. Those now middle-aged couples were once young adults starting families, living their lives, and reaching for their dreams. Their babies are now grown, and many have married and have children of their own. It seems like only yesterday, but I fully realize that over the 35+ years I've attended my church, I've also grown old right along with these other folks. And I'm very thankful for the privilege of having done so.

I am reminded that our days here on Earth pass very quickly. The Good News is that, despite our hurried days and challenging times, we have Jesus Christ to hold onto. He will never forsake us; He is perfect in every way; and He is the same yesterday, today, and forever.

There's a better day coming, and I pray that you'll remember where you are now is not your final destination. We have the option of making each new day one in which we don't focus on the negativity surrounding us, but rather we view our present difficulties in light of eternity.

May you find the Anchor for your soul and walk through today with peace in your heart and a song on your lips. You have this day. It will never come again.

Prayer: Dear Heavenly Father, we thank You for another opportunity to love and serve You. Please lead us in such a way that we will always represent You well. As time passes so quickly, we are comforted to know that this world and all of its troubles are not our home, nor is it our final destination. It is through our faith in Jesus Christ that we find the peace that passes all understanding. Thank You for loving us and caring for us. We pray these things in Jesus' name. Amen.

SUMMERTIME, DARKNESS, AND THE LIGHT OF JESUS

You are the light of the world. A city set on a hill cannot be hidden. Nor do people light a lamp and put it under a basket, but on a stand, and it gives light to all in the house. In the same way, let your light shine before others, so that they may see your good works and give glory to your Father who is in heaven.

Matthew 5:14-16 (NIV)

You know, it gets downright hot here in Texas during the summer months. I am most thankful for air conditioning, but when I was growing up, we did not have such a luxury. I spent many miserable nights lying in the darkness, sweating and getting very little sleep.

As bright as the sun is on a Texas summer day, we remember the light of Jesus Christ, which shines brighter than the noonday sun. We are called to be a beacon of hope and love in a world that often seems dark and hopeless. As believers, we have been given the gift of spreading the light and love of Jesus to those who don't yet know Him. We have an incredible opportunity to become His hands and feet. God's plan is that His light will always outshine the darkness and will never be hidden from the world, unless we fail to walk in obedience to our Lord and Savior, Jesus Christ. But when we allow the Holy Spirit to become a living presence in us, we cannot help but exhibit the change that has taken place in our hearts. This transformative light of Jesus shining through us will bring hope and positivity to a world in darkness.

Prayer: Heavenly Father, we thank You for the light of Jesus Christ in our lives. Help each one of us to spread Your light to those who need salvation, encouragement, hope, and comfort. Lead us as we tell others the excellent news of Your Son, Jesus. Let this prayer remind us of our responsibility to reflect His light and love in all areas of our lives. We pray this in Jesus' name. Amen.

KEEP ON KEEPING ON

I can do all things through him who strengthens me.
Philippians 4:13 ESV

I love how God comes through for us at the most unexpected times. He never fails to encourage us when we need it the most, and sometimes allows us to be in just the right place at just the right time so that we can see His hand at work.

One afternoon I stopped at the grocery store to pick up a few items, even though I had already bought groceries that morning. In the checkout line in front of me was a woman wearing a shirt with the above verse of Scripture written on the back. Since we had a free moment as the cashier scanned the lady's groceries, I said, "I just want you to know that you're wearing my life verse on your shirt." She smiled and replied, "Whatever would we do without our faith!" We chatted for no more than a minute or two, and although our interaction was brief, it was a rich conversation. Only God can do that!

After leaving the store and going about my errands, I then heard a Christian song on the car radio whose words offered rich spiritual encouragement and brought to mind many family members and friends who were grieving the loss of loved ones or were facing serious health issues. All had challenges before them that required strength beyond what they were physically capable of mustering, but they believed in a God who would carry them through these valleys.

If you're reading this devotional today and can identify with any of these challenges, I say to you, "Keep on keeping on." Your strength won't get you through, but God's strength will. He never runs out of what you need.

Prayer: Dear Heavenly Father, we love, worship, and adore You. It is through Your strength that we can go forward. Please help those who need extra support to seek You and You alone. Assure them that even in their sorrows and pain, You are working all things out for their good and Your glory. We pray this in Jesus' name. Amen.

THE POWER OF GOD'S WORD

So shall my word be that goes out from my mouth; it shall not return to me empty, but it shall accomplish that which I purpose, and shall succeed in the thing for which I sent it.

Isaiah 55:11 (ESV)

A couple of years ago, I undertook a project that involved typing over one hundred Scriptures to be used as gifts in a Bible Verse Jar for some dear ladies.

I was excited to begin this project, initially thinking of my own memorized Scriptures, and then discovering more in categories such as encouragement, fear, and hope. It was very uplifting to read, type, and be reminded of these Scriptures. I thought about how powerful and wonderful God's Word and the many promises found therein really are. It was not surprising that these verses of Scripture comforted me as I typed each one. I love that God's Word helps us find strength to meet each new day.

I'm going to keep these pages of printed Scriptures on my desk indefinitely because I want to memorize more verses than I already know. Having them there in front of me will no doubt give me the discipline to memorize God's Word more often. How about you? Have you ever committed to learn by heart verses from the Bible? Just as some of us memorized the old hymns as children and can still recall each word of every stanza, remembering God's Word will bring comfort at just the right time. God is so good at implanting His Word in our hearts for the here and now and for all eternity.

Prayer: Dear Heavenly Father, Your Word is a lamp unto our feet and a light unto our path. So much continues to change all around us, but You and Your Word will never change. Thank You, Father! The more we read it, the more we yearn to know You on a deeper level. Please give us wisdom as we seek Your direction in all aspects of our lives. We love You and thank You for hearing this prayer. In Jesus' name. Amen.

LESSONS FROM THE ANT HILL

And he awoke and rebuked the wind and said to the sea, "Peace! Be still!" And the wind ceased, and there was a great calm. He said to them, "Why are you so afraid? Have you still no faith?"

Mark 4:39-40(ESV)

Last Spring I discovered a colossal ant hill in our yard. I decided to eliminate this newfound ant colony, and my weapons of choice were a shovel and a bag of granules. I first exposed the ants by removing the top of the mound. As I raked the shovel across it, millions of ants instantly began running for their lives. I quickly poured the granules and my job was complete.

Sometimes we are hit with sudden disruptions, as was the case with the ants. We are going along in our particular season of life and then, out of the blue, we are struck by an unexpected life change. Our first instinct is to become fearful or try to fix the situation alone. Then we may become frenzied like a disturbed ant colony when its security has been threatened. This trauma now makes us vulnerable, and life as we know it has been forever changed.

When circumstances hit hard, what do we do? Where can we go? How do we find peace and safety during the storms that disrupt us? From experience, I have found that only through faith in Jesus Christ can we find peace during the challenges that come into our lives. He will teach spiritual truths we might never learn were we not inside the storm, and He will allow us to minister to others in a new way. Through our faith in Jesus Christ and with his help, we will be overcomers. We have the assurance that we will never walk alone, for He is always with us. That promise alone is more than enough to get us through.

Prayer: Dear Heavenly Father, thank You for helping us move to the next place or thing when our lives are disrupted and, at times, we don't know which way to go. You are our steady compass throughout each season of life, and we thank You for always being with us. Help us to honor You in all ways, all the days of our lives. We pray this in the name of our Lord and Savior, Jesus Christ. Amen.

EXCLAMATION MARK

Make a joyful noise to the Lord, all the earth! Serve the Lord with gladness! Come into his presence with singing! Know that the Lord, he is God! It is he who made us, and we are his; we are his people, and the sheep of his pasture. Enter his gates with thanksgiving, and his courts with praise! Give thanks to him; bless his name! For the Lord is good; his steadfast love endures forever, and his faithfulness to all generations.

Psalm 100 (ESV)

I love reading the Psalms both silently and aloud, singing them, and occasionally writing my own Psalm of praise to the Lord. But you know what I've noticed while reading Psalm 100? In the English Standard Version (ESV) of the Bible, there are six exclamation marks within the five verses of Scripture above. As strange as it may sound, I'm so glad that I didn't miss this little nugget. God's Word is so rich! I've read this chapter many times in my life, but it is my first time to focus on the exclamation marks - these strong and forceful utterances.

God's Word is indeed alive and active (Hebrews 4:12) and of major significance! If you read it slowly, soak in each verse, and give it some thought, I believe you will find it full of power, security, comfort, hope, assurance, and thankfulness. The Holy Spirit may even give you a different perspective because it is needed only by you today. That is the beauty of God's Word. It gives us what we need when we need it.

Prayer: Dear Heavenly Father, Your Word is amazing because You are amazing and powerful! Nothing compares to who You are and what You've done for us. Please forgive us when we fail to honor You in ways that we should. Thank You for such continuous love and care. Please help us always to represent You in the best possible light. We pledge to walk with You and seek Your supernatural help every day, in every way. Bring others to Jesus through the dear Holy Spirit as only You can do. In Jesus' name we pray. Amen.

FOREVER OURS

You are my strength, I sing praise to you; you,
God, are my fortress, my God on whom I can rely.
Psalm 59:17 (NIV)

How uplifting it is to see those who have been tested in the crucible of crisis advance in faith. I can think of many believers who are role models for me in this area of my faith walk, because their experiences demonstrate that God will ALWAYS provide the strength and encouragement we need to face life's battles or endure times of uncertainty.

God will never abandon His people, and He will forever be our hope, our stronghold, our refuge, and our strength. He loves us more than we could ever imagine, and through His Word, we can consistently draw from the well containing His never-ending supply of living water.

Enjoy this day you've been given. Pray for those around you who are currently facing their own personal crisis. Ask the Lord to make you a channel of blessing to someone today. My prayer is that out of your life, Jesus will shine.

Prayer: Dear Lord, thank You for this beautiful day created by You, for our pleasure and Your good purposes. Please help us make a difference in someone's life today. Give us an abundance of Your love, joy, peace, compassion, and kindness so that we have enough to share with others. We pray this in Jesus' name. Amen.

GOD HAS NOT FORGOTTEN YOU

I have told you these things, so that in me you may have peace.
In this world you will have trouble. But take heart!
I have overcome the world.

John 16:33 (NIV)

Do you ever experience times when it seems as though God has forgotten about you? I am pretty sure that we've all felt that way at some point. We may even think that we are insignificant in His eyes. Sometimes feelings such as this may be short-lived. At other times, the evil one may catch us at a vulnerable time and do his best to trick us into believing his lies. May we always remember that Satan is an evil instigator and the father of lies who wants to prevent us from spreading the light and love of Jesus to those we encounter. His goal is to beat us down and render us useless for the Kingdom of God.

Friends, I am here to tell you, based on the authority of God's Word, that you do matter greatly to God. He hasn't forgotten you, and He is faithful to His Word. He will guide you through life's trials, and He will give you strength to make it through this day and all the days to come.

So when you begin to feel as though you don't matter to God, all you need to do is look back and remember the miracles you have seen and the stories you've heard. Then go to God's Holy Word to find strength, wisdom, comfort, and peace. Talk to God and tell Him how you feel. Don't let the enemy cloud your vision or blur your memory. Even in the storm His strength will never fail. He is good and trustworthy! He is unchangeable! He is God and there is none like Him!

Prayer: Dear Father, we give You praise today, knowing that You will never forget us. Your eyes are always on us, and You long for a strong relationship with each of us. We praise and thank You for the many blessings that You have brought our way. We sincerely ask You to forgive us when and where we fail to walk in faith as we should. Give us Your strength and Your love as we share our faith in Jesus with those whom You place in our path. We pray this in Jesus' name. Amen.

MORE THAN ORDINARY

*Worthy are you, our Lord and God, to receive glory and honor
and power, for you created all things,
and by your will they existed and were created.*
Revelation 4:11 (ESV)

Most of the time our lives consist of ordinary moments and ordinary days. The older I get, the more I love the simpler things in life. I've come to appreciate more tranquil moments of reflection, uplifting conversations with family and friends, time with little children who see the world with such joy, and my time with Jesus.

Each day is a gift. With our focus on God, His creation, and others, we cannot help but see our day(s) through the lens of His love. Those ordinary moments will begin to take on a different meaning. Our days will be brighter and our burdens will be lighter as we recognize the One who makes each day possible. It is He who lavishes His love on us, turning our ordinary days into extraordinary moments of joy and peace.

Prayer: Heavenly Father, only You can help us take our ordinary days and make them extraordinary. Give us the strength and courage to make each day count for You. Help us to honor You in all of our ways. We pray this in the name of Jesus Christ, our Lord and Savior. Amen.

WISDOM OF A CHILD

Jesus Christ is the same yesterday and today and forever.
Hebrews 13:8 (ESV)

"The only thing that never changes about a home is the memories. Memories always last, and they follow you everywhere. No matter where you go, they will always be in your heart and walking beside you every day. Even if you don't remember, they are still there." Sophie Forston, my granddaughter, nine years old

Four years ago, my granddaughter, Sophie, shared the above thoughts with me during our devotional time. I asked her where she had heard it, and she said someone once told her that. She wasn't sure, but felt like her mom had shared it with her before she went to Heaven.

When Sophie shared this profound concept with me, we were discussing memories and the concept of change. It was during that time that her playroom at my house became more of a bedroom for a pre-teen. The uncomfortable sofa bed was replaced with a new, comfortable bed and a more luxurious mattress, and the toys she had cherished in her earlier years were organized and stored in containers. The change was very nice but it took Sophie a while to adjust.

I hope Sophie's wisdom encourages anyone who may be struggling with change(s) in their life at this time. Your Heavenly Father will give you His strength, and He will help you adjust to the differences you are experiencing. Even better, He will help you flourish and grow more than you could have imagined, just as He has done for Sophie! Our Heavenly Father desires that you trust Him in every circumstance of your life. You will never regret doing that.

Prayer: Heavenly Father, change often comes into our lives when we least expect it. Thank You for remaining the same yesterday, today, and forever. The fact that You do not change gives us comfort. We humbly ask that You help us adapt to whatever changes are needed in our lives. Give us the kind of peace that only comes from You. Help us to lean upon the everlasting arms of Jesus, for it is in that place where we will always find safety and security. We pray this in Jesus' name. Amen.

START WHERE YOU ARE

Now to him who is able to do far more abundantly than all that we ask or think, according to the power at work within us,(...)
Ephesians 3:20 (ESV)

All of us have some sphere of influence in our little corner of the world. Look around, and you'll see that God wants to work right where you are among family members, neighbors, friends, or others He puts in your path. He has gifted each of us in more ways than we can imagine and will always be beside us to lead and help us to use these abilities for the benefit of others and for Himself. He only needs our availability.

We have the potential to make a difference in someone else's life. It may be only a smile, but it's badly needed by someone who's having a tough day. You never know what another person is going through, so remember to share your smiles and positive words with everyone you encounter. God is faithful and will always show Himself strong on our behalf. Through these *Divine Appointments,* He will place others in our lives and use us for His good purposes.

Wherever you are today, you can make a difference for the Kingdom of God. He created you and me for a relationship with Himself and with others. I see no better time to show Christ's love to others than right now. Start where you are, let him take the reins, and be blessed in serving Him! It's the best thing you can do!

Prayer: Dear Heavenly Father, it is You who is our Mighty Fortress and the One who will use us for Your good purposes if only we'll give ourselves over to You. Thank You for being with us and for helping us reach out to others who need encouragement and hope. You are more than enough. We pray this in Jesus' name. Amen.

COUNT YOUR BLESSINGS

You make known to me the path of life; in your presence there is fullness of joy; at your right hand are pleasures forevermore.
Psalm 16:11 (ESV)

Do you ever think of counting your blessings daily? As a child, I learned to do just that as we sang the old hymns at church. Quite often my daddy would gather our family around the piano at home where we would joyfully sing these songs. These sing-alongs were a highlight of my formative years, and I am thankful that the enduring messages from long ago have stayed with me for a lifetime.

While singing the old songs brought revelations of God's favor in my life, there are many ways to count our blessings. We can remember that no day is guaranteed and that every experience is a gift from our loving Heavenly Father. In addition, He graciously allows us to begin anew each morning. Viewing our day with these truths in mind will no doubt cause profound gratitude to well up in our hearts.

I challenge you to look for all the blessings God has bestowed upon you. In choosing gratitude, you will arm yourself against whatever negativity the next 24 hours might bring. Any problems you face will seem more minor, challenges will seem less complex, and the good things in life will shine even brighter. I pray that you can see God's hand at work in your life and in the lives of those you love. There is no doubt that you will recognize the untold blessings that God has lavished upon you.

Prayer: Dear Heavenly Father, You are an awesome God! The blessings You shower on us are sweet moments that give us pause to acknowledge Your great love for us. We are undeserving of so much love, but You give it anyway. For that, we are eternally thankful. We love You, Lord. In Jesus' name we pray. Amen.

PRAYER

Rejoice always, pray without ceasing, give thanks in all circumstances; for this is the will of God in Christ Jesus for you.
1 Thessalonians 5:16-18 (ESV)

I believe in prayer, for I have experienced its wonder-working power, and I have felt the perfect peace that comes from it. For some who don't believe in God or the redemptive work that Jesus accomplished on the Cross, discussing the importance of prayer may sound foreign. Many who ostracize those of us who pray are spiritually blinded, thereby missing out on a beautiful relationship with our Lord and Savior, Jesus Christ. If only they could know the deep peace that passes all understanding when we take our burdens to the Lord.

I am deeply grateful to have been the recipient of many prayers over the years. I am certain the first person who ever sought the Lord on my behalf was my mother. She prayed for me before I was born and continued to do so throughout my childhood and into adulthood. Her many prayers are, no doubt, the main reason that my six siblings and I, at one time or another, gave our hearts to Jesus and began walking with Him. I am so thankful for a praying mother, and I will never take for granted the many family members and friends who have prayed for me during life's twists and turns.

How about you? Do you believe in the power of prayer? Do you often pray for others? It's incredible how one can feel the prayers that others have directed toward them. I believe that it should be an honor to pray for others each day. In addition, I believe that prayer changes things, and I am sure that it changes people.

As we go through each day, let's keep our hearts and minds in an attitude of prayer. God hears each one, wherever you are and whatever you're doing. He will always answer according to His will and plan for your life.

Prayer: Heavenly Father, what a beautiful thing it is for Your children to come before You in prayer. We do so with humility and the assurance that You hear and answer in Your own way and timing. Our trust is that You know what's best for us and that You will answer our prayers accordingly. Thank You for giving us this eternal phone line to connect with You anytime, day or night. Help us to pray for others as You bring them to our minds, even as we go about our daily activities. We pray this in Jesus' name. Amen.

REPRESENTING THE LORD

Brothers and sisters, I do not consider myself yet to have taken hold of it. But one thing I do: Forgetting what is behind and straining toward what is ahead, I press on toward the goal to win the prize for which God has called me heavenward in Christ Jesus.

Philippians 3:13-14 (NIV)

Most of us will never live on a foreign mission field, but we can serve God right where we are. He wants to use us for the good of others, which can include family, neighbors, friends, or even strangers. This service is not just about helping individuals we know or encounter, but it is also about our personal growth and fulfillment in our faith journey.

You may think that you don't have any spiritual gifts, but you would be mistaken. Each one of us has the potential to make a difference in someone else's life. God has gifted us in more ways than we can imagine. He will not waste the gifts He's given us, but we must be willing to let Him lead. If we allow it, He will develop those qualities in us that align with His perfect plan for our lives. There is immense joy and satisfaction in using these gifts for God's work.

God will place others in our lives and use us for His good purposes. I am continually amazed at how the Holy Spirit prompts us to serve someone in ways that are specific only to them. He will lead us, and all He needs is our availability. There is no better way to make Him known than by serving others. Start where you are, let Him take the reins, and be blessed in serving Him!

Prayer: Dear Heavenly Father, we strongly desire to serve You and others more and more each day. May we be the vessel who points them to Jesus through the power of the Holy Spirit. We pray this in the name of our Savior and Lord, Jesus Christ. Amen.

STEADFAST LOVE

The steadfast love of the LORD never ceases, His mercies never come to an end; they are new every morning; great is your faithfulness.
Lamentations 3:22-23 (ESV)

The Scripture above is one I've always considered to be one of my favorites. From birth to this day, God's faithfulness has been interwoven into my life circumstances–the good, the bad, and the ugly. He has been the constant source of strength and direction that I've always needed. I'm thankful for His unconditional love and care throughout every moment of my life. He has provided a shelter in every storm and a rainbow to follow each one.

Friends, there's no safer place to be than sheltered in God's love and protection. You see, His affection for us is not based on conditions—how good we are or how much we try to do to earn His approval. Rather, His love for us is steadfast and everlasting. In **Psalm 103:12 (ESV),** the Bible tells us, **"as far as the east is from the west, so far does he remove our transgressions from us."** Even though we might dwell on our past mistakes and sins, we can be assured that He remembers them no more (Hebrews 8:12). I find it amazing that He loves us that much.

Why not trust Him more today than you did yesterday and ask Him to help you take on a joy-filled life? You will never regret having done so. He is our peace, our every satisfaction, and He is the only One whose steadfast love will always be with us.

Prayer: Dear Heavenly Father, it is Your steadfast love that binds us to You like glue. Please forgive us when we fail You, and help us to forgive ourselves for any wrongs that You have already righted. Fill us with more of Your love so that we might shine the light of Jesus to a lost and dying world. We thank You for being beside us every step of the way. This we pray in the mighty name of Jesus Christ, our Lord and Savior. Amen.

THE ULTIMATE POWER SOURCE

This God is my strong refuge and has made my way blameless.
2 Samuel 22:33 (ESV)

This past winter our AC/Heating unit went out. The roads were icy because the outside temperature was below freezing, and there had been sleet overnight. Consequently, the repairman couldn't make a house call for a day or so. Thankfully, as a backup, we had a gas fireplace, a gas stove, electricity, and a smaller AC/Heating unit still working, so we knew we wouldn't freeze. Besides that, I had a few tricks up my sleeve.

Over the years, I've learned a few methods for keeping warm. One of those little nuggets involves an electric clothes dryer and electrical power. Just throw a fluffy blanket into the clothes dryer, turn it on, and let it run for a few minutes. Voila! You have a warm blanket to keep you or your loved one cozy and comfortable. My husband and granddaughter love to be treated to this special type of "luxury" when they're cold.

While pondering our light and momentary situation, I thought about another power source—a spiritual one. I asked myself these questions: *How can we remain connected to God's power source? How can we avoid costly repairs to our faith walk?*

God has already given us the necessary tools for a life of power through Jesus Christ. We can take that truth and never doubt it! I'm so thankful that as Christians, we've been given the Holy Spirit, who works to renew our minds to be more like Jesus. The comfort He brings gives us such hope and peace. He even intercedes on our behalf when we don't have the words (Romans 8:26-27). I love that! His convicting power is essential in the daily lives of all believers. Personally, I could not do without it!

Through reading and studying God's Word, daily communicating with Him in prayer, and regularly assessing our spiritual health, we can successfully navigate life's twists and turns from a biblical perspective. The Bible is the ultimate road map for living the Christian life.

What power are you plugged into today? I pray that you are connected to the ultimate and everlasting spiritual power source—God the Father, God the Son, and God the Holy Spirit—God in three persons, blessed Trinity.

Prayer: Dear God, how blessed we are to call You Abba Father. You always know what's best for Your children. We praise You for being our ultimate power source. Help us to always plug in to the One who will never leave nor forsake us—Jesus Christ. We pray this in His name and for His sake. Amen.

MOTHERS

She dresses herself with strength and makes her arms strong. She opens her mouth with wisdom, and the teaching of kindness is on her tongue. Her children rise up and call her blessed. Charm is deceitful, and beauty is vain, but a woman who fears the LORD is to be praised.

Proverbs 31:17, 26, 28, 30 (ESV)

Many of us have strong women in our ancestry. We've had praying mothers who gave us lots of nurturing and love, which played an enormous role in shaping us into who we are today.

Because of my mother's unconditional love, I had the assurance of being welcomed home, regardless of any failures and poor choices. What a comfort to know that my mother was there with her arms open wide to welcome me home. Her love and forgiveness were deep enough to see only the best in her child.

As deep as a mother's love is, our Heavenly Father loves us much more than any earthly parent could. He loves us despite our failures and bids us to come to Him for forgiveness, rest, safety, and comfort. Knowing that He loves us that much gives deep peace that nothing else can even come close to providing.

Prayer: Father God, thank You for godly mothers who poured such love into our lives and sacrificed more than we will ever know. Help us to continually look to You for guidance in our role as mothers and grandmothers. Lead us in love to be the kind of role models that You desire, so that we might gain the respect and love of our families and leave a legacy of faith and love through Jesus, our Lord and Savior. We pray this in His name. Amen.

GOD'S GOOD NEWS

*If I say, "I will not mention him, or speak any more in his name,"
there is in my heart as it were a burning fire shut up in my bones,
and I am weary with holding it in, and I cannot.*

Jeremiah 20:9 (ESV)

How great to know with complete assurance that God saves us through faith in Jesus Christ, our Lord and Savior. He specializes in dusting us off, cleaning us up, and placing His love deep inside our hearts. He forgives our every sin, so that we might have a brand-new life here on Earth and in Heaven for all eternity. This is the Good News He brings!

As believers in Jesus Christ, we can be thankful for His never-ending, unconditional affection that brings joy to our hearts, regardless of our circumstances. He is the Hope of our eternal salvation, and there's nothing that can separate us from His love.

My hope and prayer is that you'll find it too good to keep God's Good News to yourself. When we share His love with others, we will not only bless them, but we will be blessed as well.

Prayer: Dear Father, because we have experienced the change You have brought about in our lives, we cannot help but tell others what a difference Jesus has made by erasing the guilt of past failures and poor choices. Please give us more of You and less of ourselves, so that in all ways we might be true and effective witnesses for You. We pray this in Jesus' name. Amen.

GO LIGHT YOUR WORLD

When Jesus spoke again to the people, he said, "I am the light of the world. Whoever follows me will never walk in darkness, but will have the light of life."

John 8:12 (NIV)

It is a fact that spiritual darkness surrounds us everywhere. As Christians, we are called to let our light for Jesus illuminate the darkness; however, not all of us have allowed our candles to consistently burn brightly. I am disheartened by the opportunities I've missed to share the love of Jesus with others, and I am very thankful that God is patient and forgiving.

Although there may be many causes for neglecting to share the Good News, the feeling of inadequacy and the fear of rejection seem to be the reasons I hear most often. But remember, we need not fear, because we are only a vessel that God desires to use. He will prepare and equip us. All He requires is that we be willing and ready for the task(s) He sets before us.

Our challenge is to remember that because our body is the temple of God, we carry His light within us via the Holy Spirit, and we can make a difference wherever we go. May we commit to allow His light to shine forth and to approach our faith walk with optimism and in Christ's love. When we do, others will see something in us that is different.

Prayer: Dear God, as we walk through this life, please help us to let our lights shine for Jesus. We miss so many opportunities each day to share the love of Jesus with others. Even if only through a smile, each opportunity we have will make a difference in someone else's life. Thank You for helping us live out our faith daily. We take comfort in the promise of Your presence as we pray this in Jesus' name. Amen.

WHEN MORNING COMES

You do not realize now what I am doing,
but later you will understand.

John 13:7 (NIV)

Today I ran across the old hymn entitled "When Morning Comes." This song is included in a hymnal titled Sacred Selections of the Church, published in 1990. During my childhood, my dad would often sit down at the piano with a hymnal and begin playing. After a bit of a *warm-up,* he would ask my mother, my brothers, and me to join him for a time of singing some of the great gospel hymns from this book. Needless to say, these sweet memories are very special to me.

The song "When Morning Comes" also took me back to the little country church we attended when I was a child. Once a year the church sponsored an event called "All-day Singing and Dinner on the Ground." Dinner was lunch back in East Texas! To this day I remember the delicious food! My mother's fried chicken never lasted long, nor did the excellent banana pudding brought by another church member. I could not wait to consume that heavenly manna! My mouth watered all the way to the church just thinking about it! After the outdoor meal, everyone would gather inside the church again, usually with the men sitting on one side and the women and children on the other. Then for a few hours we would do nothing but sing. I can still hear the men's rich baritone and deep bass voices complementing the women's soprano and alto vocal ranges. I suspect that we children sang and made a joyful noise unto the Lord. Perhaps God was smiling down upon this little *choir* of country people at that very moment. According to the verse of Scripture found in Zephaniah 3:17, I am thinking that He was also singing along with us!

The words to "When Morning Comes" serve as a reminder to us that God is always with us to bring comfort when we face trials and sorrows in our lives. Sometimes we do not understand why bad things happen to us and our loved ones, but we can take comfort in the fact that God knows the reason.

Whatever happens, God still loves us. He will give us strength and courage to face the trials of this life and an unyielding confidence in the life to come, when we will see Jesus face to face.

Prayer: Dear Heavenly Father, although we don't always understand why things happen the way they do, we trust that You are always working out everything for our good and Your glory. Help us to keep the faith as we go through life's ups and downs, knowing that You are always with us and in control. We pray this in Jesus' name. Amen.

Tindley, Charles Albert, (1851-1933), *When Morning Comes*, (1990) Sacred Selections of the Church, Page #484.

STORMS

And he awoke and rebuked the wind and said to the sea, "Peace! Be still!" And the wind ceased, and there was a great calm.

Mark 4:39 (ESV)

Recently, my husband and I were out and about around town when we saw a strange cloud bank approaching us. A special weather statement had been issued for possible intense storms, so we decided to head home to try to avoid any bad weather. As we raced toward home, it seemed as though these beautiful but threatening clouds were chasing us, and we were neck and neck all the way home. Thankfully, we made it into the garage just in time for nothing to happen. After all of the excitement, it didn't rain a drop over our house.

Seeing these clouds roll in only to produce nothing weatherwise, I was reminded that sometimes we tend to worry about things that never happen, like the fear of personal storms that never materialize. However, they do sometimes arrive without any advance warning. Even so, God is always with us. Through every worry, through every storm, and all of the in between, He is with us!

Prayer: Dear God, how we praise You and thank You for being with us through all of the uncertainties of life. Help us to remember the many promises in Your Word that tell us we are never alone and that we need not worry. You are always with us through the good, the bad, and the ugly places of our lives. Forgive us when we fail You and when we elevate our worries above our faith. Jesus is our Rock, and we pray to always stand strong upon Him! We pray these things in His name. Amen.

WHERE IS GOD?

For I am sure that neither death nor life, nor angels nor rulers, nor things present nor things to come, nor powers, nor height nor depth, nor anything else in all creation, will be able to separate us from the love of God in Christ Jesus our Lord.

Romans 8:38-39 (ESV)

Not long ago, a family member and I discussed why some people seem to suffer the loss of so many relatives or friends in such a short time. We discussed how others sometimes feel that life is unfair, and ask the question, *Where is God in the midst of loss and uncertainty?*

Personally, I have not asked God where He is, because I know beyond a doubt that He is with me. However, I've not understood His timing many times in my life and have probably come close to asking why things happen as they do. Even in my *more mature* years, I find myself needing to lean not on my own understanding, but on His.

I do know that God is who He says He is, and that even in the wake of our own human trials, suffering, grief, and testing, He is closer than we realize. God will always be faithful to His Word, and He is merciful and compassionate. His ways and thoughts are not like ours, and His love for us is unlike anything we can imagine. Stability, peace, comfort, and assurance can be ours when we trust Him throughout the tough times.

So where is God in the midst of our pain? He is right beside us and will never forsake us. He is the same yesterday, today, and forever. Because He never changes, we can always rest in His promises. May you experience that rest and peace, even today.

Prayer: Father God, thank You for being beside us even when we don't understand. Our faith tells us that You know best, and we thank You for the security that is found in You. Rather than look for answers we will never find, help us to place our total reliance on Your sovereignty. Give us the strength to walk through our hard times with joy and gratitude, simply because of who You are! We love You and thank You for always hearing us when we pray. In Jesus' name, we pray. Amen.

CHOOSE JOY

The LORD is my strength and my shield; my heart trusts in him,
and he helps me. My heart leaps for joy,
and with my song I praise him.

Psalm 28:7 (NIV)

Over the years, I've learned there's a difference between happiness and joy. Happiness is dependent on our outer circumstances—what goes on around us. Most of the time it's temporary, at best, so we have to wait for the next "happy" moment to come along. But what about those in-between times when we're trudging along in life? When there's no happiness to be found, how do we maneuver the mundane, everyday moments? Is there an inward reserve present in us when we feel as though we're barely keeping our heads above water? Where do we find lasting happiness? We don't. But we can experience joy that outmatches happiness in an inexplicable way. True joy has to be experienced.

How comforting it is to know that we can experience joy in every situation, every pain or sorrow, every doctor's visit that brings bad news, and even in our ordinary, everyday moments in life. However, our ability to have joy in our hearts has come at a great price. As I reflect on how Jesus died for us, I am humbled to know that through His sacrifice, He paved the way for us to have eternal life. Nothing we could ever do would earn us that right, for we are very undeserving. Jesus' death on the Cross was God's ultimate gift to humanity! But to have that gift, we must invite Him to be Lord of our lives. What a wondrous exchange that is!

I am eternally thankful that my Heavenly Father loves me and that He will never give up on me. My friends, rest assured that God won't give up on you, either. Why? Because He's a forgiving Father, and He loves His creation (that's you and me) more than we could ever comprehend. He wants the best for all of us (Jeremiah 29:11). His love is amazing, and it's the perfect recipe for a joy-filled, peaceful heart.

Prayer: Dear Heavenly Father, You have provided a way for us to be joyful even in the stressful times of life. How thankful we are that Jesus came to rescue us from ourselves. In love He bore our sins on the Cross so that we might live an abundant life of joy in all circumstances. That truth is foreign to those who have not asked Him into their heart. We pray today that all will come to a saving knowledge of Jesus Christ, our Lord and Savior. We pray this in His name and for His sake. Amen.

MUSTARD SEED

He said to them, "Because of your little faith. For truly, I say to you, if you have faith like a grain of mustard seed, you will say to this mountain, 'Move from here to there,' and it will move, and nothing will be impossible for you.'"

Matthew 17:20 (ESV)

When instructing His disciples, Jesus often used a mustard seed to illustrate the importance of faith. In the Scripture I've shared, He tells us that if we have even that little amount of faith, through Him we can do great things. He also tells us not to be afraid, but to only believe. Only believe. Simple faith. As small as a mustard seed. That's all it takes. Even though small, He then has something to work with.

How strong is your faith today? To be sure, these times in which we are living are not for the faint of heart. Evil seems to be more prevalent with each passing day and our hearts break for the pain being inflicted on innocent men, women, boys, and girls. We wonder if things will ever improve. I wish I could offer an instant fix, but I can't. I can, however, offer HOPE and do my best to encourage believers to stay strong in their faith and to pray for those who have not yet decided to believe.

If you feel that your faith is small, or if you walk in fear of all that's going on in our world, take heart. Jesus specializes in giving renewed hope to those who are weary and weak in their faith. Take what faith you have, if only a little, and let Him guide and comfort you. Rest in His promises and be assured that you do not walk this road alone. He has not, nor will He ever, leave you.

The Good News today is that our faith is never too small in God's sight. He will take what little we have and multiply it, giving us strength not found on our own. He will build in us a lasting spiritual foundation that nothing will ever destroy. I am so thankful that He loves us that much!

Prayer: Heavenly Father, You know Your children all too well. At times we are burdened with life's ever-changing challenges. In our weakness, we sometimes struggle to rest in Your promises. But the hope You offer in Your Holy Word assures us that we are never alone. Thank You for loving us that much! Help us to share the Good News of Jesus Christ at every opportunity. We pray this in His name and for His glory. Amen.

A HOUSE DIVIDED

In your relationships with one another,
have the same mindset as Christ Jesus.

Philippians 2:5 (NIV)

We've all experienced moments or seasons of self-criticism and unhealthy thoughts. This way of thinking doesn't come from God, but from the enemy of our souls—the one who wants to render us useless in our work for the Kingdom of God. But the Good News today is that through our faith in Jesus Christ, we can be set free from the chains of self-criticism, self-doubt, and all the other mind games Satan often hurls our way. While he is the master of deception, knowing that no circumstance or person is beyond God's reach is reassuring. He alone knows how to help us eliminate the negative thoughts that Satan plants in our hearts and minds.

You are not alone in your journey of life, for the Holy Spirit is there to help you keep your spiritual house clean and free of unnecessary and unhealthy clutter. The labels others have given you or those you've given yourself are not permanent. It may feel that way, but they don't have to be. I'm thrilled to share with you that God is in the business of changing labels and rewriting stories! If you allow Him to, He will do a new and beautiful work in your life. He stands ready to help you conquer your worst enemy—yourself. Those negative, self-destructive, and toxic thoughts may have been born from the lies you've been told over the years, but they are no match for the love of our Heavenly Father.

Prayer: Heavenly Father, You are the mender of broken hearts and cluttered minds. You hold the keys to our spiritual health through our relationship with Jesus Christ. Thank You for changing our hearts to better resemble the heart of Jesus. We have far to go, but we know and trust that You are with us every step. We pray this in Jesus' name. Amen.

LAY YOUR BURDENS DOWN

Cast your burden on the LORD, and he will sustain you; he will never permit the righteous to be moved.

Psalm 55:22 (ESV)

Today I am reminded of the extent to which burdens can weigh us down. We've all experienced times when we've felt overwhelmed beyond our ability to cope. Our baggage sometimes feels as though we are carrying a heavy backpack around our hearts. It's tough to be in that place. But hold on! There is some Good News! The weight of our burdens and sorrows is lifted at the foot of the Cross when we choose to lay them down.

Now would be the perfect time to exchange your worries, sorrows, and encumbrances for the peace that can only come from the One who knows you better than you know yourself. When trying to solve life's challenges on your own, rely on Jesus. Whatever your deadweight may be, He is the Burden Bearer on whom you can depend through every season of your life. Even in this moment, He is waiting for you to lay your burdens down and rely on Him to get you through the hard places you are facing. Please know that I am praying for you as I write these thoughts. May the Lord bless you with a peaceful day.

Prayer: Dear Heavenly Father, there's no burden too heavy or too painful for You. Thank You for being our help and staying with us in times of overwhelming pain and pressure from life's trials. We love You, trust You, and depend on You every moment of the day. Give us rest, peace, and renewal. We pray this in the name above all names, our Savior and Lord, Jesus Christ. Amen.

GOOD FRIDAY

For God so loved the world, that he gave his only Son, that whoever believes in him should not perish but have eternal life. For God did not send his Son into the world to condemn the world, but in order that the world might be saved through him.

John 3:16-17 (ESV)

On the first Good Friday so long ago, it doesn't seem like there was anything good about it. But God had a plan, and Jesus had come to fulfill it for each of us sinners who were determined to go our own way. Not one of us was, nor will we ever be, worthy of such love.

The Cross is only the beginning of the story. With more love than I can comprehend, Jesus willingly laid down His life for humankind. The darkest day in history would soon give way to the fulfillment of His promise and Bible prophecy.

Knowing Jesus makes a profound difference in our lives. Even in tough times, especially during those times, we will experience a peace that is not understood by those who don't have a personal relationship with Him. His peace, planted deep in our hearts, enables us to say with certainty that we can face anything that comes our way because He will be there to usher us through.

We have the assurance that our Savior will always be with us and help us through life's difficulties, if we let Him. That's the best news ever! May you experience His love and peace today.

Prayer: Thank You, Heavenly Father, for the Cross. Thank You for Jesus, the One who took our place on Calvary. We can never repay that debt, but You only ask us to follow Him. We always want to do that in obedience to Your Word. Help us to be more mindful of those around us who need the Good News of Jesus Christ. We pray this in His name. Amen.

HE WATCHES OVER US

For the eyes of the LORD run to and fro throughout the whole earth, to give strong support to those whose heart is blameless toward him.

2 Chronicles 16:9 (ESV)

As a longtime employee of the local school district, I was fortunate to have had great supervisors who allowed me to do my job in the manner I was best suited. Never one to settle for mediocrity, I worked hard, took pride in my work, and always wanted to give more than what was expected of me. However, there was one thing that made me very nervous, and that was to be micromanaged.

There is one scenario in which I not only accept but also embrace being watched, directed, and guided. It's not a feeling of being micromanaged, but a deep sense of security and comfort that envelops me, knowing that my Heavenly Father is always watching over me.

If you are a believer in Jesus, be assured that there is never a moment when He is oblivious to you. He knows exactly where you are in life and what you are experiencing. I am deeply and eternally grateful that our Heavenly Father continually watches over His children, for we need a Father who loves us that much. His everlasting presence is a constant source of comfort and strength in our lives.

Prayer: Dear Father, You do not overlook one thing that we are going through, and Your eyes are always on us as we encounter each stage of our journey. Thank You for the peace that passes all understanding, for it is only through our relationship with Jesus Christ that we find a safe shelter of love and rest. Help us honor You in everything we think, say, and do. We pray these things in Jesus' name. Amen.

GARMENT OF PRAISE

to grant to those who mourn in Zion—to give them a beautiful
headdress instead of ashes, the oil of gladness instead of mourning,
the garment of praise instead of a faint spirit; that they may be
called oaks of righteousness, the planting of the LORD,
that he may be glorified.

Isaiah 61:3 (ESV)

Ever since I can remember, Christian music has been an integral part of my life, both at church and at home. More often than not, a song will run through my mind first thing every morning. It is a great way to begin my day, focusing on these timeless old hymns that are filled with rich Biblical theology and that honor the Father, Son, and Holy Spirit. If I'm having a down day, Christian music gives me the needed lift, and before I know it, I am praising our Lord and Savior for His ever-present goodness.

If your heart is heavy today, why not put on God's garment of praise. Play some Christian music, whether classic hymns, contemporary Christian music, Christian Bluegrass, or everything in between. Sing songs that have Scripture embedded in them.

Like a comfortable old coat that keeps you physically cozy, you will be kept spiritually warm through singing about God and His love. Your life will proclaim praise to our Father as your nature is renewed in Him each day. You will see your world much differently, and I believe others will notice the change in you.

Prayer: Dear Heavenly Father, our spirits are lifted when we sing these timeless old hymns and other Christian music. Please help us focus on the message in the words, not the melody or noise level. We praise You for giving us so many ways to connect with You; singing Christian music is one of the best. Thank You for helping us put on the garment of praise for the spirit of heaviness. Give us a heart that is light today because of these songs. We pray this in Jesus' name. Amen.

RESTING IN UNCERTAINTY

Peace I leave with you; my peace I give to you. Not as the world gives do I give to you. Let not your hearts be troubled, neither let them be afraid.

John 14:27 (ESV)

Many years ago my doctor discovered a tumor on the parotid gland of my neck. He recommended that I consult a specialist and prepare for major surgery to remove the tumor. Upon seeing the specialist, the need for surgery was confirmed, and I was told there was a 15% chance that the tumor would be malignant. Being the mom and sole supporter of my young daughter, I was very fearful of what possibly lay ahead for us. Before surgery my mother came to stay with us, and friends from church were scheduled to help shuttle my daughter to and from school.

The lengthy surgery was performed at the original Brackenridge Hospital in downtown Austin, Texas. During my 5-day hospital stay and as I awaited the pathology results, I focused on the goodness of God, believing that even during a time of uncertainty in my life, God had a plan and purpose. Knowing that gave me peace and rest. I was ever so thankful when the news came that the tumor was benign! To this day, I have never forgotten how God blessed me through family and friends at what was then one of my greatest times of need.

Friends, if you're currently facing a mountain that seems too steep to climb, I pray that you will rest in the knowledge that God has already paved the way for you to overcome it. Please know that He is walking beside you and oftentimes carries you. Trust Him, and He will give you His strength and help as He takes you through the uncertainties of life.

Prayer: Thank You, dear Lord, for being with us through times of uncertainty. Your presence assures us that we will never walk this road of life alone. Help us to trust that all things are working out for our good and Your glory. In Jesus' name we pray. Amen.

THE PRAYER OF JABEZ

Jabez was more honorable than his brothers; and his mother called his name Jabez, saying, "Because I bore him in pain." Jabez called upon the God of Israel, saying, "Oh that you would bless me and enlarge my border, and that your hand might be with me, and that you would keep me from harm so that it might not bring me pain!" And God granted what he asked.

1 Chronicles 4:9-10 (ESV)

Not much is known about Jabez, but we do know that he was honorable and a man of prayer. He prayed earnestly and boldly, as referenced by the above Scripture. He asked God to bless him; to enlarge his border or "territory" as some Bible translations say; to keep His hand upon him; and to keep him from evil.

It is clear that Jabez's prayer was spoken by a man who was not asking for material blessings, but those of a spiritual nature. Jabez was a man who believed in his heart that God was the ultimate power source and was very capable of answering his prayer.

I wonder if we have the kind of faith Jabez exhibited when he asked without hesitation or doubt for God's blessing. Rather than asking for material things, we could pray for our hearts to be kept pure.

The Prayer of Jabez teaches us that if we are humble and ask with the right motive, as Jabez did, God will allow us to be more productive as He carries out His plan and purpose for our lives. He will hear our prayers; His hand will guide us; He will bless us spiritually; and He will answer according to His will.

Prayer: Father God, thank You for the prayer of Jabez. Thank You for giving us the example of a man who prayed boldly—for all the right reasons. Help us to have enough faith to trust in You, knowing that You will grant our request in Your timing and according to Your will. We pray this in Jesus' name. Amen.

HE'S ALIVE!

Jesus said to her, "I am the resurrection and the life. Whoever believes in me, though he die, yet shall he live, and everyone who lives and believes in me shall never die. Do you believe this?"

John 11:25-26 (ESV)

The above Scripture speaks of the resurrection of our Lord and Savior, Jesus Christ. We Christians believe that Jesus was crucified, died, and was raised from the dead, demonstrating His victory over death and sin. True belief in the resurrection should fill us with awe and overwhelm us with a sense of peace and thankfulness. Jesus died and rose again so that we could live an abundant life and worship Him for all eternity.

For Christ-followers, hope came with His resurrection. Jesus willingly entered the mystery of death and came out alive. His first step out of the tomb changed the world forever. Were it not for His sacrifice on the Cross for all humanity, we would have no hope of eternal life. He paid the price and brought life where we once were dead. Because He lives, we can face today and all of our tomorrows with the assurance that He is in every situation. If Christ is truly risen, how can any trials of this world possibly lead to defeat?

Our eternity can be secure, and our future is bright because the tomb is empty. Pause and ask yourself if you have truly sought a living and loving relationship with Jesus Christ. If not, He waits to receive you at this moment.

Prayer: Father God, simply saying thank You for sending Your only Son to the Cross for sinners like me seems like such a feeble attempt to express our gratitude. Help me and each person reading this message to be grateful for life, for salvation, and for the hope of eternity spent with our Lord and Savior. Help us to carry His message to those who need the peace and joy that only He can give. For those who do not know Jesus as Savior and Lord, place within their hearts a desire to seek Him. Please let this be the day that their lives are transformed beyond what they could ever imagine. This we pray in the name above all names—Jesus Christ. Amen.

HEAVY LOAD

Come to me, all who labor and are heavy laden, and I will give you rest. Take my yoke upon you, and learn from me, for I am gentle and lowly in heart, and you will find rest for your souls. For my yoke is easy, and my burden is light.

Matthew 11:28-30 (ESV)

A while back, my granddaughter Sophie and I were running errands when we came to a stop at a red light. While waiting for the light to change, Sophie noticed a large gravel truck in the next lane. She was curious to know the purpose of the small, raised wheels.

Not wanting to delve into the science of these tandem/tag axle trucks, I explained to Sophie that the smaller wheels, known as drop axles, are lowered and used to help distribute the weight more evenly when the truck is carrying a heavier load than usual. After we had discussed it for a few minutes, Sophie clearly understood the reason behind the smaller wheels.

We've all carried some heavy loads during our lifetime. While the weight of our loads may vary, however much we try, we can't avoid them. Because we come from different backgrounds and circumstances, our loads are generally not the same. Some carry loads of illness, grief, guilt, sin, broken relationships, or a combination thereof. Still others have long-term burdens of unforgiveness stemming from hurts experienced during their lifetime. With chronic heaviness and inner pain such as this, we will find ourselves depleted of physical, emotional, and spiritual strength. We struggle to get through each day because a cloud of heaviness seems to follow us everywhere we go.

In our human frailties, we often try to carry these burdens on our own. But you know, it's not the least bit necessary to rob ourselves of needed strength when the answer lies elsewhere. That's why Jesus came—to carry all of our burdens, problems, anxieties, and fears. He came to relieve us of our heavy load of grief, guilt, and despair. He came to help us to forgive others who have wronged us. His is the constant strength we need to manage our heavy loads. And friends, He is so willing to do that for us.

What a relief it is when we take our burdens to the Cross, lay them at the feet of Jesus, and then get up and walk in victory! This is the only way to go. Having peace amid our burdens—one that is almost unexplainable—is an amazing thing to experience.

Why not let Him take your heavy load? Let Him bring the kind of hope to your heart that assures you will always have Someone trustworthy and able to carry all of your cares. Let Him give you the ability to walk in victory. He waits for you right here. Right now.

Prayer: Heavenly Father, how sweet it is to know that Yours is the supernatural strength we need to get through this life. You offer it to each of us through Your Son, Jesus Christ, and we are deeply grateful. Bless all who read these thoughts from my heart—thoughts meant to encourage and lift them just a little closer to You. May it be so. We pray this in the mighty name of Jesus Christ, our Lord and Savior. Amen.

GIVE HIM YOUR STRUGGLES

Cast your burden on the LORD and he will sustain you;
he will never permit the righteous to be moved.

Psalm 55:22 (ESV)

This morning, while I take in the early morning sounds from my patio, there are many things on my mind. As I hear the beautiful chorus of nearby birds ushering in another new day, this is the rhetorical question I ask myself: *What am I struggling with, or have I struggled with in the past, that needs attention?* One thing in particular stands out to me, and I take it to the Lord right then and there.

Perhaps you would want to ask yourself the same rhetorical question. No doubt your struggles are different from mine, but that doesn't matter. There is a solution, and it's found in the One who is always there to help us overcome our challenges. God knows our weaknesses, and He will help us to conquer them. He never gives up on us when we seek His help, because He specializes in mending our hearts. He remains unchanged and is always ready to bring us peace and joy. Why not talk to Him today? You will never regret it.

Prayer: Dear Heavenly Father, thank You for Jesus, our Lord and Savior, who mends our broken hearts and applies the soothing balm of His Holy and infallible Word to our wounds. We can never praise You enough for this gift of eternal life through Him. We pray this in His mighty name. Amen.

LEAVE IT THERE

Cast your burden on the LORD, and he will sustain you;
he will never permit the righteous to be moved.

Psalm 55:22 (ESV)

Are you burdened today? Do you feel the weight of those burdens on your shoulders? I have found the solution to freeing myself of the unnecessary weight of things I cannot control is in giving everything to Jesus, including my heavy backpack of burdens and sorrows. Jesus came that we might have an abundant life, and we can't live abundantly if we are carrying around a sack full of heartaches, regrets, and worries.

Over the years, I have given many burdens to the Lord, and He has yet to disappoint me by refusing to carry them. I have total assurance that He hears, listens, and answers—sometimes in ways I don't understand, but I trust. I simply believe and trust.

Sometimes it's not easy to let go of our burdens, but it is the right thing to do. With God's help, we will always feel the weight being removed when we lay our cares at the foot of the Cross. Our shoulders will feel lighter, and our hearts will be made brighter.

Why not give Him your burdens today? Take them to the Cross of Jesus and leave them there. As the timeless old hymn says, "If you trust and never doubt, He will surely bring you out. Take your burden to the Lord and leave it there."

Prayer: Dear God, thank You for allowing us to bring our burdens to You. Thank You for Jesus! Without Him, we would be weighted down with burdens, sorrows, grief, sin, and guilt. Please continue to do Your good work in us and change us from the inside out. Help us to serve You all the days of our lives. We pray this in Jesus' name. Amen.

Source: Tindley, Charles A., Leave It There, 1916, *United Methodist Church Hymnal*, Page 522, Public Domain.

THE RACE BEFORE US

Brothers, I do not consider that I have made it my own. But one thing I do: forgetting what lies behind and straining forward to what lies ahead, I press on toward the goal for the prize of the upward call of God in Christ Jesus.

Philippians 3:13-14 (ESV)

Sometimes life gets tough, and we grow tired; consequently, our spiritual endurance often suffers. Maybe this has happened at some point in your walk with the Lord. Because we are all still under construction, spiritually speaking, God consistently leads, teaches, and guides us toward becoming mature believers.

My prayer is that we will run our race with endurance, leaving a legacy of faith for all who come behind us. May we light the path to God's never-ending love, as we continue to share His Word at home and around the world with those who don't yet know Him.

Finally, may we also be reminded that our Wonderful Counselor, Mighty God, Everlasting Father, and the Prince of Peace will never, ever leave us to run our race alone. Friends, that is gloriously Good News!

Prayer: Dear Heavenly Father, thank You for leading us along life's journey. Sometimes it's a great adventure, and at other times we struggle with the cares of life. It is You who stands with us through it all. In You, we find our help, peace, and rest. Thank You for Your never-ending love. We pray this in Jesus' name. Amen.

A HEART OF LOVE

It was fitting to celebrate and be glad, for this your brother was dead, and is alive; he was lost, and is found.

Luke 15:32 (ESV)

The story of the prodigal son illustrates how excited the young man's father was when he came home. The father was not concerned that his son had wasted his life on foolish things. All he knew was that his son, once lost, was now coming home.

God watches and waits for His children who have strayed from His presence. He longs for us to come home and find the rest in our souls that He intended all along. He is there to bathe us with His unconditional love. Can't you see His face when one of His lost ones makes their way toward home? It is, no doubt, the face of a proud father who loves that child deeply and longs for the closeness they once had.

God's heart for us is pure love. Therefore, He will never reject us and always waits for us with outstretched arms when we run to Him.

Prayer: Dear Father, You are good and ever faithful! Thank You for loving us unconditionally. Please help us receive Your love and then pass it on to others as we are prompted. Through the power of Your Holy Spirit, we want to make a difference in someone's life today. We pray this in the name of our Lord and Savior, Jesus Christ. Amen.

THE ULTIMATE FIND

For this son of mine was dead and is alive again; he was lost and is found.' So they began to celebrate.

Luke 15:24 (NIV)

Our security alarm system had been acting up for three or four weeks. I called the alarm company, and a lovely lady helped me troubleshoot the issue. Within a few minutes, most of the alarm issues were corrected through a series of technical maneuvers. However, I was informed that one of the sensor batteries on a nearby window needed to be replaced. Recalling that I had purchased batteries for the window sensors a year or two ago, I proceeded to look for them in the most unlikely place: the kitchen junk drawer. As I was unloading and clearing out the drawer, hoping to find the needed battery, I found something that had been lost for six or seven years—a Brighton ring purchased in the early 2000s at a small gift shop in East Texas. The ring wasn't expensive, but it held sentimental value to me. When I held this long-lost treasure in my hand, I was reminded of my most significant find of all time—Jesus Christ.

We who are followers of Jesus can rejoice that He pursued us, found us just as we were, and called us to Himself. We were lost sheep in need of a Shepherd, and He offered us green pastures, peaceful rest, and restoration for our souls.

Can you imagine the celebration in Heaven when someone on Earth invites Jesus Christ into their heart to be their Lord and Savior? **Luke 15:10 (NIV)** encourages us with the following truth: **"In the same way, I tell you, there is rejoicing in the presence of the angels of God over one sinner who repents."** While we can't fully grasp what these moments in Heaven look like, we can be confident that such divine love and unbridled joy exceed our wildest imagination.

Prayer: Heavenly Father, thank You for our Ultimate Find—our faith in Jesus Christ. There is no greater discovery and none more important than knowing Him as Lord and Savior. You are generous, merciful, and full of grace. Please grant us a heart and head full of wisdom so that we might serve You to the fullest each day we live. We pray this in Jesus' name. Amen.

CHRIST'S AMBASSADORS

Therefore, my beloved brothers, be steadfast, immovable, always abounding in the work of the Lord, knowing that in the Lord your labor is not in vain.

1 Corinthians 15:58 (ESV)

Many times I have felt inadequate to serve the Lord in the manner to which He was calling me, and I've felt insignificant in my little corner of the world. I truly am inadequate and insignificant when it comes to matters of a spiritual nature. Still, when I empty myself daily of the fear and self-doubt that Satan likes to hurl at me and put on the armor of God, then I am ready for the spiritual task ahead.

Wherever you are in your walk of faith, God wants to use you. He will equip you specifically for the assignment He has for you. You may not think you are capable, but with His help, you are! He will never turn away one who desires to serve Him.

We are Christ's ambassadors, and we're the only means He has here on earth to spread the Good News. He will gladly use us in our place of influence, both for our good and His glory! I am thankful that He never gives up on us, and that He will take care of the details. We only have to be willing.

Prayer: Dear Heavenly Father, You are forever worthy of our praise. Thank You for calling us to be Your children. We can never adequately express what our faith in Jesus Christ means as we live out life daily. Thank You for always supplying just what we need when we need it. We pray this in the name of Jesus Christ, our Savior and Lord. Amen.

MOVING FORWARD

Let the word of Christ dwell in you richly, teaching and admonishing one another in all wisdom, singing psalms and hymns and spiritual songs, with thankfulness in your hearts to God. And whatever you do, in word or deed, do everything in the name of the Lord Jesus, giving thanks to God the Father through him.

Colossians 3:16-17 (ESV)

God's perfect plan for us is that we would always be moving forward in our faith, constantly growing spiritually in our knowledge of who He is, ever seeking and living out His plan for our lives, and strengthening our relationship with Jesus Christ. But all too often, life gets in the way. We are distracted from that *perfect* spiritual walk. **Mark 14:38** and **Matthew 26:41** give us the words of Jesus when He told His disciples to **"Watch and pray(...)" "The Spirit indeed is willing, but the flesh is weak."**

Many things can hinder the progress in our faith. Because of those roadblocks, sometimes our walk becomes cloudy and hazy. We cannot seem to get to where God is, even though the desire is there. We may have unconfessed sin in our lives that will hinder our closeness with the Lord. We may also harbor unresolved guilt, hurt, anger, resentment, insecurities, fears, anxieties, and other negative factors that will affect us. Satan wants nothing more than to keep us distracted and discouraged so that we will not be able to serve God to the fullest.

Wherever we may be stuck, restricted, or limited in our walk with the Lord, the great news is that joy is just around the corner from whatever weighs us down. Our journey with the Lord is a step-by-step, day-by-day walk, and that is how God can work best in our lives. As we begin to move in His direction and come to Him each day seeking His strength and guidance from the Holy Spirit, He will always provide us with the spiritual nourishment we need and continually refresh us.

Prayer: Dear Heavenly Father, only You can give us the strength to move forward and grow in our faith. Today, we seek Your will and wisdom above all else, and ask that You guide us to live out our faith passionately, sharing the Good News of Jesus Christ as we navigate life's complexities. We pray this in Jesus' name. Amen.

SEASONS

*For everything there is a season, and a time for
every matter under heaven.*

Ecclesiastes 3:1 ESV

During the winter months in Central Texas where I live, we seldom have ice storms or snowy weather. When we do get a patch of snow or ice, it makes the news headlines! Children become friskier, pets love getting outside, and most folks like me want to stay in and keep warm.

I've never been one to embrace cold weather. Winter, for me, is merely a prelude to my favorite season—Spring. The allure of warmer weather, the melody of birds in harmony, the sight of budding and blooming trees, the fragrance of beautiful flowers, and the lushness of green grass are the things that draw me out of winter's hibernation. Spring, with its promise of new life, is a season of hope and anticipation.

For just a moment let's talk about our own seasons of life that sometimes get rough. How can we learn to persevere through the hard times? The Scripture above tells us that God has a purpose for everything we go through. We may not see it, feel it, or even want it, but God has a good plan for us (Jeremiah 29:11). When we trust Him with every fiber of our being, He will bring joy when there seems to be none. He will strengthen us and use us for His good purposes, giving His peace and security amid life's uncertain circumstances. And He will always be with us. We have His Word on that.

Prayer: Dear God, Thank You for the seasons of life. Whatever each one brings, please help us to view our circumstances with the hope and assurance that You are with us. We pray that You will give us peace and comfort today, as only You can do. We pray this in Jesus' name. Amen.

WHEN YOU DON'T KNOW WHAT'S NEXT

For we are co-workers in God's service;
you are God's field, God's building.

1 Corinthians 3:9 (NIV)

Recently, our church members voted to sell the current church campus and relocate to two new areas. We witnessed God's miraculous work when another church, with numerous locations, submitted a generous offer to purchase our entire church property. We have until the end of 2026 to vacate, relocate one campus to a new location, and begin construction on another at an alternative site.

The news of the potential sale of our church property came as no surprise, as it is a journey we've been on for a couple of years. Our pastors have clearly heard from the Lord, and while the logistics are being worked out in God's timing, we know that God, His Word, and His great love for us will not change. We are assured that He will guide us through this time of uncertainty, and we believe that He already knows the way and is leading us to new streams in the desert.

Are you in a season of uncertainty? May I tell you that our Heavenly Father does not leave us even when we aren't sure of what's next. We can be confident that He will be with us wherever we are, always providing guidance, comfort, and support in times of change. Hold on to Him and the many promises found in His Word. You will rest securely in knowing that He is in control and will work out your situation for your good and His glory.

Prayer: Dear Heavenly Father, You are the only One we look to in the challenging and uncertain places of our lives. You already know what is in store for our church, its staff, and its members. You see the path each person reading this devotional is on. Please give us comfort in knowing that You only want what is best for us. We humbly ask that You plant seeds of love and wisdom deep in our hearts so that we might make Jesus known wherever we go, for we are Your Church. We pray all this in the mighty name of Jesus Christ, our Savior and Lord. Amen.

HEAVENLY SUNSHINE

Because of the LORD's great love we are not consumed,
for his compassions never fail. They are new every morning;
great is your faithfulness.
Lamentations 3:22-23 (NIV)

One early morning after dropping my granddaughter off at school, I stopped at one of the little lakes in our neighborhood to take pictures. On cool, clear mornings, a thin covering of fog and a beautiful sunrise appear over the water.

When I reached the spot, a faint layer of fog still clung to one end of the little lake, enhancing the beauty of the scene. As I looked to the East, I was greeted by a magnificent early sunrise, a sight that filled me with awe and inspiration.

As I stood in this picturesque spot, I was keenly aware that each new day is a gift, and I'm deeply grateful for the opportunity to bask in the heavenly sunshine that emanates from the Cross. It's a spiritual experience that fills me with reverence and gratitude.

I'm wishing you a day filled with the same heavenly sunshine that I've been blessed to experience. May we all be reminded that the Son shines over us, whatever the weather conditions or our personal situations may be. What peace to know that Jesus is the Master of it all.

Prayer: Dear Heavenly Father, You are so generous to give us beautiful sunrises and sunsets. Thank You for reminding us that the beauty we see in nature is from Your hand. We pray this in Jesus' name. Amen.

REST, RELAX, LISTEN

(…)but the LORD was not in the wind. After the wind there was an earthquake, but the LORD was not in the earthquake. After the earthquake came a fire, but the LORD was not in the fire. And after the fire came a gentle whisper.

1 Kings 19:11b-12 (NIV)

We are sometimes overrun with the noise of the world and the busyness of our own daily lives. It can often be a challenge to sit still and spend needed time with the Lord. More often than not, I am hard-pressed to merely sit still! My day begins early, and I usually don't stop until bedtime. I have to be intentional in setting aside my spiritual quiet time, although my mind never strays too far from thoughts of a spiritual nature or comforting songs. But it is in these quiet moments with the Lord that we never fail to gain His peace and comfort deep in our hearts. Remaining in His presence gives us the needed strength for the day and sets us on a course of keeping Him at the forefront of our thoughts and actions.

Have you taken time to listen for Him today? Have you placed your burdens on His shoulders instead of dragging them around on your own? I can testify to the fact that God is BIGGER, WISER, and STRONGER than we will ever be. Our thoughts and ways are pitiful compared to His. How thankful we can be for His willingness to speak to us through these moments as we listen for His still, small voice.

Today why not rest your mind, relax, and listen. Open God's Word and read of the life-giving water so freely offered for humanity. Sense His presence in the midst of where you are and be ready to meet the day head-on, knowing that He is beside you every step of the way.

Prayer: Dear Heavenly Father, forgive us when we get caught up in the *busyness* of life. It is so easy to be distracted away from time spent with You, yet we know full well what it takes to bring rest to our hearts. Being still before You allows us to receive Your covering of peace and contentment. Please help us to act on what we know, rather than being distracted by the world. Thank You for being such a loving Father. We pray this in the name of Jesus Christ, our Lord and Savior. Amen.

WHERE DOES YOUR FAITH LIE?

And without faith it is impossible to please him, for whoever would draw near to God must believe that he exists and that he rewards those who seek him.

Hebrews 11:6 (ESV)

As you read the above Scripture on faith, I pray that you will be overwhelmed with gratitude for your faith in Jesus Christ and how it has shaped your life.

As Christians, are we perfect? Heavens NO! Have we made mistakes that we deeply regret? Most of us would say YES, because we live and learn His ways as our faith in Christ develops. But our faith assures us through God's Word that we are deeply loved and accepted by our Heavenly Father, not because of what we've done to earn salvation, but because of what Jesus did for us and all of His creation on the Cross. I am so thankful that we can say with assurance that He has never once let us go through a day without His presence. We can be incredibly grateful for His patience with us on days when we haven't relied on His help, instead choosing to do things in our own strength.

Where does your faith lie today? In government, money, materialism, and others, only to name a few? While we do hope for better days ahead, I know by experience that anything we rely on other than God's sovereignty will disappoint us and leave us feeling anxious, frustrated, and empty.

May God bless each one who reads this today. I pray that you will remain strong in your faith and find the rest you need as you navigate this thing called life.

Prayer: Dear God, we can never thank You enough for Your wonder-working power in our lives. Without faith in Jesus, we wouldn't know which way to turn, and surely, we'd go in the wrong direction without Your leadership. Thank You for loving us that much! Help us to always give praise and honor to You in all that we do and say. Forgive us when we fail to do the things we should, whether by commission or omission. May we always be found near Your heart. We pray these things in Jesus' name. Amen.

CLEARED PATHS

He restores my soul. He leads me in paths of
righteousness for his name's sake.
Psalm 23:3 (ESV)

There are some beautiful nature paths in my neighborhood which I enjoy from time to time. For this girl who was raised in the country, I love feeling as though I'm back in my element, even if it's for just a little while. These paths that I walk always seem to enhance my closeness to the One who created Heaven and Earth.

When I reflect on the planning that led to these nature paths being where they are today, I am reminded that God has already gone before me, clearing my path. He knows the twists and turns that my life has taken and any that lie ahead. He knows the plans that He has for me from birth to death. My responsibility is to trust that He is leading me toward something beautiful, because He is.

Isn't it wonderful to know that we are safe in the gentle Shepherd's arms at all times, and that even though our paths haven't always been straight, God has been working out all things for our good and His glory? He is an expert at working with us. The great news is that He takes us right where we are. He will always make something beautiful of our story so that we might testify to His never-ending love and care for us.

Prayer: Dear God, it is through Your great power that we can take the love of Jesus to those around us. Thank You for clearing our paths of any brush and weeds that would hinder us from being effective witnesses to others. Help us to stay strong and never give up our passion for serving You. We pray this in the name of Jesus Christ, our Lord and Savior. Amen.

STORMS COME AND GO

I have told you these things, so that in me you may have peace.
In this world you will have trouble. But take heart!
I have overcome the world.

John 16:33 (NIV)

Are you currently experiencing storms in your life? If you aren't, you will be. My former pastor, who is now retired, once said that every person we meet is either going through, coming out of, or about to go into difficulties. Scripture is clear that trouble and trials will be a part of our lives.

Through experience, I have come to understand that we must remain steadfast in God's Word throughout all seasons of life. We are to remember His promises. Although we may not feel or see activity, we can be assured that God is working. We should never doubt that He has our best interests at heart, even though we may not understand. While we can't see God's big picture, I believe we must adopt a childlike faith that says, *"No matter what, I trust You, God." "Whatever the plan, I trust You."* And we must hold firm to that each day, listening for the still, small voice that leads us. That is enough to bring us peace and joy and to help us survive the storms of life.

When you grow discouraged and weary or want to quit, I pray that you will go to the Lord with your burdens. Stay in His Word, holding on to the many promises He gives that bring hope and strength. Then pray that He will lead you to trusted Christians who will encourage you, pray with you, and walk with you through all seasons of your life.

Prayer: Dear God, thank You for being the constant source of our strength and for giving us everything we need to navigate the difficulties of this life. We know that one day You will make everything right. Help us to trust You when life gets hard. This we pray in the name of Jesus Christ, our Lord and Savior. Amen.

IN CELEBRATION OF

SHELLY RENA STRICKLAND FORSTON

May 25, 1967 –
November 13, 2016

DON'T BE AFRAID

When I am afraid, I will trust in you. In God,
whose word I praise, in God I trust; I will not be afraid.
Psalm 56:3-4a (ESV)

It's a terrible thing to be fearful. When my daughter Shelly was around 9 years old, she went through a time of being terrified of dying. The trigger for her fear was the sudden death of one of her teachers. No amount of talking or trying to reason with Shelly helped ease her mind. She lost a lot of sleep during those days and nights, as did I. A family doctor told me to ignore Shelly at night when she wanted to come into my bedroom to be consoled, because he believed that Shelly was only seeking attention. I am thankful that the Mama Bear in me took over and did not take his advice past one night. After a miserable and heartbreaking time for both of us, I decided to seek counseling for Shelly.

Following weekly visits with Shelly, the counselor determined that my daughter was perfectly normal and not otherwise disturbed, except for the trauma from that one event that she seemed to be currently suffering. Slowly but surely, this overwhelming fear passed for my sweet girl, and it was a tremendous relief to see her return to her normal behavior. Throughout the ensuing years, I watched Shelly grow up unafraid of anything she encountered in life. Even when she was diagnosed with pancreatic cancer, she told me that she was sad but not afraid to die. Her strong faith in Jesus Christ carried her through that painful and traumatic journey and on to Heaven.

God's Word tells us not to fear, because He is always with us. Although the days in which we are now living can cause us to become fearful, we know that fear is not from God. Rather, it is a tool that Satan uses to try to discourage us and to render us useless for God's work.

When life looks scarier than ever before, may we always remember that God didn't bring us this far in our faith journey to abandon us. He promises to be with us in all circumstances. May we always choose faith over fear as we face the challenges in this life. We serve a God who can do no less than be faithful and true to His Word. Praise His name for that!

Prayer: Dear Heavenly Father, You are a God of great promises, and Your Word is powerful beyond our comprehension. Help us to remember the many times "fear not" is repeated in Your Word. Give us great faith over fear and strength for our journey as we walk in Your ways. We pray this in Jesus' name. Amen.

A PERSONAL STORM

Fear not, for I am with you; be not dismayed, for I am your God; I will strengthen you, I will help you, I will uphold you with my righteous right hand.

Isaiah 41:10 (ESV)

Springtime in Texas often brings severe storms. A few years ago, our city experienced an F2 intensity tornado. Although the local television station meteorologists were closely monitoring the severe storms in the area, *our* tornado appeared seemingly out of nowhere just moments before striking. Over 600 homes were severely damaged, with 19 of those homes being destroyed. Even though extensive damage to properties occurred, we praise the Lord that there were no serious injuries or fatalities.

As much as we'd like to avoid them, storms of life sometimes pop up out of nowhere. We may be going along just fine, and all seems right in our world. Life is good. Suddenly our lives are shaken to the core, testing every ounce of faith, courage, strength, and perseverance within us.

Our family's storm came in early June 2015, when our daughter Shelly was diagnosed with pancreatic cancer. We watched her suffer deeply for 17 1/2 months before Jesus called her home. During that time, we entered into uncharted waters emotionally, physically, and spiritually.

Shelly's illness and death took an unimaginable toll on me. I say this not for pity, but simply as a fact. I was left with a broken heart, unlike anything I had ever experienced. In my dark valley, I realized that God still had a plan for my life, which included sharing with others what Jesus had done for me, even in the depths of despair, and how He can do the same for them if they will only trust Him.

If you are facing a situation today that seems impossible to maneuver, I want to encourage you to turn your worries and heartaches over to Jesus. Whatever you do, don't quit! Through His endless love and mercy, He is the same yesterday, today, and forever. There is never a situation in life that He can't handle. Give Him your burdens. Give Him your sadness. Give Him your grief. Give Him your uncertainties and insecurities. Give Him EVERYTHING!

Jesus waits for you to knock on His heart's door. He is ready and willing to open the door.

I want to urge you to go forward because Jesus walks beside you. And on those days when you are too weary to walk, He'll carry you! I guarantee it! Better still, He and His Word guarantee it!

Prayer: Dear Heavenly Father, were it not for You, we would sink into the depths of despair when troubles and challenging situations surround us. Thank You for being our comfort and strength in each season of our lives. We love You and ask these things in the name of our Lord and Savior, Jesus Christ. Amen.

FINDING REST IN GRIEF AND SORROW

The Lord is my shepherd; I shall not want. He makes me lie down in green pastures. He leads me beside still waters. He restores my soul.

Psalm 23:1-3a (ESV)

November 2016 is a time I'll never forget. My precious daughter Shelly was nearing the end of her earthly life and was about to see Jesus face-to-face. That alone should have brought comfort and peace, but for those who loved Shelly and would be left behind to mourn, it was a time of great sadness and sorrow.

Shelly was courageous as she fought against an unforgiving beast called pancreatic cancer. She fought hard, kept the faith, and encouraged others even in the valley of the shadow of death. She'd say, *"God is good. He has a plan. Everything is going to be okay."*

Scores of prayers went up for Shelly from around the world, and they were felt by Shelly and us. But healing did not come in the way we had asked. God had a longer-lasting plan—to give Shelly His PERFECT healing. Shelly's last season of life came to her in God's perfect timing, but much too soon for her family and friends.

It has been said that a mother never gets over the loss of a child. Based on my own experience, I will testify to the accuracy of that statement. God does, however, help us to be more than conquerors through it all. His presence is with us continuously if we call on Him, and He carries us on days when we're stuck and can't seem to move forward. He helps us manage our grief rather than let it manage us.

If you're struggling with grief and sorrow over the loss of someone you love, hold on to the One who will comfort you as only He can. As much as you loved that person, God loved them more. You can move forward by realizing that and remembering the many promises found in His Word. It's sometimes slow, but your relationship with Jesus will grow as you trust and depend on Him daily. He loves you and will see you through.

Prayer: Heavenly Father, it is You who has numbered our days. I thank You for the gift of my daughter and the precious memories of our years together. Please help those who are grieving from the loss they are feeling at this moment. Give them peace and comfort in knowing that You will take them through their sorrow to a much brighter day, where they will also make a difference in the lives of others who are hurting. We pray this in Jesus' name. Amen.

SEE YOU LATER

I give thanks to you, O Lord my God, with my whole heart,
and I will glorify your name forever.
Psalm 86:12 (ESV)

On November 17, 2016, 150 pink and purple balloons were released at the cemetery as we said our final "see you later" to our sweet Shelly. It was a beautiful sight as the balloons slowly drifted upward. We felt the hope of the grand reunion we'd have with Shelly and other loved ones and friends someday. As Shelly's mother, it was my way of returning her to the Lord, who so graciously loaned her to me for a season. Humanly, I didn't want to do that, but spiritually, my faith gave me the strength to take that step. A few days later, just around the corner from Shelly's house and miles from the cemetery, a friend found one of the balloons in her yard. Somehow, that brought us comfort as we believed God had given us another reminder that Shelly was safe with Him.

It is incredible to think how good our God is through these times. We trust and believe that His plan is best, even though we don't understand His timing. He is not restricted, nor does He operate on our schedule. We will understand that part better someday, but I don't think that it will be important to us then.

If you are currently in the midst of a challenging season, please hold onto the One who holds all things together—Jesus Christ. He will give you His love, strength, and a strong purpose to go forward. Whether you feel it or not, He is leading you out of your wilderness right this minute. Trust Him and you will never be the same. I am praying for you.

Prayer: Dear Heavenly Father, thank You for the promise of our eternal home where we will one day be reunited with our loved ones who believed and trusted in Jesus. Without You, life would be hopeless, but as we continue to trust You, we have nothing to dread or fear, but everything to gain. We pray this in Jesus' name and for His sake. Amen.

SAFELY HOME

Today I gazed upon your face,
My child of God's amazing grace.

I thought of all I'd like to say,
If we were given one more day.

One more day to share the love,
That God gave us from Heaven above.

But you're not here, I fully know,
And where you are, I can't yet go.

But while I'm here, I'll think of you,
Of how you have been made anew.

From head to toe, you radiate,
God's love in you, amazing grace!

No pain you'll have forevermore;
No worries like you had before.

In Heaven above, you're safely there,
Eternal life with saints you share.

Thank God for His amazing grace,
You'll live forever; you've won the race!

God gave us all a choice to make,
To live for Him, His gift to take.

It's sad to see the world these days,
So many lost He came to save.

So while we're here on earth to live,
Our faith alone to them we'll give;

And pray they hear from God above,
Accept His gift of endless love.

Until that day God calls us home,
We pray the lost will cease to roam.

That they will know His love so free,
And walk with Him eternally.

In Memory: Shelly Rena Forston, May 25, 1967 - November 13, 2016

A MOTHER'S TRIBUTE

I have fought the good fight, I have finished the race,
I have kept the faith.

2 Timothy 4:7 (NIV)

I believe that a mother's love is deeper than anything except God's love. When my precious daughter, Shelly, went to Heaven, my heart was shattered, but I am so thankful that I know the mender of broken hearts. I cherish each moment we shared during Shelly's 49 years of life.

As a child and young girl, Shelly was always so bubbly and happy. Throughout her life, she and I were mostly inseparable. However, it was during her illness that I saw clearly the strength she possessed as an adult. Because of her unwavering faith in God, Shelly reflected His character. The Fruits of the Spirit – love, joy, peace, patience, kindness, goodness, faithfulness, gentleness, and self-control – were evident in her life. Although I knew Shelly possessed these fruits, they became more obvious through her time of suffering.

Shelly was a true blessing and inspiration to me, and she will forever live in my heart until we meet again where we will be together for eternity. She took a big part of my heart with her to Heaven. I miss our time together, phone conversations, the many texts, and the hugs so very much! The memory of her beautiful smile always helps me soldier through the sad days of missing her.

The Good News today is that Shelly is now forever whole with no more cancer, pain, sadness, or worries. She fought the good fight, finished the race, and is now home where she was created to be – forever with her Lord and Savior Jesus Christ.

If you're going through a season of grief from the loss of a loved one, please know that you are not alone. You are loved unconditionally and God's specialty is mending broken hearts. He will never leave you, so stick with Him! Your life will not be the same, but if you let Him, our Heavenly Father will see you through. He will help you use your pain for the good of others and His glory. In the process, you will experience healing, one step at a time. Slowly, you'll begin to see more light than darkness.

Prayer: Father God, we turn to You through our hard places in life. You have never disappointed us or left us to grieve alone. Resting in You is the only direction we will ever desire to turn. Thank You for Your comfort and peace. We pray this in Jesus' name. Amen.

OUTSIDE MY WINDOW

But, as it is written, "What no eye has seen, nor ear heard,
nor the heart of man imagined, what God has
prepared for those who love him."

1 Corinthians 2:9 (ESV)

I was sitting at my desk working on a Bible study lesson when a flutter passed by the corner of my eye. Outside my window was a beautiful Monarch butterfly. I stopped writing to take a few pictures, because it was the first Monarch I had seen on the butterfly plant in months. My immediate response was, *"Hi, Shelly!"* You see, ever since my daughter went to Heaven, I've had that instant reaction when I see a butterfly.

I sometimes think of how much Shelly is missing, but as I write this, the above verse of Scripture comes to mind, and my heart is lifted. The things of this world no longer constrain Shelly. She's not worrying about all that's happening down here, but is safe, secure, well, and more joyful than we could ever imagine. She's with her Lord and Savior, and that's more than enough. After all, that's the goal of every Christian and the desire of our Heavenly Father—that all would come to know Jesus Christ as their personal Lord and Savior, so that they might spend eternity with Him when their time on Earth is over.

As you read this, I pray there will be in your heart a HOPE that far surpasses anything this world throws at you! God is a good Father. He gives us His best in times of plenty and in times of need. We can always depend on Him, regardless of where we are in our life's journey.

Prayer: Dear Heavenly Father, thank You for sending reminders such as butterflies our way. In doing so, we are given the assurance that You see every detail of our lives. You know our individual struggles, sorrows, and pain. It is through Your great love and our faith that we make it through the hard days. We know that You are always with us and that You will never leave or forsake us. For this and so much more, we are eternally grateful! These things we pray in the name of Jesus Christ, our Lord and Savior. Amen.

THANKS, MOM

The LORD appeared to us in the past, saying: "I have loved you with an everlasting love; I have drawn you with unfailing kindness."
Jeremiah 31:3 (NIV)

While tackling the dreaded task of cleaning one of my bookshelves, I spotted a small devotional book that my daughter, Shelly, had given me on Mother's Day a few years earlier. The most beautiful message was written inside, expressing her thanks and love for me. It warmed my heart to know that Shelly saw me as the most wonderful mother and grandmother in the world. Seeing and reading this sweet message in her own handwriting brought a mix of sadness and joy. Sadly, my precious daughter had gone to Heaven the year before after fighting a valiant battle with pancreatic cancer. Upon discovering the book, I took a break, sat down on the floor, had a good cry, and read a few of the inspirational messages.

The above verse of Scripture, which was found at the beginning of the book, is very uplifting. As Shelly's mother, I loved and comforted her as long as she was alive. That's what our Heavenly Father does for us, and I am so thankful for the comfort that He has given me and will continue to provide throughout my lifetime. As believers in Christ, we belong to Him now and forever. He loves us much more than we will ever know and will always stand beside us, carry us when we can't walk, and never leave us!

Today could be a sad day for you. I pray that it isn't, but if you're a mom and are grieving the loss of a child, please know that God loves you with an everlasting love. If you've lost a beloved family member or friend, rest assured that Jesus is there to wipe the tears from your eyes and your heart. If life's circumstances have knocked you down, please understand that your Heavenly Father knows every hurt you feel. He is waiting to comfort you and will lead you through your grief or other hurt one step at a time. He will never leave you nor forsake you. You can trust Him with your tears, your past, your present, and your future. He will always care for His children because He can do no less.

Prayer: Father, there is no one like You! Our comfort, peace, and joy come from the relationship we have with our Lord and Savior, Jesus Christ. Thank You for making a way for us to become Your children through belief in Him. Please help us to comfort others who might be going through their own season of grief. We pray this in His name. Amen.

KEEP YOUR FOCUS ON GOD

Peace I leave with you; my peace I give to you. Not as the world gives do I give to you. Let not your hearts be troubled, neither let them be afraid.

John 14:27 (ESV)

"God's peace will be with us through every circumstance. Our struggles in life will change, but our focus should remain the same. God is the author of our story, and He is not yet finished writing it. That IS the Good News of the day." Carolyn McDaniel Canizales, November 2010

The paragraph above is a little excerpt from something I wrote 15 years ago. I LOVE that the things of God NEVER change. Our circumstances come and go, but He remains the Great I Am!

When I wrote those thoughts, I had no idea how my life would change five years later. I did not know that my only biological child, my daughter Shelly, would be diagnosed with pancreatic cancer and fight a valiant battle, only to succumb to its ravages. I did not know the depth of grief I would experience.

I also did not know the healing and blessings that would come to me during and after this traumatic season of my life. God has been so good in restoring joy to my heart. As I interact with the little ones in our family who have been born since Shelly's illness and death, I see that God continues to write a beautiful legacy for Shelly. He has also lavished His love upon our family by giving us wonderful friends who have stood by us through thick and thin.

We aren't meant to know what's ahead. If we did, we could not bear it. While there are circumstances I'd rather have skipped, truthfully the hard times have served to bring me closer to my Lord and Savior, Jesus Christ. Realizing I cannot make it on my own, I lean even more into His strength and guidance. That's exactly where He wants me to be, and I'm so thankful for that.

Friends, whatever you are going through today, please don't let your circumstances pull you away from a strong dependence on God. In His love and power, He beckons you to trust Him daily for things seen and unseen. In your dependency on Him, you will gain awareness of the needs and cares of others. He will use you to comfort and encourage them. The closer you get to Him, the more you will realize that He has been there all along.

Prayer: Dear Heavenly Father, You are the perfect One to save, love, strengthen, help, and guide us. Please be with those who are hurting from life's difficulties today. Help us to be good listeners and encouragers to them as we walk life's road. We pray this in Jesus' name. Amen.

PERSEVERING

Blessed is the man who remains steadfast under trial, for when he has stood the test he will receive the crown of life, which God has promised to those who love him.

James 1:12 (NIV)

Persevering is not something we enjoy thinking about or going through, because it always involves some hardship. But in this imperfect world, we will experience trials and tribulations if we live long enough. When faced with adversity, we have two choices: to trust in God and keep our vision fixed on Him or to quit and abandon hope.

When my daughter Shelly began her battle with pancreatic cancer, she persevered until the Lord took her home. Her faith and witness to her Lord and Savior only grew richer and stronger as she neared the valley of the shadow of death. It was heartbreaking, yet amazing. As Shelly persevered, so did her family. While the outcome wasn't what we would have chosen, God knew best, and we trusted Him during our own time of persevering.

If you are going through a hard season, please remember that God has much more in store for you. His plan has always been for our struggles and hardships to become blessings and rewards if we persevere!

Prayer: Dear Heavenly Father, in the midst of life's struggles and hard times, You hold the keys to our comfort and peace. Through Your great power, we can persevere through times we would rather not face. We have learned from Your Word and by experience that these times come to strengthen our faith. Thank You for being with us through all seasons of life. We pray this in Jesus' name. Amen.

IN CHRIST ALONE

The steadfast love of the LORD never ceases; his mercies never come to an end; they are new every morning; great is your faithfulness.

Lamentations 3:22-23 (ESV)

I sometimes wear a purple wristband in memory of my daughter, Shelly, who is safely home with our Lord. The wristband says, *"Wage Hope. Fight Pancreatic Cancer."*

Today I am reminded of the hope we have through our relationship with Jesus Christ. It is found in the assurance that no matter what we face, He is with us. This assurance brings comfort as nothing else can. Once we become His child, we have the promise that He will never leave us, and we will have life everlasting when our time here on Earth is over.

If your world seems somewhat hopeless today, please don't give up. The security we have in Christ brings many possibilities. When we come before Him in humble sincerity, we will receive renewed strength to help us maneuver each season of our lives. When we pray fervently, our faith in Christ grows and rises to a higher level. We can rest in the knowledge that He will meet us at our point of need and give us strength for today and bright hope for tomorrow! What a great way to find rest as we begin our day, knowing that it is in Christ alone where our true worth is found.

Prayer: Dear Heavenly Father, thank You for the promises we have in Jesus. May we share His light and love with all whose path we cross today, especially those whose hearts are breaking. May the Holy Spirit guide us and give us divine appointments as we go about our daily activities. We pray this in the name of Jesus Christ, our Lord and Savior. Amen.

WHERE IS GOD DURING HARD TIMES?

When he calls to me, I will answer him; I will be with him in trouble; I will rescue him and honor him.

Psalm 91:15 (ESV)

Have you ever wondered where God is during hard times, sorrow, or pain? Do you wonder if He is just sitting there letting you endure the trauma you feel? Do you think you need to go searching for Him? Allow me to share what I've discovered.

One day, several years after my sweet daughter Shelly had gone to Heaven, I sat down and listed all the blessings and ways that God had helped to get us through such a traumatic time in our family. For me, it was comforting to recount the many ways His loving hand had worked on our behalf, even amid the pain and deep sadness of those 17 1/2 months of Shelly's illness and the ensuing months and years after her passing. While my heart will always hurt because of Shelly's absence, and I will have moments of deep grief, I know there will always be shelter from the hard places in life. Simply put, my hope is in the Lord Jesus. I will never be alone, for He is always with me.

Back to the beginning question: *Where is God during our hard times, sorrow, or pain?* He is right beside us! I have found that the only thing we can be certain of during the difficult seasons that come into our lives is that, through faith and trust in Jesus, we will experience God's presence, peace, and faithfulness. He is with us every step of the way and will bring comfort to our hearts. This truth remains above all else: God's peace will be with us through every circumstance. Our struggles in life will change, but our focus should remain the same.

God is the author of our story, through all seasons. Wherever your station in life, if you're alive, He's not finished writing your story. That reality in my life is the Good News of the day, and I'm looking forward to the next chapter!

Jehovah Shalom - The LORD is Peace.

Prayer: Heavenly Father, how thankful we are that You are our peace. You are with us. Even though there are times of great sorrow and pain when we might not sense Your presence, Father, we know, based on Your Word and our total trust in You, that Your presence goes before us; we could not make it without knowing that. Help us share Your love and light with those we encounter in our daily lives. May we all be good representatives of Jesus Christ, our Lord and Savior. We pray this in His name. Amen.

POEMS FROM MY HEART

THE OLD ROCKING CHAIR

If the old rocking chair could say a few words,
There'd be some sweet stories of talks with the Lord
Of singing and praying, gently stroking the hair
Of the three precious children God placed in her care.

Holding her babies so close to her breast
She silently prayed, asking God for sweet rest
Through long sleepless nights for a worn, weary mother
The chair has been rocking two girls and their brother.

Rocking and singing to this little one
She smiled and thanked God for the gift of her son.
Two daughters had taken their turn in the chair
For many a night, sweet peace was found there.

Deep down in her heart this dear mom won't forget
The love that she felt when each baby she met.
How special they are, and forever will be
The old rocking chair has helped her rock three.

Children are such precious gifts from above
That old rocking chair was just filled with His love.
She learned how to trust and be still when He's near,
He'll ease all her burdens and calm all her fears.

I, too, have spent time in this old rocking chair
Singing, praying, and stroking their hair.
These three precious children have brought me such joy,
These two little girls and this one little boy.

I love them so much, much more than they know,
And I pray they serve Jesus wherever they go.
A new mom is taking the old rocking chair
Sweet memories to make that her family will share.

The old rocking chair still has plenty of worth
To be used once again when its owner gives birth
To babies so sweet, brought down with great love
Created by God, sent from Heaven above.

For Heather Mosby, my beautiful granddaughter, a dedicated mother and strong woman of faith who radiates God's love daily, and to all mothers who sacrifice so profoundly in the daily care of their children. You are not forgotten.

HOME

"Home is where the heart is," I've often heard it said.
"All that's really needed is a place to lay your head."

For some a home feels empty – no warmth to even measure.
No thoughts of what to make it, no memories to treasure.

But home is so much greater than just a place to be.
Home should be a shelter from the storms of life we see.

It's more than just a simple place we find ourselves to live,
It's where we often share the things that God would have us give.

My home should be a refuge, and I've tried to do my best
To make a place where love abounds and offers needed rest.

It was my childhood home, though not a perfect place.
That shaped me as I am today and helped me run this race.

Seven little children, two daughters and five sons,
Were taught to follow Jesus, to be His faithful ones.

We siblings loved each other, our mother led the way.
She pointed us toward Heaven where we would live some day.

A MORNING PRAYER

It's morning, Lord, and I've come to say,
How thankful I am for a brand-new day.

You've blessed me with the gift of sight.
You're prompting me to share Your light.

Please guide and use me as You please,
I pray for wisdom on my knees.

To seek Your ways, my heart desires.
Rain down Your passion; send Your fire.

I want to serve with all of my might,
Be strong in battle and armed to fight.

You warriors march; these days are dark,
Your children need to light the spark,

That gives bright hope for days to come,
When God will reign, the Holy One.

And when we're strong with joy and love,
We'll humbly praise the One above.

FOUR O'CLOCK

Right around the hour of four
That's when my thoughts begin to soar.

To no avail, I seek more rest
With morning light, to be my best.

But sleep won't come, so I give in
And let my time of prayer begin.

I first thank God for this new day
Then ask Him what He'd have me say,

To bring some hope to all in need
To share His love, to plant a seed.

I give my thanks for all He's done,
For what He gave to send His Son.

I think of those in pain and ill,
Of stormy seas, they've had their fill.

I hope they know that He is there
With every step, their load He'll bear.

He will not leave them in their grief
But shares His strength to bring relief.

So thank You for this wake-up call
Four o'clock—not bad at all!

It gives me time to start my day
Just You and me, sweet time to pray.

I'll take this time with special care
To give You thanks for being there.

For helping me always to see
Through this clear lens You've given me.

THE TABLE

The house is so quiet, the table is clear
Totally opposite from this time last year.

No children, no laughing, no one will be here
Nor customs of past that we've always held dear.

But one thing remains when plans go astray,
There's something so lasting, I've just got to say.

The things that will last remain in our hearts
And important they are, for they never shall part.

A Savior was born on that Bethlehem night
To show us the way, to give us His light.

He came down to Earth for you and for me
To offer new life abundant and free.

The world forever this baby did change;
He gave us His love that forever remains.

His life for mine, I can't comprehend
But His light to my heart He freely did send.

So today if you're feeling somewhat alone,
Be encouraged, my friend, God gave us His song.

For Jesus is with you from cradle to grave,
He came down to Earth, God's children to save.

Without Him, I ask you, what would we see?
No hope, no joy, no peace there would be.

We'd miss that He came, to save our lost souls,
We'd stumble in darkness, no light to behold.

What's really important to you and to me?
I hope that it's Jesus whose child you will be.

Though your table be empty, His blessings abound.
When you're quiet and still, His love can be found.

Though your table be empty this moment in time
Don't worry, my friend, for Jesus doth shine.

He shines on those places your heart longs to fill
He'll give you these moments to sit silently still.

Then thank Him sincerely for blessings untold
His love knows no end, and it never grows old.

I wrote this poem in late 2020 during the Pandemic when we were unable to gather with our family and friends for our annual Christmas Eve celebration.

PRECIOUS MEMORIES

The old hymns have always lifted my soul,
Like "Precious Memories" and "Never Grow Old."

Mere children we were when we learned how to sing,
These songs of great meaning to which I still cling.

Our activities ceased when Daddy would call
To Mother and children, "Please come one and all.

Stop what you're doing and gather around,
Our fine-tuned piano with its beautiful sound."

Both Mother and Dad played piano by ear;
Happy times for us children, it was special to hear.

We'd sing every line of those songs that we loved;
Raising our voices to Heaven above.

The words of a song speak louder to me
Than a sermon on Sunday whose points total three.

A powerful preacher my pastor may be,
But the words of the songs are what speak to me.

The words of these hymns still abide in my heart,
They've nourished my soul with the joy they impart.

How thankful we are to receive such a gift,
These anointed old hymns....for our souls they do lift.

A PSALM OF GOD'S MERCY

LORD, Your love and mercy surround me!
Each day my strength comes from You!
I call on You, and You hear my plea,
I speak Your name, and You bring life to me.
My hope is in You.

You are my God; there is no other!
I will trust You all of my days.
My lips will continually praise You.
Because of Your great love and mercy,
I shall ever praise You.

You dwell continually in my heart and mind.
Your praise is on my lips and in my heart.
How I praise You for Your mercy and forgiveness!
How I praise You for Your grace, guidance, and joy!
How I praise You for Your love!

Throughout the day, my thoughts turn to Your love for me;
It is a love that You gave me when least deserved;
It is a personal love like no other.
It is a love made possible by Your son, Jesus.
It is a love You gave freely to all who will receive.

Jesus, You are the Light of the world

In whom there is no darkness.

Jesus, You are the hope of the world

In You, there is eternal life.

Jesus, You are the Light of my life.

This personal Psalm was written as an assignment for my Bible Study Fellowship (BSF) class. These words remain deeply ingrained in my heart. My prayer is to always remember the gift of God's mercy and never-ending love for His children. May you do the same.

BROKENNESS

When brokenness strikes like a thief in the night,
Intent on destroying our peace and Your light,
When these moments come, Lord, to whom should we turn?
Your wisdom is needed to help us discern.

There's no doubt we know what the answer will be,
For Your help alone, Lord, is all that we need.
The perfect solution is looking to You,
To give us Your strength and to fill us anew.

We wait on You, Lord, draw us near to Your heart,
From Your peace and love may we never depart,
We give You our lives, though sinful and flawed,
Forgiveness is given, on Your name we have called.

The hard times, the good times, we place in Your care,
Deep from our hearts, the great sorrows we bear.
Those things we can't fix, Lord, we give them to you,
To help us, to heal us, to carry us through.

Although we can't fathom Your plan all the time,
Securely we're held by our Savior sublime.
Assurance we have that our Jesus is real,
For deep in our hearts, His sweet peace we do feel.

*I wrote the above poem after reading Psalm 31:7 (ESV), "I will rejoice and be glad in your steadfast love, because you have seen my affliction; you have known the distress of my soul."

GRANDCHILDREN

A grandchild is someone for whom there's great love;
One who has come as a gift from above.

You've always been part of their many life stages,
And these memories you'll keep whatever their ages.

But what do you do when they're feeling so blue,
Worn down by the antics of only a few?

There's sadness and hurt in their eyes, you can see,
And the pain that you feel brings you down to your knees.

A grandparent's role in a precious child's years,
Is to pray and encourage, to alleviate fears.

To love and defend when their young hearts are breaking,
Though deep in your soul, your own heart is aching.

You fervently pray for these children, so dear;
To trust in the One who's eternally near.

To learn to forgive and get past all the pain;
To know in their hearts that it won't always rain.

To understand life has its good days and bad,
And grasp that their moments won't always be sad.

Your prayers are that God will protect and defend,
These innocent ones with deep love, He did send.

There's no other way but with faith from above,
To trust that our God, in His infinite love,

Will give quiet rest as they travel through life,
And show them the road that will cause them less strife.

These days are so hard with a culture run wild,
When a grandmother's heart hurts for a dear child.

So what do we do when their tender hearts break?
We put them in God's hands; His love there to take.

We pray they'll choose light, and from darkness they'll shrink,
And from God's Living Water, they'll joyfully drink.

He has great plans for each grandchild, you see,
He loves them as much as He does you and me.

Please remember throughout your long busy day,
That you may be the only one who will pray.

For these dear grandchildren are sent from above,
So pray for them always and show them God's love.

DEEP FAITH

A deep faith in Christ is so often borne
From trials that leave us sad, sick, and worn.

Hard things come along we can't understand,
But through all the pain, we hold Jesus' hand.

With deep faith in God through each scary storm,
We learn not to fret as our lives He transforms.

The more that we trust, the more He will move,
Deep into our lives to comfort and soothe.

He'll give us the strength and courage to stand;
Find others like us and take hold of their hand.

To help someone else on life's weary way;
To give them new hope for a much brighter day.

This world was so lost that God sent His son,
To live in our midst and redeem everyone.

He taught us the truth in word and in deed,
He died in our place to set us all free.

The third day he rose, His mission complete;
Will victory we choose or no faith and defeat?

When we allow Jesus in our lives to reign,
We have blessed assurance that Heaven we'll gain.

What peace and contentment this knowledge does bring,
In Heaven above, His praises we'll sing.

As Jesus sustains us through all of life's woes,
Our faith becomes deeper; our love overflows.

Let's trust in His goodness to carry us through;
Our home He's preparing for me and for you.

HE'S WAITING

I've walked some mighty long roads in my life
And I've been held hostage by worry and strife.

I've traveled through sadness, sorrow, and pain
Convinced that my eyes would always see rain.

I've hidden the fact that my heart was well broken
Engaging in life without hurts being spoken.

I longed for true peace and contentment to be
Deep in my heart, something special for me.

Others I'd seen had a sweet peace so real
And I knew they had something I wanted to feel.

Then Jesus came in as quick as a wink
And gave me new life that caused me to think.

How he'd been there with me all the day long
And He was the One who gave me this song.

It's a song that I've carried for many a year
And I'll always be thankful for something so dear.

This song I'll keep singing as long as I can
Of how He has changed me and shown me His plan.

He helps me to see those who are sad and alone
Just like I once was, til He gave me a song.

He helps me to tell them that life does have pain
But in trusting the Son, they will have Heaven's gain.

That His ways are all perfect; His plan is the best
And that He will lead them to valleys of rest.

Friend, if you're walking a lonely dark road
He wants to relieve you of your heavy load.

Trust Him today and find all that and more
For He's waiting to enter your lonely heart's door.

It's all up to you, will you let Him come in?
You have to decide – will you stay where you've been

Or open the door and your Savior you'll meet
And forever you're privileged to sit at His feet.

But please don't delay; life goes by so fast
Believe in the Son, you'll have treasure that lasts.

THE DOVE

This morning as I sip hot tea,
There's something lovely that I see.

Outside my window, there it sits,
A peaceful dove upon the fence.

This dove begins his day anew,
So very much like me and you.

He coos until his heart's content,
His song, no doubt, is heaven-sent.

He sings his special hymn of praise.
To God, the maker of his days.

The dove appears to be at ease,
And sings to God about his needs.

He has no thoughts of worldly cares,
His heavenly song is what he shares.

Oh, may we each learn from the dove,
Take time to sing and feel God's love.

Make time for others as you go,
The love of God they need to know.

Ask God to fill you with His light,
So those in darkness can have sight.

Thank You, God, for the dove You shared,
To remind us of Your loving care.

To cheer my heart and give me peace,
To know God's love will never cease.

FAITH ALONE

Life is filled with ups and downs
Sometimes peace just can't be found.

We search for what we cannot find
And worldly things oft' come to mind.

We find that things don't satisfy
They leave us feeling drained and dry.

And still, we thirst for something more
We wonder what is next in store.

When empty hearts cannot be filled
It's God alone, our minds will still.

He sent His Son to save from sin
All who believe, He'll take us in.

He brings us what we're searching for
And gives new life forevermore.

Unveils our eyes so we can see
Adopts us, so His child we'll be.

He fills our hearts with His great love
And gives us peace from Heaven above.

This world alone will leave us weak
We'll never find that which we seek.

Our trust and hope must always rest
In Christ alone; He gives His best.

It is His strength that sees us through
He brings sweet peace and life anew.

So if you're searching and don't know
What to do, which way to go,

It's faith alone that fills your heart
With love and peace right from the start.

PARKING LOT TESTIMONY

I'll never forget that October day
When through an old parking lot I made my way
To meet some friends who were waiting for me
To be on our way for others to see.

I suddenly saw her with windows rolled down.
In an old car she sat, the color was brown.
She looked so alone as she stared into space.
Worry was etched in the lines on her face.

Politely I smiled and walked briskly on by,
But something within me started to cry.
"You must go back, 'cause she seems pretty bad!
Tell her you noticed she's looking so sad."

My friends were informed they'd now need to wait.
It appeared I'd been called to a God ordained date
With someone in need and hurting inside
Who needed God's Word in which to abide.

Walking back to her car, I prayed Lord, be my guide.
Give me words, give me peace, please be by my side.
I returned to the car without a word spoken,
Just looking at her, I could tell she was broken.

Her eyes filled with tears, and I saw right away,
The hope that God gives was needed that day.
I stepped to the window and told her my name,
I prayed she would listen as Jesus I claimed.

Standing there for a moment, I knew what to say
"Would you like some fresh hope, fresh hope for today?"
The wording, the question, I'd not used in the past
It was surely from God to her heart so downcast.

She said she knew Jesus and loved him a lot,
But that autumn morning she felt quite distraught.
As she shared her life story so sad it did sound,
She said she was drifting, her feet off the ground.

She needed much hope on that day, she confessed,
For her life circumstances had left her distressed.
As I listened intently my heart felt a love
With great depth and compassion from Heaven above.

I told her that Jesus would always be there
To love her and help with her burdens to bear.
His love and His grace would both beckon her near,
She'd rest at His feet never needing to fear.

To Him she'd submit all her worry and pain,
And from start to the finish, in her life He would reign.
At the end of our sacred time spent together,
We joined hands to pray that this storm she would weather.

We asked for God's strength, His wisdom, His plan
His light for her path as her new walk began.
I left this dear sister a Bible to read
And prayed that solely on God's Word she would feed.

For more reasons than one be aware, look around.
On this autumn day, a sad lady I found
To encourage, to listen, to join hands and pray
To give her God's Word filled with Hope to convey.

This poem was written based on my participation in the Gideons International Austin Scripture Blitz, Austin, Texas, October 2019.

WHO'S IN YOUR BOAT?

A crowd had amassed by the seashore that day
They longed to hear more of what Jesus would say.

Disciples were there lending Jesus a hand
To Him, they'd committed to preach in the land.

While hearing Him teach, the crowd gathered 'round,
More likely than not, there wasn't a sound.

He had much to share with these ones He held dear
To show them the Way to salvation, so near.

He taught all day long, they launched out to sea.
Out into the waters they called Galilee.

The crowd had pressed in for most of the day
Tired Jesus was sleeping, lulled by the boat's sway.

A storm came from nowhere and quick as a wink,
His friends became fearful that the boat would soon sink!

So Jesus got up and admonished the sea
The waves and wind stopped, and the storm ceased to be.

Those men in the boat, a staunch trustworthy band
Were awed as the weather obeyed His command.

How often have you had to face your own storm
With no one around to protect you from harm?

Just like the disciples, you fear what's ahead,
Your boat might go under, sink quickly like lead.

As Jesus commanded the wind and the waves
He'll do what it takes, His dear people to save.

Sisters and brothers, I ask you today,
Has Jesus been trying to show you the Way?

Has He lovingly bid you to trust Him alone?
To give you a reason to sing a new song?

Don't be disheartened, I tell you for sure
That He'll carry your load and give strength to endure

Those hard times in life when you feel so alone
It's during those times when He'll bring you that song.

His love and protection are there for the taking
He mends our sad hearts whenever they're breaking

He gives us the peace we are longing to know
And shows us His path, the direction to go.

So, friends, look to Jesus to calm all your fears
He'll always be with you and dry all your tears.

He'll be there to quiet the storm in your heart.
He'll give you His love and never depart.

I learned a good lesson a long time ago
It's best to ask Jesus to sleep in my boat.

Based on Mark 4:35-41

HOPE

There is a hope the world doesn't know,
A way to move forward, the best way to go.

They're missing the mark, the true meaning of life,
If only they'd stop and let go of their strife.

If they could just see the One who is there,
He's ready and willing His Good News to share.

The God of the ages, a whisper away,
Is waiting and watching day after day.

His Word full of love may be there on a table,
But has never been read, even though they are able.

What will it take, oh tell me, dear friend,
To convince them to see that His love has no end?

The beginning, the present, He's always been there
To give them His heart, to show that He cares.

He's present each time they have struggled and wept,
If only they knew every promise He's kept.

They've traded His peace for a life filled with worry,
Running around in too big of a hurry.

They've hoarded their treasures on Earth for today,
The things they have valued will all pass away.

They've missed the true joy deep down inside,
That comes when we know Him, a joy we can't hide.

Many years on this Earth, I've been blessed here to be,
And I'm happy to say that I know He loves me.

How thankful I am that we never shall part,
And He'll always reside down deep in my heart.

He gave me a Hope for others to see,
It was planted within when Jesus saved me.

That Hope has sustained me through sunshine and rain,
Has given me joy amidst sorrow and pain.

I want them to know Him--to trust in His name,
I pray for them daily, His truth they'll proclaim.

TWISTS AND TURNS

Life has many twists and turns,
Important lessons we must learn.

Some are good, some are bad
Some are happy, some are sad.

Some we welcome, some we don't
Some we definitely did not want.

But through it all, we find our way,
We find the strength to watch and pray.

We thank God for another day,
And seek His guidance on our way.

May we live for Him alone,
And share our hearts on our way home.

One thing we always come to know
It's through the trials our faith will grow.

With more of Him and less of us;
It's Him alone that we must trust.

So when you think what life has dealt
Remember this, your pain He's felt.

He's been there with you all along,
To comfort, carry, and keep you strong.

He longs to write a beautiful story
Of hard times conquered, all for His glory.

It's up to us to let Him lead,
For through great love, He did bleed.

He gave His life so we could show
A dying world, which way to go.

Don't give up, don't stop now,
For soon before Him all will bow.

MORNING'S FIRST LIGHT

There's something distinct about morning's first light,
A new day has come; I have passed through the night.

I always thank God for another new day,
For giving me rest and for being my stay.

I ask Him to help me reach those far and near;
That lives would be changed as the Gospel they hear.

My first plea should be, "Help me serve You today.
Please lead us to others on life's weary way."

By word or by deed may I serve someone else,
Lord, show me Your plan; help me give of myself.

Awaken my mind to an awesome new day;
Lord, guide me anew as I go on my way.

You've given this day with the morning's first light,
To show me the way from the darkness of night.

Although I don't know what this new day will bring,
I pray that to God my whole being will sing.

WE'RE NOT HOME YET

Our present life can wear us down,
But there's a hope that can be found.

For as we walk from day to day,
Within God's plan we need to stay.

If we abide close to His side,
Our earthly needs He will provide.

Divine encounters will abound
As Gospel seeds we spread around.

For those who've borne a heavy load,
There are more seeds for you to sow.

We share the truths about our Lord
Who loves and wants us all on board.

Let's run the race and not forget
Though life is short, we're not home yet!

ROOTED IN HIS LOVE

Dear Lord, we gather in this place,
To learn and grow and seek Your face.

For every year sent from above,
We thank You, Lord, for Your great love.

We pray Your Word will light our way,
And give us strength for each new day.

Help us to stay on bended knee,
To live a life pleasing to Thee.

Give us more of Your great power;
Guide us, Lord, in this dark hour.

O loving Savior, let us be,
Your servants now built up in Thee.

Lord, give us roots down deep and sure;
That we might stand strong and secure.

To be a bold yet caring voice,
To those who've made an unwise choice.

That they will turn to You alone,
And trust Your Son to make them strong.

Let others see a brand-new light,
That called them out of darkest night.

May they be rooted in Your love,
Reflect Your light from up above.

This prayer today we humbly bring;
To You, O Lord, our voices ring.

To stay the course You lead us through,
With less of us and more of You.

So, build us up and let us be,
Always devoted Lord to Thee.

ACKNOWLEDGMENTS

The Resting Place:
Finding Hope, Peace, and Joy in All Circumstances

My Heavenly Father: First and foremost, I want to thank God for equipping me with the ability to share my faith in Christ through these devotions and poems. May all who read them find rest, hope, peace, and joy in all circumstances, and may they be strengthened with a deeper connection to their faith. **Ephesians 2:4-5**

Ray Canizales, my husband: As I reflect on our many years of serving the Lord together, I am filled with gratitude that God has taken us safely through times of uncertainty, grief, and sorrow. Through it all, we have grown together in our love and commitment to one another, and our faith, trust, and reliance on God's strength rather than our own. Thank you for your love and support throughout my writing journey and for encouraging me to step out in faith. I love you very much and look forward to making many more wonderful memories together. **Jeremiah 29:11**

Heather and Zachary Mosby, my granddaughter and her husband: The love and encouragement you have given me to follow my writing dreams mean more than you will ever know. On hard days, you continually reminded me that God had a purpose for my writing and that it was He who had given me this method of sharing the Good News of Jesus Christ. Thank you for loving me, believing in me, and for your generosity in sharing directly in my dream of publishing this book, all to the glory of God! All my love and prayers to you and your precious family. **Philemon 1:7**

Sophie Forston, my granddaughter: As your full-time babysitter from 11 weeks old through the age of 9, it is only natural that you have influenced my writing significantly. As we shared in everyday adventures, nature walks, nightly devotionals, and conversations about Jesus and His love, I collected a lot of writing material in my memory bank. You have greatly inspired me, and I cherish all the memories we have made. My prayer for you is that you will continue to grow in your faith and become a mighty woman after God's own heart. I love you more than you will ever know and am so proud of you. **Philippians 1:6.**

My family members – children, grandchildren, great-grandchildren, extended family, and dear friends, far and near: Each of you holds a very special place in my heart, and I would not be who I am today without you in my life. Your love, respect, and support have been a constant source of strength and inspiration. My greatest desire is to pass on the deep faith God has given me to each of you, not only through my writing, but also by the way I live my daily life. My prayer for you is that you will be God's faithful and obedient servants in all things. You are deeply loved, and your role in my life is invaluable. **Proverbs 3:5-6**

Judy Ferguson, dear friend, sister in Christ, and editor of this project: My greatest desire was to find someone who would help to fine-tune these devotions without changing the message that God had given me. You have faithfully and carefully done that and so much more with love and respect. Thank you for being sensitive and obedient to where the Lord was leading, for being willing to join in, and for being a friend who consistently offered humor, laughter, and encouragement when it was needed the most. **Psalm 16:11**

Peyton Sepeda, WildCreativePublishing.com: The first time we spoke, I knew it was no accident that God had led me to seek you out for this project. There was a great deal I didn't know about preparing to publish a book, but you made the process go very smoothly. Without your skill, experience, and support, this book would not exist. Your excellence is noted and greatly appreciated. I pray that the Lord will bless you and your family in ways you can only imagine. May He give you great success in all things, according to His will for your life. **Philippians 4:13**

www.ingramcontent.com/pod-product-compliance
Lightning Source LLC
Chambersburg PA
CBHW061558120626
46550CB00004B/1531